D0207665

# FEMINISM, THE FAMILY, AND THE POLITICS OF THE CLOSET

# Feminism, the Family, and the Politics of the Closet: Lesbian and Gay Displacement

CHESHIRE CALHOUN

OXFORD
UNIVERSITY PRESS

# OXFORD
UNIVERSITY PRESS

Great Clarendon Street, Oxford OX2 6DP

Oxford University Press is a department of the University of Oxford.
It furthers the University's objective of excellence in research, scholarship,
and education by publishing worldwide in

Oxford  New York

Athens  Auckland  Bangkok  Bogotá  Buenos Aires  Calcutta
Cape Town  Chennai  Dar es Salaam  Delhi  Florence  Hong Kong  Istanbul
Karachi  Kuala Lumpur  Madrid  Melbourne  Mexico City  Mumbai
Nairobi  Paris  São Paulo  Singapore  Taipei  Tokyo  Toronto  Warsaw

with associated companies in  Berlin  Ibadan

Oxford is a registered trade mark of Oxford University Press
in the UK and in certain other countries

Published in the United States
by Oxford University Press Inc., New York

British Library Cataloguing in Publication Data

Data available

Library of Congress Cataloging in Publication Data
Calhoun, Cheshire
Feminism, the family, and the politics of the closet: lesbian and gay displacement/
Cheshire Calhoun.
p. cm.
Includes bibliographical references (p.) and index.
1. Lesbian feminism—United States.   2. Lesbian feminist theory—United States.
3. Lesbians—United States—Identity.   4. Sexual orientation—Political aspects—United States.
5. Oppression (Psychology)—Political aspects—United States.   6. Lesbians–United
States—Political activity.   7. Gay men—United States—Political activity.   I. Title.
HQ75.6.U5 C35 2000      305.48′9664—dc21      00–040073
ISBN 0–19–829559–6

1 3 5 7 9 10 8 6 4 2

Typeset in Minion by
Cambrian Typesetters, Frimley, Surrey
Printed in Great Britain
on acid-free paper by
T J International Ltd
Padstow, Cornwall

# *Preface*

Writing philosophy has always been, for me, a way of bringing some greater amount of conceptual clarity to puzzling issues in everyday life. This book is no exception. I am one of the not so small group of people who switched sexual orientation from heterosexual to lesbian in mid life. Feminism had, in many ways, enabled me to think critically about women's intimate relations with men and to call into question the assumption that a normal, healthy, mature life trajectory for women must include an intimate relationship with a man. It had not, however, prepared me to live life as a lesbian. After thirty-seven years of living with heterosexual privilege, I was stunned at how difficult it was to present myself publicly as a lesbian. I was also deeply unaccustomed to having my most important, intimate relationships treated as mere friendships or imitations of 'real' romance. Feminist work, however, had largely failed to provide me with a conceptual scheme for clearly seeing and articulating the shape that the subordination of lesbians and gays takes. Indeed, while reading Susan Moller Okin's *Justice, Gender, and the Family*, I was forcibly struck by how much I knew about the structure of women's oppression from reading feminist work and how structureless my grasp of lesbian and gay subordination was.

The aim of this book is to explore the distinctive features of lesbian and gay subordination. Paying attention to the distinctive structure of lesbian and gay subordination means, in part, resisting the temptation to view lesbian experience through feminist eyes that are on the lookout for evidence of gender oppression. In Chapter 1, I suggest that this will mean that feminist theorizing must make a methodological shift from thinking that heterosexism is just a byproduct of sexism to thinking of lesbian and gay subordination as a separate axis of oppression. In Chapters 2 and 3, I argue that feminist theorizing about gender oppression has worked to conceal, rather than reveal, lesbian specificity; and I try to determine what it is in feminist thinking that makes it difficult to see the lesbian in the feminist subject 'women'. Paying attention to the distinctive structure of lesbian and gay subordination also means trying to get a grip on just how social practices work to subordinate lesbians and gays so that it is possible to get a clearer picture of what needs to be done politically. Chapter 4 is my attempt to isolate the structure of lesbian and gay subordination. Chapters 5 and 6 address what is, for me, the most frustrating dimension of lesbian life and the dimension that needs to be politically prioritized, namely, the denigration of same-sex intimate relationships that claim to constitute marriages or families.

Most of the chapters in this volume have appeared in a somewhat different form in a variety of philosophical, feminist, and legal journals and books. Each essay was originally written with the previous one in mind. Together they represent an eight year process of trying to clarify for myself the difference that being lesbian makes.

I am grateful to Claudia Card, Morris Kaplan, Richard Mohr, and Ed Stein for their friendship and ongoing support of my work. They provided me with opportunities to present portions of this present book to university audiences and to the Society for Lesbian and Gay Philosophy. I thank my dissertation director, Bob Solomon, for teaching me that it is better to be bold and controversial than carefully correct. Dennis D'Angelo's skilled, thoughtful, and painstaking work on the final drafts of the manuscript made completing this book possible. I owe him a very large debt of gratitude. My institution, Colby College, Waterville, ME, provided, through sabbatical funding and its progressive and open-minded conception of academia, a wonderful place to do this work. Finally, I would like to thank my parents, Jack and Edith Calhoun, who taught me the importance of thinking for oneself and who, throughout many years of generous support, made possible an academic career in philosophy.

C. C.

*Colby College, Waterville, ME*
*April 2000*

# Contents

# 1
# Introduction: Centering Sexual Orientation Politics

This book is devoted to two different but interrelated questions about centering sexual orientation politics. The first is the question of the extent to which lesbian theorizing occupies the center of feminist theorizing about women. In raising this first question, my aim is to unsettle the comfortable assumption that because feminist thought is about women, and because so much of existing lesbian theorizing has been conducted within a feminist frame, lesbians are already securely at the center of feminist theory in a way in which women of color or poor and working class women have not been. I will suggest instead that the specifically lesbian features of lesbian lives persistently slip from view in feminist theory. In order to keep lesbian specificity in view, feminist theorizing needs to give up the idea that heterosexism is nothing but a byproduct of sexism; and it needs to work out the basic structure of lesbian and gay subordination.

The second question is the question of what the political center of lesbian and gay liberatory activity should be. In raising this second question, I aim to unsettle the common assumption that lesbian and gay politics should be centered first around combating the socio-legal structures that regulate sexual activity and second around securing protection against the material costs of discriminatory practices. Prioritizing challenges to sexual regulations makes sense if one assumes that gays and lesbians are primarily stigmatized for their sexual object choice. I will suggest instead that the stigma of being lesbian or gay emerges from a century's worth of constructing the identities 'lesbian' and 'homosexual' as types of persons whose deviancies are not limited to sexual object choice. Looking at the multiple deviancies attributed to lesbians and gays suggests that marriage and family issues need special priority in a lesbian and gay politics. The second standard goal of lesbian and gay politics—securing protection against the material costs of discriminatory practices—makes sense if one assumes that lesbian and gay subordination directly parallels race and gender oppression. I will argue that it does not because gays and lesbians can largely evade the material costs of discrimination. This does not necessarily mean that pursuing anti-discrimination protection should not be central to lesbian and gay politics. What it does mean is that we need a better account of why that protection is so important.

In this chapter, I simply want to lay out some of the groundwork for later chapters. Later chapters will focus on specific ways that feminist scholarship drops lesbians from view—even while talking about lesbians. Later chapters will also focus on the specific shape of lesbian and gay subordination. Here, I want to defend the general methodological strategy of treating lesbian and gay subordination as a distinct axis of oppression that intersects with gender, race, and class axes of oppression. Readers unfamiliar with lesbian feminist work may find this puzzling. Surely it is obvious that gays and lesbians are penalized specifically on the basis of their sexual orientation. Does this not imply that heterosexism differs from sexism and classism and racism? Well, yes and no. Lesbian feminist theorists recognize that lesbians (and gay men) suffer a distinctive set of social penalties; but they also typically trace those penalties back to gender oppression and regard homophobia and heterosexism as just one among many specific ways that sexism gets enacted. Section I of this chapter lays out the general arguments for *not* treating heterosexism as simply one among many byproducts of gender oppression.

Section II introduces what I take to be the two central features of lesbian and gay subordination. First, the principal, damaging effect of a heterosexist system is that it *displaces* lesbians and gays from both the public and private spheres of civil society so that lesbians and gays have no legitimated social location, not even a disadvantaged one. Second, the principal ideologies rationalizing lesbian and gay displacement are: (1) that there are two and only two natural and normal sex/genders, (2) that lesbian and gay sexuality is excessive, compulsive, and disconnected from romantic love, and (3) that for a variety of reasons lesbians and gays are fundamentally unfit for marital and familial life. Throughout this book, my analyses of lesbian and gay subordination include remarkably little mention of *sex*. This may strike readers as odd. Lesbianism and homosexuality are, after all, *sexual* orientations, and lesbians and gays are socially penalized because what they do sexually is thought by many to be pathological or immoral. Later chapters will, in quite specific ways, take issue with this idea that gay and lesbian subordination emerges straightforwardly out of cultural aversion to same-sex sexual activity and desires. Here, I simply want to introduce the idea that lesbianism and homosexuality are stigmatized sexualities because of the way that same-sex sexuality has been culturally connected to other, more deeply stigmatizing characteristics.

My approach throughout this book is a social constructionist one. That is, in order to understand the nature of lesbian and gay subordination, I think it is crucial to work from a detailed description of our dominant cultural understanding of what it means to have a lesbian or gay identity. I conclude this chapter, in Section III, with some general remarks on how this book fits into the essentialist-constructionist controversy.

## I. Feminism and Lesbian Theory

Of all liberatory academic discourses, feminist thought has been the most self-critical. Feminists have been acutely and distinctively alive to the risk of producing theories that, while ostensibly about women generally, are in fact tacitly about only the most privileged women. Very early in the history of second wave feminism, black women objected to feminism's failure to problematize the relation between black and white women, to invoke the experience of black women as the ground of theory construction, and to orient feminist politics around anything except those issues that were most salient to middle class white women. Black feminists insisted that feminist theorizing, if it hoped to be genuinely about all women, needed to move issues of race and class from the margins to the center.[1] This required making a key shift in feminist methodology. First wave and early second wave feminism approached the analysis of women's situation through the lens of a single system of oppression—gender oppression. Because analyses that focused only on gender relations in fact dropped women of color and poor and working class women out of the picture, taking a different methodological tack seemed warranted. The most promising methodological strategy for bringing nonwhite and nonmiddle class women from the margins to the center was to move away from an exclusive focus on only one system of oppression—gender oppression—and to begin thinking in terms of multiple, interlocking systems of oppression. The key shift in feminist method, then, was to begin from the assumption that there are multiple, conceptually distinct systems of oppression that in actual social arrangements intersect to produce race and class-specific experiences of gender oppression. Theorizing that attends to the *intersections* of conceptually distinct systems of oppression became, and continues to be, at least the regulative ideal of contemporary feminist work even if race and class issues often continue in practice to occupy the margins of feminist work.

Lesbians of all races and economic classes could have voiced a parallel complaint and pushed a parallel methodological solution. Both first wave and second wave feminism were conducted from a specifically heterosexual viewpoint. The relation between heterosexual and nonheterosexual women was not problematized. Heterosexual women's experience, and not lesbians' experience, provided the ground for theory construction. And feminist politics were virtually exclusively centered around those issues that were most pressing for heterosexual women, such as educational and employment discrimination on the basis of sex, inadequate access to contraception and abortion, gender dominance within heterosexual intimate relations, and heterosexual pornography. The marginalization of lesbians within feminist thought might naturally have been thought to be a product of exactly the same problematic methodology that marginalized black women—the exclusive focus on gender oppression. And the solution might naturally have been thought to be the same—a shift to thinking about the ways that gender oppression intersects with a conceptually distinct system of lesbian and gay subordination. None of

---

[1] That image was crystallized in the subtitle of bell hooks' widely read book, *Feminist Theory: From Margin to Center* (Boston: South End Press, 1984).

this in fact happened. This is not to say that lesbian feminists have never protested heterosexual bias in feminist work. It is, however, to say that that protest had a distinctively different character. Black feminists protested by emphasizing their *difference* from white, middle class feminists. Lesbian feminists, particularly of the 1980s, protested by emphasizing the potential *commonalities* or continuum between lesbians' and heterosexual feminists' experience, especially their valorization of woman-loving and their resistance to compulsory heterosexual interaction with men. Black feminists protested by underscoring the racial and class *biases* encoded in dominant feminist theorizing. Lesbian feminists protested by underscoring the *incompleteness* of dominant feminist theorizing's resistance to gender oppression when it failed to call into question heterosexuality itself. Black feminists took the problem with feminist theorizing to be both methodological and social. Methodologically, feminist theorizing was too narrowly focused on only one system of oppression; and the narrow focus was itself a product of many feminist theorists' racism and classism. Lesbian feminists took the problem to be neither methodological nor particularly social. If lesbians were at the margins of feminist theorizing it was only because feminists had not extended their analyses of gender oppression far enough; and it was not heterosexual feminists' heterosexism that barred them from doing so as much as it was simply an uncritical adoption of cultural ideology about the naturalness and immutability of one's sexual orientation. In short, the marginal position of lesbians was not taken to be problematic for feminism in the way that the marginal position of women of color and poor and working class women was.

I think this was a mistake. One of my central aims in this book is to argue that specifically lesbian oppression cannot be either adequately described or politically addressed without a shift in methodology. In particular, lesbian and gay subordination needs to be taken as a conceptually distinct axis of oppression that intersects with systems of gender, race, and class oppression. Chapters 2 and 3 are devoted to making the case for that claim. In Chapter 2, I focus on the failure of 1980s lesbian-feminism to account for the specifically lesbian experience of oppression. In Chapter 3, I turn to the ways that, in the 1990s, feminist theorizing that is governed by the ideal of tracing intersections between different forms of oppression has not treated heterosexism as one of the axes of oppression and thus has also failed to account for specifically lesbian experience of subordination. If what is needed in order to bring lesbians from margin to center in feminist theorizing is attention to lesbian and gay subordination as a separate axis of oppression, then we will need an account of the basic contours of that axis of oppression. I try to pinpoint those contours in Chapters 4, 5, and 6.

Because so much of this book is devoted to the thesis that lesbian and gay subordination is not simply a byproduct of male dominance, but is itself a separate system of oppression, it is worthwhile saying a bit more about this claim. What do I mean when I refer to a 'separate' axis of oppression? Why has it generally been thought to be unnecessary to describe heterosexism (lesbian and gay subordination) as a separate axis? Why is it methodologically important to treat heterosexism as a separate axis?

What distinguishes oppression or subordination from merely unequal treatment in a particular sphere is by now fairly well articulated. 'Oppression' and 'subordination' refer to social systems. One cannot claim to be oppressed simply because one is treated in a disadvantagingly unequal way in a particular sphere of human activity. Men, for example, cannot claim to be oppressed simply because they are not given equal priority in child custody decisions. Nor can students claim to be oppressed simply because they are not granted equal academic freedom with professors. Both treatments may be wrong or unfair, but this fact by itself does not make the treatment oppressive or subordinating in the sense in which racist or sexist treatment is oppressive or subordinating. Oppression and subordination depend on the cultural articulation of basic social identities that are taken to be: (a) relatively or completely immutable features of persons, (b) determinative of their psychological, moral, physical, and intellectual capacities, and (c) in polar opposition to an Other identity where polarity of evaluation (good-bad, respectable-unrespectable, superior-inferior, natural-unnatural) is central. Such identities are basic in the sense that they serve as the basis for a systematic organization of social life and social relations. And it is organization of a particular sort. An interlocking set of practices based on the assumption that one social type is deficient in relation to its polar Other produces a pervasive reduction of one group's political status, self-determination, life chances, resources, physical safety, and control over cultural products.[2] These interlocking practices also produce pervasive and important benefits, privileges, and liberties for the other social group. For a variety of reasons, oppressive systems are extremely difficult to intervene in. One obvious reason is that they are systems. Men's right of sexual access to women, for instance, is encoded in dating and marital practices, advertising images, pornography, prostitution, women's responsibility for pregnancy, and the like. Piecemeal or quick-fix efforts to address oppression, such as censoring pornography, are thus unlikely to have a substantial effect. The importance and scope of benefits accruing to the dominant group also produce a vested, if often unconscious, interest in preserving the system. Thus, attempts to intervene in oppressive systems often result in oppression taking new forms rather than in an overall reduction of oppression itself. For instance, affirmative action policies aimed at increasing racial minorities' access to professional occupations, while in fact making those occupations more accessible, have also been used in cultural discourse to reaffirm basic social beliefs about black inferiority and inability to compete on

---

[2] For an enormously helpful discussion of the forms that oppression takes see Iris Young's 'The Five Faces of Oppression', *Justice and the Politics of Difference* (Princeton: Princeton University Press, 1990).

their own merits. Finally, because oppression is connected to the way that we view our most basic social identities and most fundamental ways of organizing social life, oppressive systems generate ideologies about the naturalness, divine authorization, and scientific validity of differential treatment. This works both against seeing that oppression is taking place at all and against justifying alternative, less oppressive arrangements.

Although accounts of oppression along these lines are now commonplace, what is not commonplace are criteria for *individuating* systems of oppression.[3] That gender, race, and class are connected to separate systems of oppression is, more often than not, treated as an obvious fact. Their assumed separability provides the *starting* point for analyses that then look at their intersection. Once we move beyond these three systems, it becomes much less clear how we are to go about counting systems of oppression. Heterosexism occupies a particularly problematic place. On the one hand, heterosexism looks very much like a free standing system of oppression. Heterosexism is an interlocking set of practices built on the distinction between what appear to be basic identities—heterosexual versus gay and lesbian—whose effect is the pervasive reduction of lesbian and gay life chances, self-determination, political status, physical safety, and control over cultural products. On the other hand, heterosexism looks very much like a *component* of gender oppression. Heterosexism appears to be part of a broader array of interlocking practices built on the distinction between the identities 'man' and 'woman'. The social penalties visited upon lesbians and gay men for their gender and sexual deviance appear to be simply a special case of the systematic penalization of *anyone* who departs from the gender and sexual norms that support male dominance and female oppression. Are heterosexism and sexism two systems or one, the one being gender oppression?

I am not sure what a conclusive answer to this question would look like. I do, however, think there are good conceptual and pragmatic arguments for treating sexism and heterosexism as two separate systems.

One might begin with a thought experiment. Imagine a society that is not structured around male dominance. It might be a society that draws no gender distinctions but still emphasizes male–female sexual differences. Or it might be a society that draws masculine-feminine gender distinctions but either inverts our evaluative order (so that the society is female-dominant) or treats the two genders as equal though different. Could that society have a stringent taboo on homosexuality and lesbianism? Could social practices and social relations be systematically structured around heterosexuality? Could those practices work pervasively to the detriment of lesbians and gays and to the benefit of heterosexuals? It seems to me that the answer to all three questions is yes. Heterosexism would, of course, have to take a quite different form.

---

[3] I owe this point to Ann Ferguson, 'Cheshire Calhoun's Project of Separating Lesbian Theory from Feminist Theory'. *Hypatia* 13 (1998): 214–22.

The very notions of heterosexuality, lesbianism, and homosexuality would have to be socially constructed differently. In a gender-undifferentiated society, for example, gender deviance could not occupy a central role in what it means to be homosexual as it does in our society; and in a gender-inverted society, being lesbian would likely be more severely penalized than being gay. But in principle there seems to be no more reason to deny that one could have heterosexism in a gender-egalitarian society than to deny that one could have racism in a gender-egalitarian society.

What may make it tempting to say that there could not be heterosexism without sexism is that it is hard to see what the *point* of heterosexism would be if it were not aimed at preserving the gender distinctions and sexual relations that support male dominance. Gayle Rubin's early piece, 'The Traffic in Women,' is useful in clarifying what that point might be.[4] There, she argued that the sex/gender system gets off the ground when a society installs the male–female couple as the most basic economic unit. A sexual division of labor within the household makes the male–female couple more economically viable. That sexual division of labor, however, depends on producing differently gendered types of persons who are suited to assume their particular labor. Anatomical sex difference is thus turned into gender difference. A sex/gender system that depends on the male–female couple as the foundational social and economic unit will also need to construct strong taboos against lesbianism and homosexuality. Although Rubin adds to her account an explanation of how the sex/gender system comes to be male-dominant (namely, through the traffic in women to establish new kinship relations), the taboo on same-sex sexuality is, in her account, not *essentially* connected to male dominance. Thus, heterosexism is not essentially connected to sexism. *Any* society, even a gender-egalitarian one, that makes the male–female couple foundational will be one in which stigmatizing lesbianism and homosexuality has a point.

Heterosexism can, of course, have more than one point. I do not mean to deny that heterosexism plays a substantial role in sustaining male dominance. I do mean to assert that this is not the only possible point heterosexism might have. In Chapter 5, I will argue that a central point of lesbian and gay subordination is to preserve the heterosexual marital couple's foundational place within the social structure. The United States Congressional debates about the Defense of Marriage Act (DOMA), which is a focus of that chapter, make it quite clear just how much preserving that foundational place provides the point of lesbian and gay subordination. Throughout this book, my aim is also to call more clearly into view the full scope and importance of the benefits that heterosexuals, as a class, receive. Those benefits, I will argue, are sufficiently

---

[4] Gayle Rubin, 'The Traffic in Women', in *Toward an Anthropology of Women*, ed. Rayna Reiter (New York: Monthly Review Press, 1975), 157–210. For a somewhat more extended discussion of Rubin, see my 'Taking Seriously Dual Systems and Sex', *Hypatia* 13 (1998): 224–31.

large to explain why heterosexual men and women would have a deeply vested interest in maintaining a system of heterosexual dominance even in the absence of male dominance.

The possibility of heterosexism serving multiple points undercuts one very tempting argument against treating heterosexism as a separate system of oppression. That argument begins from the observation that heterosexism serves male dominance and concludes that heterosexism is *nothing but* a byproduct of male dominance. Consider, for example, Andrienne Rich's ground-breaking piece, 'Compulsory Heterosexuality and Lesbian Existence'. There, Rich argued that heterosexuality is not clearly a natural orientation for women.[5] It is, instead, systematically enforced through a wide variety of practices that make women sexually accessible to men and that conceal and penalize the lesbian option. It is thus a mistake for feminists, particularly heterosexual feminists, to treat a heterosexual orientation simply as a natural fact outside the scope of feminist political critique. Practices that enforce male right of sexual access to women, including the taboo on lesbianism, constitute the center of women's oppression. Given the central role that heterosexism plays in all women's oppression, including the specific subordination of lesbians, it is then tempting to conclude that heterosexism is nothing but a product of male dominance. The inference, however, does not follow. What Rich's argument shows is only that challenging male dominance is, in our own society, a *necessary* condition for eliminating the subordination of lesbians and gay men.[6] That is, lesbians and gay men cannot interrupt the system that subordinates them unless they adopt a broadly feminist agenda. The argument does not, however, show that eliminating gender oppression is *sufficient* for liberating lesbians and gays. This is because the male right of sexual access may not be the only driving force behind heterosexism. Thus, the claim that there is only one system of oppression (gender oppression) rather than two (gender and sexual orientation oppression) cannot be established simply by showing that heterosexism and male dominance are interconnected. To establish a single system one would have to show, in addition, that there is no other possible basis for the extensive social control of lesbians and gays. In particular, one would have to argue that heterosexual women and men, as a class, do not derive benefits from lesbian and gay subordination that are of sufficient magnitude to motivate the transformation, rather than elimination, of heterosexist practices were gender equality to be achieved.

Two analogies with feminist thinking about class and race are useful here. Consider, first, the history of specifically Marxist theorizing about women's oppression. Marx and Engels, and subsequently second wave Marxist femin-

---

[5] Adrienne Rich, 'Compulsory Heterosexuality and Lesbian Existence', in *The Signs Reader: Women, Gender, and Scholarship*, ed. Elizabeth Abel and Emily K. Abel (Chicago: University of Chicago Press, 1983), 139–68.

[6] Ann Ferguson clarifies this distinction between necessary and sufficient conditions for lesbian and gay liberation in 'Cheshire Calhoun's Project of Separating Lesbian Theory from Feminist Theory'.

ists, tried to argue that women's oppression is a byproduct of oppressive economic class relations. Fairly early on in second wave feminism, the defects of this approach became apparent. Why think that women would automatically be liberated through the elimination of economic classes or that their oppression would be reduced in tandem with improved, more egalitarian worker conditions? After all, within a single class, women are subordinate to men. Moreover, the benefits to men of male dominance are sufficiently great that it seems more reasonable to suppose that male dominance is independently motivated and is more likely to simply undergo transformation rather than elimination were more egalitarian economic relations established. Finally, in fact, improved economic conditions, such as the family wage, worked in favor of male dominance rather than undercutting it.[7] Thus, as Heidi Hartmann has argued, even if capitalism and patriarchy often work together in such a way that one can show how capitalism contributes to male dominance, it does not follow that capitalism and patriarchy are not two separate systems. Just as it behooved feminists to ask whether their interests were being adequately advanced by Marxist class critiques, it behooves lesbians to ask whether their interests are being adequately advanced by feminist gender critiques. A central aim of this book is to open up the critical space for asking and beginning to answer that question.

Turning now to the second analogy, consider how inflected with gender the images and practices are that support racial dominance. Black men's inferiority, for example, gets promoted through constructions of black men as both hypersexual and thus threateningly excessive embodiments of masculinity and as emasculated within the family by unfemininely strong black women. Our conception of racial differences is so heavily inflected with images drawn from the domain of gender oppression that it is difficult to imagine what a construction of racial difference would look like absent gender-subordinating images. However, it seems obviously implausible to argue that because one can give a gender analysis of racially subordinating practices and stereotypes, racial oppression is *nothing but* a byproduct of gender oppression. Even if gender readings of racist practices are possible, those readings do not exhaust the content of racist practices. By the same token, it does not follow from the fact that much of lesbian and gay experience can be analyzed through the lens of gender oppression that one cannot also give an analysis through the lens of lesbian and gay subordination. It is thus methodologically important to resist 'nothing but' inferences of the form 'Lesbians and gay men are socially penalized for their gender insubordination, therefore heterosexism is nothing but a form of gender oppression'. This may be true. Its truth, however, is not established by the fact that one can give a gender analysis of lesbian and gay experience.

[7] Heidi Hartmann, 'The Unhappy Marriage of Marxism and Feminism', in *Feminist Frameworks*, 2nd edn, ed. Alison M. Jaggar and Paula S. Rothenberg (New York: McGraw-Hill, 1984), 172–89.

So far, I have been trying to establish one simple conceptual point. It is a negative one. The possibility that sexual orientation subordination is a separate axis of oppression cannot be ruled out simply by showing that heterosexism and male dominance are connected. Let me now turn to more positive methodological and pragmatic arguments for employing the assumption that lesbian and gay subordination and gender oppression are two separate axes of oppression. In particular, I want to forestall the objection that any attempt to isolate lesbian and gay subordination from gender oppression is methodologically a bad idea, because in social practice, different systems of oppression do not operate independently of one another; they are interpenetrating.

It is certainly true that in actual social practice and experience, different systems of oppression do not operate entirely separately. Racial dominance of east Asians, for example, gets played out via gender images of east Asian men as effeminate and thus inferior in relation to Caucasian men; it also gets played out via sexual orientation images of east Asian men as questionably heterosexual and thus deficient in relation to Caucasian men. Taunting east Asian men with the jeer 'faggot' thus simultaneously invokes systems of race, gender, and sexual orientation dominance.[8] Neither the specific experiences of oppression suffered by some particular people nor the full meaning of specific social practices can be adequately analyzed without bringing to bear an understanding of multiple systems of oppression. It would thus seem that it is methodologically a bad idea to try to specify lesbian and gay oppression in abstraction from race, gender, and class oppression. The particular experiences of particular people are not fully describable in terms of a single system of oppression.

At one level, this is absolutely right. An exhaustive socially critical analysis of any particular experience of oppression or any particular subordinating social practice cannot be done without invoking multiple systems of oppression. Some care, however, needs to be taken in what we infer from this. It does not mean that racial dominance has no specificity apart from class dominance or that heterosexual dominance could not have any specificity apart from gender dominance. That is, it does not follow from the fact that multiple systems of oppression converge to give particular practices a complex texture of meaning that one cannot *conceptually* distinguish racial dominance from gender dominance from sexual orientation dominance. Nor does it follow that there is no good methodological reason for doing so.

One might think about the possibility and point of conceptually distinguishing separate systems on analogy with that of distinguishing conceptually distinct features of good writing. A good piece of writing is one that at the least is grammatical, has no spelling errors, does not mix metaphors, is clear,

---

[8] The example is drawn from Cynthia Peterson, 'Envisioning a Lesbian Equality Jurisprudence', in *Legal Inversions: Lesbians, Gay Men, and the Politics of Law* (Philadelphia: Temple University Press, 1995). 118–37, 122.

and has some narrative or logical order. In any piece of writing, these desiderata do not occur separately. Any one paragraph is likely to satisfy a number of the criteria for good writing. The fact that this is so, however, does not make it impossible to point out which of the criteria are being satisfied where and how. Good grammar may be used in clear prose, indeed may be essential to it; but good grammar and clear prose remain conceptually separable features of a piece of writing.

By the same token, for any particular social practice or experience of oppression where multiple systems of oppression are at work, we can point out those features that make the experience or practice racist, sexist, classist, and so on. Consider, for example, what Patricia Hill Collins has called 'controlling images' of black women—the mammy, the matriarch, the Jezebel, and the welfare mother.[9] Without denying that these are racist images, we can say a lot about what makes these images gendered images, how they are connected across racial lines to other gendered images, and how they function in a general pattern of black and white women's oppression. The mammy image, for example, trades on broad cultural associations between women and domesticity, between women and self-sacrificing virtues, and between motherhood and asexuality. Similarly, without denying that these are sexist images, we can say a lot about what makes these images raced images, how they are connected across gender lines to other raced images, and how they function in a general pattern of racial oppression of both black women and black men. The mammy image, for example, trades on broad cultural associations between being black and failure to establish an adequate family of one's own and between being a good black and being a devoted, faithful servant of whites.

Not only *can* different systems of oppression be conceptually separated, but there is a good methodological reason for trying to tease out the basic structures of different systems of oppression. One cannot even begin to give a complex analysis of the interpenetration of race, sex, and class unless one has first attempted to delineate the basic structures of, say, racial oppression in abstraction from other forms of oppression. One might reasonably think, then, that one also cannot give a complex analysis of the interpenetration of lesbian and gay subordination with race, class, and gender oppression unless one has first attempted to delineate the basic structures of lesbian and gay subordination in abstraction from racism, sexism, and classism. The abstract concept of lesbian and gay subordination makes it possible to answer the question: 'What is specifically heterosexist about this practice or this experience?'

In Chapter 3, my primary aim will be to show how this point has been largely lost in feminist theorizing about lesbians that begins from the assumption that

---

[9] Patricia Hill Collins, *Black Feminist Thought: Knowledge, Consciousness and the Politics of Empowerment* (New York: Routlege, 1990).

feminist analyses must attend to the intersections of race, class, and gender. Race, class, and gender get taken as the exclusive systems of oppression with the result that there is nothing specifically lesbian for them to intersect with. Although dropping lesbian and gay subordination from the list of intersecting axes might be justified by showing that heterosexism is nothing but a byproduct of male dominance, dropping lesbian and gay subordination out of the picture cannot be justified by a methodological appeal to the importance of attending to multiple axes of oppression. That method conceptually depends on there being separable axes to intersect. Thus, that method cannot be used as a rationale *not* to inquire whether heterosexism is itself a separate axis.

To my mind, the most compelling reason for treating lesbian and gay subordination as a separate axis of oppression is a straightforwardly pragmatic one. Here, it will be helpful to call back into view exactly why second wave feminists came under such pressure to thematize race and class. At the time that it was published, Betty Friedan's *The Feminine Mystique* was a path-breaking feminist work.[10] So too was Mary Daly's *Gynecology*.[11] Both, however, in different ways seriously failed to address all women's oppression even while claiming to do so. Friedan's pinpointing 'the problem that has no name' resonated with middle class white women's experience of gender oppression. But it clearly presupposed that women were all located in a relatively moneyed family that could afford to keep the wife out of the paid labor force and in full-time child rearing and domestic labor. Moreover, it presupposed that absent male dominance, all women would have access to meaningful paid labor in the public sphere. From the point of view of black women who confronted a racial division of labor and from the point of view of poor and working class women who did not have the luxury of experiencing 'the problem with no name', but instead entered the paid labor force out of economic necessity, *The Feminine Mystique* was clearly not about their experience of gender oppression.

Taking a different tack from Friedan, Daly in *Gynecology* ruthlessly exposed the extent and nature of patriarchal ideology and invited women to free themselves from internalized gender oppression by reconceiving both social practices and scholarly production as lethal for women. Again, her emphasis on accurately naming the contours of social reality and engaging in a largely conceptual rebellion against patriarchy resonated with white, middle class women, particularly women connected with academia. But from the point of view of women for whom material rather than ideological barriers were most salient, a strategy of naming anti-woman practices, reconceiving women's experience, and transvaluing patriarchal values was clearly not addressed to solving their experiences of gender oppression.

What I want to note about both examples is that there was no *conceptual*

---

[10] Betty Friedan, *The Feminine Mystique* (New York: Norton, 1963).
[11] Mary Daly, *Gynecology* (Boston: Beacon, 1978).

reason why a feminist who set out to describe women's oppression using only the lens of gender oppression would necessarily fail to describe the forms that gender oppression takes for women of color and poor and working class women. After all, black women who complain that they are disproportionately placed in the division of labor as domestic workers are pointing out a fact about the *gender* division of labor. Poor and working class women who complain that they lack the material resources of male peers and are inadequately positioned to care for and support their children are pointing out a fact about the *gendered* distribution of income and responsibility for children. Race and class are certainly relevant to the complete explanation of why different women end up being differently located in patriarchal systems; and understanding the structure of racial and class oppression makes it possible to diagnose the specifically racist and classist dimensions of some women's experience of gender oppression. But even without appeal to race and class as separate axes of oppression, a straightforward gender analysis should not have dropped women of color and poor and working class women out of the picture. Had those feminist writers who were later charged with race- and class-biased accounts begun with a broad base of empirical information about *all* women it would have been clear from the onset that not all women suffered from the problem with no name, that paid labor was not liberating for all women, and that much of women's oppression is a function of their material conditions rather than ideology. The problem of bias to which the method of using separate but intersecting axes of oppression was introduced as a solution was *not* largely methodological. The problem was a practical one. Those producing feminist accounts were almost exclusively white and middle class. The temptation to use their own social location as the vantage point for viewing all women was enormous. The familiarity of white, middle class women's experience, combined with the fact that in a racist and classist culture white, middle class women are constructed as the norm for women, made it highly likely that women of color and poor and working class women would drop out of the picture even though there is nothing about a gender analysis that necessitates the equation of women's oppression with white, middle class women's oppression. Adopting a different method that begins from a set of axes of oppression was in this case primarily a pragmatic move. For the purposes of targeting the variety of factors that sustain women's oppression, the lenses of race and class were not *conceptually* necessary. But for practical reasons deriving from who was producing theories, using those lenses was *pragmatically* necessary as an antidote to the accidental importation of race and class bias into feminist theorizing.

In short, even were it not possible to show that racial dominance and class dominance are separate axes of oppression, there would nevertheless be good pragmatic reasons for adopting a methodological strategy that treats them as separate axes. Lesbians, I will be arguing in Chapters 2 and 3, have also tended to drop out of the feminist picture even in work that is ostensibly about lesbian experience. For example, in the 1980s, heterosexual women's experience of woman-loving was installed as the norm for all woman-loving, including that of lesbians. And throughout the 1980s and 1990s, heterosexual women's experience of gender deviance from the category woman was installed as the norm for all gender deviance, obscuring lesbians' historical relation to a third gender category, the not-womanly invert. Because being heterosexual, like being white and middle class, are socially constructed as the norm for women, there is a real danger that lesbian specificity will drop out of feminist theorizing unless some methodological strategy is adopted that compels attention to lesbian versus heterosexual difference. Thus, even if one remains skeptical that heterosexism is anything more than a byproduct of male dominance, there is nevertheless pragmatic reason to adopt the methodological strategy of treating lesbian and gay subordination as a separate axis of oppression.

## II. Lesbian and Gay Politics

I said at the beginning of this chapter that this book is devoted to two different questions about centering sexual orientation politics. The first is the question of whether and how lesbian theorizing can be centered in a feminist frame. So far, I have been defending the legitimacy of the methodological strategy I will be employing in later chapters, namely, treating lesbian and gay subordination as a separate axis of oppression.

The second question, which is equally thematic, is the question of which political issues belong at the center of a lesbian and gay political agenda and why they belong there. Two strategies are commonly used both to locate which issues are politically important and to explain why addressing them would improve the standing of lesbians and gays. I will employ both strategies in later chapters. What will be new, I hope, are some of the conclusions I arrive at.

The first strategy for locating central political issues is to look for the most serious *effects* of lesbian and gay subordination and then target policies and practices that produce those effects. So, for example, it is commonly claimed that anti-gay employment policies have the serious effect of diminishing lesbian and gay access to income and status by comparison to heterosexuals' access to these same things. If the material costs of discrimination are sufficiently pervasive and serious to constitute an injustice, then securing anti-discrimination protection belongs on a lesbian and gay political agenda. Just how central securing anti-discrimination protection should be to a lesbian and gay politics would depend on how serious one takes the effects of discrimination to be when compared to other policies and practices that also have detrimental effects on gays and lesbians as a group.

The second strategy for locating those issues that belong on a lesbian and gay political agenda is to begin by determining what *ideological representations* of lesbians and gays are used to rationalize the subordinating treatment of lesbians and gays. Policies and practices predicated on those ideologies can then be targeted for political challenge. For example, gay men (and to a lesser extent lesbians) are commonly stereotyped as having poorly controlled sexual desires. Some youth organizations like the Boy Scouts of America use this stereotype to rationalize barring gay men from youth leadership positions. Family courts have also used this stereotype to rationalize not awarding custody to divorcing parents who are gay or lesbian. A gay and lesbian politics should challenge such policies and practices that are based on ideological representations, because it is unfair to treat members of a social group differently on the basis of merely alleged, but in fact nonexistent, differences. In addition, one of the most direct ways of disrupting stigmatizing ideological is to eliminate the policies and practices that reflect and reinforce that particular mistaken representation.

In Chapters 4 to 6, I will be using both of these strategies to argue that anti-discrimination protection, same-sex marriage, and opposition to policies that restrict lesbians' and gay men's access to children belong at the center of a lesbian and gay politics. These are not novel conclusions. However, in reaching those conclusions I will be arguing that we need to rethink *which* effects of subordination and *which* rationalizing ideologies belong at the center of lesbian and gay political arguments. It is generally taken for granted that the relevant serious effects of lesbian and gay subordination are broadly *material* effects (in terms of income, status, education, housing, health care, and the like), and thus that a liberatory political agenda needs to be centered on remedying the material costs of subordination. Arguments for laws protecting lesbians and gays against discrimination, are consequently centered on documenting the material costs of discrimination. It is also generally taken for granted that the primary ideological representations used to rationalize the unequal treatment of lesbians and gays are ones that stigmatize lesbian and gay sexuality. As a result, discussions of sexuality and critiques of sexual regulations, particularly anti-sodomy laws, end up at the center of lesbian and gay political arguments; and historians, anthropologists, and sociologists who aim to produce scholarship that will have a liberatory effect end up focusing on other cultures and time periods that have not stigmatized same-sex sexual practices.

One of my main aims in this book, particularly in Chapter 4, is to challenge the pervasive assumption that the principal serious effect of discriminatory policies is that they undermine lesbians' and gays' material welfare. Centering political concern on the material costs of discriminatory treatment obscures its most serious effect—the displacement of lesbian and gay identities from the public sphere and the displacement of lesbians and gays from a protected private sphere. A second main aim of this book is to challenge the pervasive assumption that gays and lesbians are stigmatized exclusively or primarily for their sexual object choice. Centering political concern around the stigmatizing of same-sex sexuality obscures what I think are more damaging ideological representations—namely, the multiple representations of lesbians and gays as outlaws to the family. In this chapter, I simply want to lay some introductory groundwork for later arguments by, first, briefly introducing the notion of displacement that will be central throughout this book, and second, describing the ideological representations of lesbians and gays which I think, in fact, motivate and rationalize the subordinating treatment of lesbians and gays.

Gender and race oppression impose serious material costs on women and racial minorities. If one assumes that lesbian and gay subordination is directly analogous to gender and race oppression, it makes sense to assume that lesbian and gay subordination also imposes material costs. But, as I will argue in Chapter 4, lesbian and gay subordination is *not* analogous to gender and race oppression. Lesbian and gay identities can be closeted. One's gender or race typically cannot. Because lesbian and gay identities can be closeted, lesbians and gay men can often evade the material costs of discriminatory policies in a way that those who have more visible identities cannot. Thus, if there is a good reason for insisting that lesbians and gays not be treated discriminatorily, that reason is *not* that nondiscriminatory treatment would equalize lesbians' and gays' material position. In Chapter 4, I will argue that, unlike race and gender oppression, the primary serious effect of lesbian and gay subordination is not material disadvantage so much as it is the *displacement* of lesbians and gays from civil society.[12] Discriminatory policies that penalize openly lesbian and gay persons have the effect of requiring everyone to present themselves as heterosexual if they are to have full access to the public sphere. Discriminatory policies thus have the effect of displacing lesbian and gay identities from the public sphere. In addition, lesbians and gay men are displaced from the private sphere through anti-sodomy laws and policies that impose barriers to the formation of lesbian and gay marriages and families.

In contrasting being *disadvantagingly placed* in a way that produces material costs with being *displaced*, I am not suggesting that lesbian and gay subordination has no material costs or that securing anti-discrimination coverage does not belong on a lesbian and gay political agenda. Nor am I suggesting that race and gender oppression never involve the displacement of raced or gendered identities from the public sphere. Minority raced images *are* quite often displaced from cultural visibility. Nor am I suggesting that there are no

---

[12] I have been using the term 'subordination' rather than 'oppression' to refer to lesbians' and gay's political position precisely in order to avoid implying a strong analogy between lesbians and gays on the one hand, and women and racial minorities on the other. Because sexual identity can be closeted, and thus the force of discriminatory policies evaded, 'oppressed' seems the wrong description. In Marilyn Frye's classic description, '[t]he experience of oppressed people is that the living of one's life is confined and shaped by forces and barriers which are not accidental or occasional and hence avoidable, but are systematically related to each other in such a way as to catch one between and among them and restrict or penalize motion in any direction'. *The Politics of Reality* (Freedom, CA: Crossing Press, 1983), 4.

other forms of oppression characterized more by displacement than by being disadvantagingly placed. Anti-Semitism is very much like lesbian and gay subordination in the sense that it requires the closeting of Jewish identity as a condition of full access to the public sphere. What I am suggesting is that if our interest is in determining which issues belong at the *center* of lesbian and gay politics and why they belong there, it is important not to assume uncritically that a lesbian and gay politics should be centered on the same equity issues that have been central to gender and race politics or that the reasons for stressing these equity issues are the same.

Let me turn now to the question of which rationalizing ideologies should be of central concern in lesbian and gay political arguments. The idea that stigma attaches directly to same-sex object choice is a natural enough thought. After all, the defining trait of the identities 'lesbian' and 'gay' seems obviously to be the orientation of desire and activity toward members of the same sex. Lesbian and gay subordination appears, then, to be the direct result of systematically organizing social life around the division of people into two, differently evaluated types—those whose sexual desire and activity is oriented toward members of the opposite sex and those whose sexual desire and activity is oriented toward members of the same sex. The stigmatizing of same-sex sexual object choice as unnatural, pathological, and morally abhorrent produces a set of regulations aimed at controlling or eliminating same-sex sexual interaction and the persons whose defining trait is the desire to engage in same-sex sexual interaction. If one assumes that hostility to same-sex sexual object choice is the primary factor motivating lesbian and gay subordination, it makes sense to put challenges to sexual regulations, especially to anti-sodomy laws, at the center of lesbian and gay politics and to do so for the purpose of legitimating same-sex sexual object choice.

I think this view is mistaken. I will suggest in ensuing chapters that same-sex sexual object choice comes to be stigmatized only because same-sex sexuality is culturally interpreted as inherently connected to *other* more fundamentally stigmatizing characteristics of lesbian and gay identity—three, in particular. First, we as a culture assume that there are two and only two natural, normal, nonpathological sex/gender categories—'woman' and 'man'. However, as I will argue in the next chapter, the orientation of sexual desire and activity toward the opposite sex is partially constitutive of the sex/gender identities 'man' and 'woman'. Gays' and lesbians' sexual orientation toward members of the same sex dislocates them from these two sex/gender categories. Lesbians are not-women. Gays are not-men. It is this latter ideology that explains why same-sex sexuality is so stigmatizing. Engaging in same-sex sexual activity marks one out as an inferior sort of person only if raises doubts about one's manhood or womanhood. Heterosexuals, for example, can often engage in same-sex sexual activity without similar stigma because their heterosexual orientation links them securely to the category 'woman' or 'man'. Lesbians and gays who engage in exactly the same sexual activity are vulnerable to being stigmatized because that activity is culturally read as a sign of their failure to be either real women or real men.

Lesbian and gay sexuality is also stigmatized because it is culturally interpreted as being *qualitatively* different from heterosexual sexuality. Since the popularization of psychoanalytic theories in the mid 1900s, lesbians and gays have been culturally imagined to be prone to pathological sexual excess and a neurotic obsession with sexual gratification. As I will argue in Chapter 6, such sexual excessiveness was taken to mean, among other things, that lesbians and gay men are incapable of sustaining long-term intimate relationships founded on marital or romantic love. Once lesbians and gays are thought to be psychologically incapable of romantic and marital love, it then makes sense to *reduce* lesbian and gay identities to purely sexual identities that have nothing to do with romance, marriage, family, and parenting. Heterosexuality, by contrast, retains a very strong cultural connection with the most esteemed forms of intimate relationships. What makes same-sex sexuality so stigmatizing, then, is not the sheer fact that desire is focused on a same-sex partner. Rather, lesbian and gay sexuality comes to be deeply stigmatizing because it is culturally construed as a kind of sexuality that consumes one's psychology, driving out ennobling emotional attitudes like romantic and marital love.

Finally, taken together, lesbians' and gay men's failure to occupy a nonpathological sex/gender category and their possession of an excessive sexuality makes them fundamentally unfit to participate in the foundational institution of society—the family. Lesbianism and homosexuality represent, in the cultural imagination, a threat to family life. Being neither fully men nor women, gay men and lesbians cannot be counted on to raise properly gendered children. Possessing excessive sexual desires, gay men and lesbians cannot sustain stable marital relationships, nor can they be counted on to refrain from seducing children. These ideological represenations of lesbians and gay men as outlaws to the family are what make same-sex sexuality so stigmatizing.

In sum, a lesbian and gay politics needs to be centered on challenging policies and practices that are predicated on the assumptions that: (1) there are only two natural, normal, nonpathological sex/gender categories, (2) lesbian and gay sexuality differs qualitatively from heterosexual sexuality in being more excessive and compulsive, and (3) lesbians and gays are fundamentally unfit for marriage and family.

Implicit in what I have just said is a rejection of the view that gay and lesbian identities are properly defined simply in terms of the orientation of sexual desire and activity. This narrow or 'simple' definition drops from view too much of the culturally elaborated content of the identities 'lesbian' and 'gay'. As a result, this narrow definition invites a mislocation of lesbian and gay politics. In particular, narrowly defining lesbian and gay identity in terms of sexual object choice makes it seem politically reasonable to focus on legitimatizing same-sex *sex*. Gay historical and anthropological work, for example, often seems to take its political task to be showing that other cultures and time periods have not stigmatized sexual activity between men or between women. But if the contemporary stigma of lesbianism and homosexuality attaches in part to lesbians' and gays' presumed unfitness for participation in the family, then gay historians and anthropologists need to question whether their narratives of cultures that have not penalized same-sex *sexual* activity—but have nevertheless organized marriage and parenting around heterosexuals—are as liberatory as they take them to be. They also need to question whether their narratives of cultures that assume that there are only two (normal) sex/gender categories and that tolerate same-sex sex in 'real' men are as liberatory as they take them to be. Finally, the popular assumption that pursuing same-sex marriage rights is less radical and thus less critical to lesbian and gay politics than pursuing liberalized legal and educational policies with respect to same-sex sex needs to be critically reassessed.

In addition, the assumption that being sexually oriented toward members of the same sex is the defining trait of lesbians and gay men, has obscured the politics of theorizing about lesbians within a feminist frame that takes its subject to be women. Feminists have been able to assume uncritically that lesbians and heterosexual women are equally *women*, differing only in their sexual object choice. By contrast, I will be arguing in Chapter 2, and even more so in Chapter 3, that because lesbian identity is partially constituted by failure to fit within the sex/gender binary 'woman' and 'man', feminist theorizing needs to take more seriously the question of whether theorizing about *women* ultimately excludes lesbians from the picture.

My point, of course, is not that same-sex sexual object choice is irrelevant to lesbian and gay identity. It is, rather, that the orientation of sexual desire and activity does not exhaust the content of the identities 'lesbian' and 'homosexual' as they have been socially constructed over the past century. Locating the ideologies that rationalize lesbian and gay subordination requires a more expansive account of the cultural content of these identities.

## III. Identity, Essentialism, Constructionism

The term 'identity' is ambiguous. 'Identity' can refer to the social category that people take themselves to occupy, or are taken by others to occupy (e.g. a lesbian, a professor, a woman). Identity in this sense can be contested. We can dispute whether or not an individual really does occupy a particular social category. Questions about identity in this sense sometimes take a normative form, for example: 'Who counts as a *real* lesbian?' 'Identity' can also refer to the subjective experience of living with a particular identity and to the subjective meaning that that identity has for oneself. In this case, questions about identity are typically questions about what it has meant to the individual to live life, say, as a lesbian and how she interprets what having a lesbian identity does and does not involve. Lesbian autobiographies and narrative-based studies of lesbians are about identity in this sense.[13] They give us detailed accounts of the multiplicity of experiences of being lesbian and conceptions of lesbianism, including descriptions of how lesbian identity is differently inflected by one's class, race, religious, and ethnic identities.

In this book, I am not concerned with 'identity' in either of these senses. My concern is with the *culturally authorized* conception of how lesbianism and homosexuality differ from heterosexuality. Although lesbians and gays have influenced that conception, they have not been in a position to authorize or culturally disseminate their own developed understandings of what it means to be lesbian or gay. The culturally authorized conception has instead emerged largely from within medical, psychiatric, and scientific work. Government policy, laws and legal reasoning, literature, the media, and religion have also had a hand in constructing the culturally authorized conception of lesbianism and homosexuality. That conception shapes and is reinforced by routine social practices, such as the practices of closeting lesbian and gay identity and of discriminating against lesbians and gays.

The culturally authorized conception plays both a negative and positive role. Negatively, it supplies the ideological rationales for lesbian and gay subordination. In Chapter 6, for example, I will examine three phases in the historical construction of lesbian and gay identity that have rationalized treating lesbians and gay men as outlaws to the family. Positively, the culturally authorized conception makes lesbians and gay men 'legible' in the first place. That is, it is possible to read individuals' behavior and self-presentation as lesbian or gay rather than heterosexual only because there are culturally authorized conceptions of lesbian and gay difference. In Chapter 3, for example, I will suggest that reading individuals as lesbian or gay depends on being able to see them as falling outside the sex/gender binary 'man' and 'woman'.

My concern with the cultural content of our conceptions of lesbianism and homosexuality as it has developed since the end of the 1800s places me squarely in the social constructionist camp. Social constructionists take sexuality to be a social fact about persons, not a natural fact. On this view, there is no such thing as sexuality *simpliciter*. Rather, cultures create the possibility of being sexual by supplying 'sexual' with a culture-specific meaning; and different cultures may construct substantially different scripts for being sexual. Homosexuality and lesbianism, too, are social, not natural facts, about persons. By supplying meaningful content to a concept of homosexuality, and a script for enacting a homosexual identity, a culture creates the opportunity for individuals to be homosexual in much the same way that a culture can create the opportunity for individuals to be a peasant or a Democrat. Understanding what it means to be sexual or to have a sexual

---

[13] Kath Weston's *Render Me, Gender Me*, for example, is about identities in this sense (New York: Columbia University Press, 1996).

orientation, then, is always a matter of understanding how a particular culture or a particular time period understands those possibilities. Capturing the complex cultural content of 'sexual' or 'sexual orientation' requires complex definitions of these notions. Essentialists, by contrast, assume that sexuality and sexual orientations are natural facts about persons. So, for example, if a person is lesbian, she would be lesbian no matter which culture or time period she were transported to. And, since having a sexual orientation, on the essentialist view, does not depend on whether or not the culture has a conception of homosexuality or heterosexuality, there may in fact have been homosexuals in all cultures and all time periods. Since what it means to have a sexual orientation is not culture-specific, a simple definition such as 'persistent desire for persons of the same sex/gender' may suffice.[14]

My approach in this book is a constructionist one with one qualification. While constructionists contest, as I do, the utility of using narrow definitions of lesbians' and gays' identity, they have not always contested essentialists' narrow focus on *sex*. David Halperin, for example, does not reject essentialist definitions because they drop from view lesbians and gays different sex/gender categorization or their construction as outlaws to the family. He objects because, in his view, the very concept of a sexual orientation is a modern, western invention.[15] Medical and psychiatric discourses beginning in the late nineteenth century invented the idea of a sexual orientation that constitutes a deep feature of one's personality. The invention of distinct personality types connected to sexual object choice, he argues, provided the cultural opportunity to *be* lesbian or homosexual. By contrast, as I suggested in the previous section, I want to challenge the assumption underlying both essentialist and some constructionist views that sexual object choice is *the* defining feature of lesbian and gay identities.

The constructionist approach to lesbian and gay identity has often seemed to pose an insuperable barrier to doing lesbian and gay history and anthropology. It entails that if a culture does not share our detailed conception of lesbian and gay identity there are no lesbians and gays in that culture. Absent real lesbians and gays to study, no lesbian and gay history or anthropology can be done. As a result, key players in standard gay history and anthropology must be eliminated. For example, it would seem that on a constructionist view the sexual man–boy relationships of Ancient Athens should *not* be described

[14] For very helpful overviews of the essentialism-constructionism debate, see Daniel R. Ortiz, 'Creating Controversy: Essentialism/Constructivism and the Politics of Gay Identity', *Virginia Law Review* 79(1993): 1833–57; Edward Stein, 'The Essentials of Constructionism and the Construction of Essentialism', *Forms of Desire: Sexual Orientation and the Social Constructionist Controversy*, ed. Edward Stein (New York: Routledge, 1992); Edward Stein, *The Mismeasure of Desire: The Science, Theory, and Ethics of Sexual Orientation* (Oxford University Press, 1999).

[15] David Halperin, 'Is There a History of Sexuality?' in *The Lesbian and Gay Studies Reader*, ed. Henry Abelove, Michele Aina Barale, and David M. Halperin (New York: Routledge, 1993), 416–31. See also Jonathan Katz, *The Invention of Heterosexuality* (New York: Dutton, 1995).

as homosexual relationships. This is because, as Morris Kaplan puts it: 'Athenians of the fifth century did not understand themselves as defined by their desires for objects of a specific gender or biological sex. What mattered was the political and social status and age of the object of desire, as well as the sexual practices in which the citizen engaged'.[16] Nor are the Native American *berdache*, who function as members of the opposite sex, obvious players in a constructionist history, since their gender difference from their sexual partners disqualifies them from being culturally read as different from 'heterosexuals'. Indeed, it may turn out that there are no lesbians or gays at all outside western society since the late nineteenth century.

This unfortunate upshot of the constructionist approach makes essentialism more appealing. As I said above, essentialists assume that there really is some natural fact about persons that makes them oriented toward same-sex sexual activity even if that natural fact is not cross-culturally recognized and elaborated. Historical and anthropological records might then be searched for evidence of the existence of persons who have this natural property, just as we might search for evidence of hemophilia or epilepsy in cultures that do not recognize these medical conditions.

While invoking the essentialist's narrow definition of lesbian and gay identity may get us around the main problem with constructionism, it leaves in place the very problem that motivated constructionism in the first place. There is certainly something odd about subsuming under the identity categories, 'lesbian' and 'gay', people who, from their own culture's perspective did not differ from (what we would call) heterosexuals in their culture. Cultures simply do not always attach significance to the fact that a sex partner is anatomically similar. In some cultures, for example, the fact that males have sex with other males does not mark them out as sexually different from males who do not, provided that they occupy the dominant position and do not permit penetration of themselves. In others, they are not marked out as different so long as one is a man and one is a boy. In others, lack of difference from 'heterosexual' males is preserved by adopting a masculine gender role in relation to a femininely gendered male. In our own culture, some men claim that they are heterosexual because they are only occasionally having sex with other men or because the males they are having sex with are drag queens who are 'real women'. Thus, what one does while having sex, how often one has sex with anatomically similar people, what the relative ages of the two people are, and what the gender roles of the two people are may be the significant factors distinguishing sexual actors—*not* the fact that a person is regularly having same-sex sex.

The solution to this particular dilemma over whether essentialism or constructionism is the preferred basis for doing history and anthropology is,

[16] Morris B. Kaplan, *Sexual Justice: Democratic Citizenship and the Politics of Desire* (New York: Routledge, 1997), 54.

I think, to rethink what the point of doing lesbian and gay history is. It is a political one. When we look across cultures and time periods at persons who, if transported to *our* culture would qualify as lesbian or gay, we discover a politically significant fact. There has never been a universal taboo on same-sex desire as we understand it. Many cultures regard sexual interaction between men as compatible with being heterosexual. Some cultures, notably ancient Greece have valorized what *we* see as man–boy homosexuality, ranking it over what *we* see as heterosexuality. Other cultures, for example in New Guinea and Melanesia, have prescribed sexual interaction between men and boys as a necessary transition to heterosexual adulthood. Similarly, there has never been a universal taboo on same-sex romantic intimacies. Native American and some African cultures have institutionalized what to *our* eyes look like same-sex marriages. The nineteenth-century Boston marriages institutionalized what to *our* eyes look like lesbian partnerships. What studies like Kenneth Dover's history of Greek homosexuality[17] or histories of same-sex marriage underscore is the parochialism, and from a global point of view arbitrariness, of our culture's obsessive aversion to sexual interaction and intimate partnerships between men or between women. Seen in this light, contemporary sodomy laws, proscriptions on gays and lesbians in the military, bars to same-sex marriage, and legal toleration of discrimination against gays and lesbians seem insupportable. They cannot be justified by appeal to the naturally abhorrent nature of same-sex sex. The historical and cross-cultural record suggests that there is nothing natural at all in our culture's intolerance.

Gay history and anthropology thus serve as valuable political tools when they begin from our contemporary, western, complex definition of lesbian and gay identity and then search the historical and cultural records for people who, if transported to our culture, would be categorized as lesbian or gay. What matters is not, for example, whether the Greeks regarded man–boy sexual interaction as homosexual. What matters is that we do. Only by looking at how people that we 'read' as lesbian or gay were treated can gay history and anthropology reveal the arbitrariness of our contemporary hostility to lesbianism and homosexuality. Deciding whom to include in gay and lesbian history and anthropology by asking: 'Whom can *we* read as gay or lesbian?' need not distort the historical or anthropological record so long as we are self-conscious about what we are doing. That individuals get into gay and lesbian histories and anthropologies because we read them as gay or lesbian does not entail that historians and anthropologists should not also attend to how these individuals would have been categorized and complexly described from their own culture's perspective. In short, constructivists can do history and anthropology. Doing so, however, requires adopting the fiction that our own categories can be applied across cultures and across time periods to determine

---

[17] Kenneth Dover, *Greek Homosexuality* (New York: Vintage, 1980).

who is gay or lesbian. That is, it requires treating our identity categories as though they pick out a transtemporal and transcultural essence. In doing so, we employ *fictional essences*, since the persons picked out may well not be read by their own culture and time period as bearing the traits that we attribute to lesbians and gays.

# 2

# Separating Lesbian Theory from Feminist Theory

Heidi Hartmann once said of the marriage of Marxism and feminism that it 'has been like the marriage of husband and wife depicted in English common law: marxism and feminism are one, and that one is marxism'.[1] In this and the following chapter, I want to suggest that lesbian theory and feminism are at risk of falling into a similar unhappy marriage in which 'that one' is feminism. The focus here will be largely on lesbian feminist theorizing in the 1980s. In the next chapter, I will argue that 1990s feminism, which is committed to articulating differences between women, nevertheless fails to make room for fully *lesbian* feminist theorizing.

Although lesbian feminist theorizing has significantly contributed to feminist thought, it has also generally treated lesbianism as a kind of applied issue. Feminist theories developed outside the context of lesbianism are brought to bear on lesbianism in order to illuminate the nature of lesbian oppression and women's relation to women within lesbianism. So, for example, early radical lesbians began from the feminist claim that all male–female relationships are dominance relationships. They then argued either that the lesbian is *the* paradigm case of the patriarchal resister because she refuses to be heterosexual[2] or that she fits on a continuum of types of patriarchal resisters.[3] In taking this line, lesbian theorists made a space for lesbianism by focusing on what they took to be the inherently feminist and anti-patriarchal nature of lesbian existence. Somewhat later, lesbian theorists were less inclined to read lesbianism as feminist resistance to male dominance.[4] Instead, following the trend that feminist theory itself took, the focus largely shifted to women's relation to women: the presence of ageism, racism, and anti-Semitism among lesbians, the problem of avoiding a totalizing discourse that speaks for all lesbians without being

---

[1] Heidi Hartmann, 'The Unhappy Marriage of Marxism and Feminism', in *Feminist Frameworks*, 2nd edn, ed. Alison M. Jaggar and Paula S. Rothenberg (New York: McGraw-Hill, 1984), 172–89, 172.

[2] See e.g. Charlotte Bunch, 'Lesbians in Revolt', in *Passionate Politics, Essays 1968–1986* (New York: St. Martin's Press, 1987), 161–7; and Monique Wittig, *The Straight Mind and Other Essays* (Boston: Beacon, 1992).

[3] Adrienne Rich, 'Compulsory Heterosexuality and Lesbian Existence', in *The Signs Reader: Women, Gender, and Scholarship*, ed. Elizabeth Abel and Emily K. Abel (Chicago: University of Chicago Press, 1983), 139–68.

[4] For instance, Jeffner Allen states in her introduction to the anthology *Lesbian Philosophies and Cultures* (Albany, NY: State University of New York Press, 1990, 1–11), 'The primary emphasis of this book is *lesbian* philosophies and cultures, rather than lesbianism considered in relation to or in contrast to, patriarchy, or heterosexuality', p. 1.

sensitive to differences, the difficulty of creating community in the face of political differences (e.g. on the issue of sadomasochism), and the need to construct new conceptions of female agency and female friendship.[5] All of these are issues that had their birthplace in feminist theory. They became lesbian issues only because the general concern with women's relation to women was narrowed to lesbians' relation to fellow lesbians. Once again, lesbian thought became applied feminist thought.

Now, there is nothing wrong with using feminist tools to analyze lesbianism. Indeed, something would be wrong with feminist theory if it could not be usefully applied to lesbianism in a way that both illuminates lesbianism and extends feminist theory itself. And there would surely be something lacking in lesbian thought if it did not make use of feminist insights. My worry is that if this is all that lesbian-feminism amounts to then there is no lesbian *theory*. Lesbian theory and feminist theory are one, and that one is feminist theory. What more could one want?

When Hartmann complained that Marxism was like the husband in English common law, her point was that because traditional Marxism lacks a notion of sex-class, and thus of patriarchy as a political system distinct from capitalism, it must treat women's oppression as a special case of class oppression. Marxism is of necessity blind to the irreducibly gendered nature of women's lives. A parallel complaint might be raised about feminist theory. To the extent that feminist theory lacks a concept of heterosexuals and nonheterosexuals as members of different sexuality classes and thus of lesbian and gay subordination as a political structure separable from patriarchy, feminist theory must treat lesbian oppression as a special case of patriarchal oppression and remain blind to the irreducibly lesbian nature of lesbian lives.

Lesbian-feminism has been for several reasons at high risk of doing just that. First, the most extensive analyses of heterosexuality available to feminists are those developed in the late 1970s and early 1980s by Charlotte Bunch, Gayle Rubin, Adrienne Rich, Monique Wittig, and Kate Millett.[6] Heterosexuality, on this account, is both product and essential support of patriarchy. Women's heterosexual orientation perpetuates their social, economic, emotional, and sexual dependence on and accessibility by men. Heterosexuality is thus a system of male ownership of women, participation in which is compulsory for men and especially for women. The lesbian's and heterosexual woman's relation to heterosexuality on this account are fundamentally the same. Both experience it as the demand that women be dependent on and accessible by men.

---

[5] See e.g. the anthology, *Lesbian Philosophies and Cultures*, as well as Sarah Lucia Hoagland's *Lesbian Ethics: Toward New Value* (Palo Alto, CA: Institute of Lesbian Studies, 1988) and Janice G. Raymond's *A Passion for Friends* (Boston: Beacon, 1986).

[6] Charlotte Bunch, ' "Lesbians in Revolt", Learning from Lesbian Separatism', 182–91, and 'Lesbian-Feminist Theory', 196–202, in *Passionate Politics*; Gayle Rubin, 'The Traffic in Women', in *Toward an Anthropology of Women*, ed. Rayna Reiter (New York: Monthly Review Press, 1975), 157–210; Kate Millett, *Sexual Politics* (New York: Doubleday, 1969); Rich, 'Compulsory Heterosexuality and Lesbian Existence'; Wittig, *The Straight Mind*.

Both are vulnerable to penalties if they resist that demand. Thus, heterosexuality is equally compulsory for heterosexual women and lesbians; and compulsory heterosexuality *means* the same thing for both. There is no specifically lesbian relation to heterosexuality.

Second, lesbian feminists have had to assert their differences from gay men and thus their distance from both the political aims and the self-understanding of the gay movement. The gay rights movement has suffered from at least two defects. On the one hand, in focusing on lesbians' and gays' shared status as sexual deviants, the gay rights movement was unable to address the connection between lesbian oppression and women's oppression. On the other hand, it tended to equate gay with gay *male* and failed to address the patriarchal attitudes embedded in the gay rights movement itself.[7] Making clear the difference between lesbians and gay men meant that lesbian feminists' focus had to be on the experience of lesbians in a patriarchal culture, *not* on their experience as deviants in a heterosexist culture.

Third, the fact that to be lesbian is to live out of intimate relation with men and in intimate relation with women encourages the reduction of 'lesbian' to 'feminist'.[8] Early radical feminists were quite explicit about this, claiming that lesbians are the truly woman-identified women. Contemporary lesbian feminists, recognizing that lesbians may share patriarchal attitudes toward women, resist such grand claims. But even if lesbian-feminism is no longer at risk of equating being lesbian with being a true feminist, the danger remains that it may equate lesbian issues with feminist issues. If what count as lesbian issues are only those visible through a feminist lens, then lesbian issues will simply be a special class of feminist ones.

Finally, the historical circumstances that gave birth to lesbian-feminism had a decided impact on the direction that lesbian-feminism took. The first major lesbian feminist statement, 'The Woman Identified Woman', was a direct response to Betty Friedan's charge that lesbians posed a 'lavender menace' to the women's movement.[9] In the view of Friedan and many members of the National Organization for Women (NOW) the association of feminism with lesbianism, and thus with deviancy, undermined the credibility of women's rights claims. Threatened with ostracism from the women's movement, the Radicalesbians argued in 'The Woman Identified Woman' that

---

[7] See e.g. Marilyn Frye's critical assessment of the gay rights movement in 'Lesbian Feminism and the Gay Rights Movement: Another View of Male Supremacy, Another Separatism' in *The Politics of Reality* (Freedom, CA: Crossing Press, 1983), 128–52, as well as John Stoltenberg's 'Sadomasochism: Eroticized Violence, Eroticized Powerlessness' in *Against Sadomasochism*, ed. Robin Ruth Linden *et al.* (San Francisco: Frog in the Well, 1982), 124–30.

[8] Bunch, for example, observes that '[l]esbianism and feminism are both about women loving and supporting women and women revolting against the so-called supremacy of men and the patriarchal institutions that control us' ('Lesbian-Feminist Theory', in *Passionate Politics*), 196.

[9] For brief historical discussions of this event, see Shane Phelan's 'The Woman-Identified Woman', in *Identity Politics: Lesbian Feminism and the Limits of Community* (Philadelphia: Temple University Press, 1989), 37–58, and Terralee Bensinger's 'Lesbian Pornography: The Re/Making of (a) Community', in *Discourse* 15 (1992): 69–93.

lesbians, because they love women and refuse to live with or devote their energies to the oppressor, are the paradigm feminists.[10] The political climate of the
1970s women's movement thus required lesbian feminists to assert their allegiance to feminist aims and values rather than calling attention to lesbians'
differences from their heterosexual sisters. It was neither the time nor the place
for lesbians to entertain the possibility that lesbian and gay subordination
might itself be a political system and that heterosexual women and men, as a
consolidated and powerful class, might have strong interests in maintaining a
system of heterosexual privileges. In affirming their commitment to opposing
patriarchy, lesbian feminists instead committed themselves to a specifically
feminist account of the interests motivating the maintenance of institutionalized heterosexuality. Specifically, men have patriarchal interests in securing
sexual/emotional access to women, and heterosexual women have complici-
tous interests in securing access to a system of male privileges. This move effectively barred lesbian feminists from asking whether heterosexual women and
men have, as heterosexuals, a class interest in constructing heterosexual sex as
the only real, nonimitative sex, in eliminating historical, literary, and media
representations of lesbians and gay men, in reserving jobs, public accommod-
ations, and private housing for heterosexuals only, in barring lesbians and gay
men from access to children in the educational system, children's service organizations, and adoption and artificial insemination agencies, in reducing
lesbianism and homosexuality to biologically or psychodevelopmentally
rooted urges while propagating the myth of a magical heterosexual romantic
love, and in securing for the married heterosexual couple exclusive pride of
place in the social world. Nor could or did lesbian feminists ask whether these
privileges, taken as a set, could provide a sufficient motivating interest for
maintaining lesbian and gay subordination even in the absence of patriarchy.

For all four reasons, treating sexual orientation on a par with gender, race,
and economic class (i.e. as a distinct and irreducible dimension of one's political identity) did not come naturally to lesbian feminist thinking throughout
the 1980s. But separating sexuality politics from gender politics is exactly what
needed to happen if there were to be a specifically lesbian feminist theory
rather than simply feminist theory applied to lesbians. A lesbian feminist
theory would need, among other considerations, to focus on what is distinctive about the lesbian's relation to heterosexuality, to the category 'woman', and
to other women. That is, it would need to put into clear view the difference
between being a lesbian who resists heterosexuality, who resists being a
woman, and who resists loving men rather than women and being a feminist
who resists the same things.

In what follows, I will be continuing the argument introduced in Chapter
1, that, like patriarchy and capitalism, gender oppression and lesbian and gay

[10] Radicalesbians, 'The Woman Identified Woman', in *Radical Feminism*, ed. Anne Koedt *et al.* (New
York: Quadrangle, 1973), 240–5.

subordination are two, in principle, separable systems. Even where they work together, it is possible conceptually to pull the patriarchal aspects of social relations apart from their heterosexist ones. In arguing for the conceptual separability of lesbian and gay subordination from gender oppression, I hope to establish two main points in this chapter. First, lesbianism ought not to be read solely as a resistance to patriarchal male–female relationships. One misses a good deal of what it means to live life as a lesbian as well as much of the political significance of lesbian practices by doing so. Second, even if empirically and historically lesbian and gay subordination and gender oppression are completely intertwined, it does not follow from this fact that the end of gender oppression will bring about the end of lesbian and gay subordination.[11] Heterosexism may simply take new forms adapted to fit changed social conditions. Thus, it is a mistake for feminists to assume that work to end gender subordination will have as much payoff for lesbians as it would for heterosexual women. Only a political strategy that keeps clearly in mind the distinction between gender oppression and lesbian and gay subordination— as well as the potential for conflict between feminist and lesbian political strategies—could have such a payoff.

In making this argument, I will take the category 'woman' and the institution of heterosexuality in turn. My aim in both cases is to illustrate the difference between being a lesbian and being a feminist, and between lesbian politics and feminist politics.

## I. The Lesbian Not-woman

Monique Wittig ends 'The Straight Mind' with the assertion, 'Lesbians are not women'.[12] Wittig denies that 'man' and 'woman' are natural categories, arguing instead that the two sex-classes—men and women—are the product of heterosexual social relations in which 'men appropriate for themselves the reproduction and production of women and also their physical persons by means of a contract called the marriage contract'.[13] Thus, '[i]t is oppression that creates sex and not the contrary'.[14] Lesbians, however, refuse to participate in heterosexual social relations. Like runaway slaves who refuse to have their labor appropriated by white masters, lesbians are runaways who refuse to allow men to control their productive and reproductive labor within a nuclear family. Thus, Wittig observes:

Lesbianism is the only concept I know of which is beyond the categories of sex (woman and man), because the designated subject (lesbian) is not a woman, either economically, or politically, or ideologically. For what makes a woman is a specific

---

[11] I thank Ann Ferguson for pointing out that capitalism and patriarchy are empirically and historically intertwined, even if conceptually separate, and for suggesting that the same might be true of the heterosexual and patriarchal aspects of male/female relationships.

[12] Wittig, 'The Straight Mind', in *The Straight Mind and Other Essays*, 21–32, 32.

[13] Wittig, 'The Category of Sex', in *The Straight Mind*, 1–8, 6.          [14] Ibid. 2.

social relation to a man, a relation that we have previously called servitude, a relation which implies personal and physical obligation as well as economic obligation ('forced residence', domestic corvée, conjugal duties, unlimited production of children, etc.), a relation which lesbians escape by refusing to become or to stay heterosexual.[15]

Wittig's explanation here of what bars lesbians from the category 'woman' claims both too much and too little for lesbians as well as reads lesbianism from a peculiarly heterosexual viewpoint. To say that only lesbians exist beyond sex categories (in Wittig's particular sense of what this means) claims too much for lesbians. If to be a woman just means living in a relation of servitude to men, there will be other ways short of lesbianism of evading the category 'woman'. The heterosexual celibate, virgin, single-parent head of household, marriage resister, or the married woman who insists on an egalitarian marriage contract all apparently qualify as escapees from the category 'woman'.[16]

Although Wittig does remark that runaway wives are also escaping their sex-class, she clearly thought that lesbians are in some special sense *not women*. But her own analysis does not capture lesbians' special deviancy from the category 'woman'. There is indeed no conceptual space in Wittig's framework for pursuing the question of how a heterosexual woman's refusal to be a woman differs from a lesbian's refusal to be a woman. It is in that failure that she claims too little for lesbians. Because lesbians and heterosexual resisters must have, on her account, the same relation to the category 'woman', there can be no interesting differences between the two. This, I think, is a mistake, and I will argue shortly, and more extensively in the next chapter, that lesbians are in a quite special sense not-women.

Finally, to equate lesbians' escape from heterosexuality and the category 'woman' with escape from male control is to adopt a peculiarly heterosexual viewpoint on lesbianism. The fact that heterosexuality enables men to control women's domestic labor is something that would be salient only to a *heterosexual* woman. Only heterosexual women do housework for men, raise children for men, have their domicile determined by men, and so on. Thus, from a heterosexual standpoint lesbianism may indeed appear to offer a liberating escape from male control. But from the standpoint of a woman unaccustomed to living with men (i.e. from a *lesbian* standpoint), lesbianism is not about a refusal to labor for men. Nor is heterosexuality experienced primarily as a form of male dominance over women, but instead as heterosexual dominance over lesbians and gay men. Nor is the daily experience of lesbianism one of liberation, but instead one of subordination within a system that privileges heterosexuals.

[15] Monique Wittig, 'One is Not Born a Woman', in *The Straight Mind*, 9–21, 20.
[16] This point has been made by a number of authors including Marilyn Frye ('Some Reflections on Separatism and Power', in *The Politics of Reality*, 95–109); and Kathryn Pyne Addelson ('Words and Lives', *Signs* 7 (1981): 187–99).

Because Wittig looks at lesbianism from a (heterosexual) feminist perspective, asking how lesbians escape the kinds of male control to which heterosexual women are often subject, she misses the penalties attached to lesbians' exit from heterosexuality. Indeed, contrary to Wittig's claim, the lesbian may as a rule have *less* control over her productive and reproductive labor than her married heterosexual sister. Although the lesbian escapes whatever control *individual* men may exercise over their wives within marriage, she does not thereby escape control of her productive and reproductive labor either in her personal life with another lesbian or in her public life. To refuse to be heterosexual is simply to leap out of the frying pan of individual patriarchal control into the fire of institutionalized heterosexual control over both the public and private spheres. Wittig's claim that 'lesbianism provides for the moment the only social form in which we can live freely' vastly underestimates the coercive forces brought to bear on the lesbian for her lesbianism.[17] She may be unable to adopt children or be denied custody of and visiting privileges to her children. In order to retain her job, she will most likely have to hide her lesbianism and pretend to be heterosexual. She will likely be punished for public displays of affection. She may be denied the housing of her choice or be forced to move from her home as a result of harassment by neighbors. If she is uncloseted, she will find herself abused or subjected to lascivious interest by heterosexual men. Even if she is no longer at risk of being burned at the stake or subjected to clitoridectomy or electroshock, she may still be subjected to 'therapies' that insist that she cannot be both lesbian and a healthy, mature adult. She will be labeled a dyke and scrutinized for symptoms of mannishness in her anatomy, dress, behavior, and interests. She will not see her lesbian sexuality or romantic love for another woman reflected in the public media. And both because there are no publicly accessible models of lesbian relationships and because such coercive pressure is brought to bear against lesbian relationships, sustaining a stable personal life will be more difficult for lesbians than it is for heterosexual women. The lesbian may be free from an individual man in her personal life, but she is not free.

What these criticisms suggest is, first, that the political structure that oppresses heterosexual women is patriarchy; but the political structure that most acutely oppresses lesbians is more plausibly taken to be heterosexual dominance. Second, these criticisms suggest that heterosexual women's (especially heterosexual feminists') and lesbians' relation to the category 'woman' are not the same.

From a feminist point of view, the problem with the category 'woman' is not so much that there is one. The problem lies in its specific construction within patriarchal society. 'Woman' has been constructed as the Other and the deficient in relation to 'man'. To 'woman' have been assigned all those traits that would both rationalize and perpetuate women's lack of power in relation

---

[17] Wittig, 'One is Not Born a Woman', in *The Straight Mind*, 20.

to men. Women are weak, passive, dependent, emotional, irrational, nurturant, closer to nature, maternal, and so on. This is to say, that from a feminist point of view, the problem with the category woman is that 'woman' has been equated with subordination to men. The feminist task, then, is to rupture that equation. With the exception of early liberal feminists' recommendation of androgyny and possibly some contemporary attempts to deconstruct 'woman', the feminist project has *not* been the elimination of the category 'woman'. Instead, the project has been one of reconstructing that category. That reconstructive project has had two phases within feminism. The first phase tried to reconstruct the category 'woman' so that it could no longer be used to rationalize male dominance. So, for example, some feminine traits were rejected, others, such as nurturance, were revalued and/or redefined, and some masculine traits (e.g. strength) were appropriated with or without redefinition.[18] The more recent phase has been devoted to reconstructing the category 'woman' employed within feminism itself so that it cannot be used to rationalize white, middle class, college-educated, heterosexual, Christian women's dominance within feminism.[19] This latter reconstruction has required the postulate of multiple categories of 'woman' to capture the intersection of gender with other political identities.[20]

The feminist experience of her relation to the category 'woman', thus, has been the experience of *being* a woman in a male-dominant, as well as racist and classist, society, which imposes on her a conception of what it means to be a woman that she rejects. Her refusal to be a woman has extended only to a refusal to be the kind of woman that a patriarchal, racist, and classist society demands that she be. And that refusal has gone hand in hand with claiming the category 'woman' (or categories of 'women') for herself and insisting on a revised construction of that category.

This is not the lesbian relation to the category 'woman'. Although mistaken, I think, in her reasons, Wittig was correct to say that to be lesbian is to exit the category 'woman' altogether. It is to be ungendered and unsexed within a binary scheme of 'woman' and 'man'. As I will explain at greater length in the next chapter, the beginnings of our contemporary concept of the lesbian emerged at the turn of the century with the invention of a third sex category, that of the invert. The construction of lesbians as a third sex that inverts the 'natural' gender for women by enacting masculinity on a female body has, as I will argue in Chapter 6, since been overlain with additional meanings, especially those of sexual pathology and excess. For the moment, however, what is

---

[18] Joyce Trebilcott neatly summarizes these reconstructive strategies in 'Conceiving Women: Notes on the Logic of Feminism', in *Women and Values: Readings in Recent Feminist Philosophy*, ed. Marilyn Pearsall (Belmont, CA: Wadsworth, 1986), 358–64.

[19] See, e.g. Marilyn Frye's 'A Response to *Lesbian Ethics*: Why Ethics?', in *Feminist Ethics*, ed. Claudia Card (Lawrence, KS: University Press of Kansas, 1991), 52–9; and Elizabeth V. Spelman's *Inessential Woman: Problems of Exclusion in Feminist Thought* (Boston: Beacon, 1988).

[20] Elizabeth V. Spelman argues elegantly for the necessity of multiple categories in *Inessential Woman*.

important to call into view is the fact that lesbians were originally conceptualized as beings who occupy a middle position between men and women. Lesbians (and gays) became conceivable by imagining a type of person for whom failure to fit into a binary scheme was their defining trait. Late nineteenth and early twentieth century sexologists' theories instituted, at the same time that they pathologized, a middle position between 'man' and 'woman'. Later psychoanalytic theories of lesbianism and homosexuality, in their telling of the developmental story of lesbianism, also instituted, at the same time that they pathologized, a new category of psycho-sexual personality that did not neatly fit into the sex/gender binarism of 'man' and 'woman'.

What makes a woman a woman and a man a man are the 'relations of coherence and continuity among sex, gender, sexual practice, and desire'.[21] That is, the category 'woman' is constructed along at least three dimensions: female anatomy, feminine genderization, and heterosexual desire for men.[22] From the late nineteenth century on, lesbians were conceptualized in relation to sex/gender binarism by imagining a kind of person who, while still having some link to the category 'woman', nevertheless violated the unity of female anatomy, heterosexual desire, and gender behavior. In particular, she might be suspected of not being a real woman along all three dimensions. Neither anatomy nor desire nor gender links her securely to the category 'woman'. She is, first of all, a being whose female anatomy is suspect. Early modern anatomists connected tribadism with possession of an enlarged clitoris.[23] Later, sexologists emphasized the physical masculinity of the lesbian, including the possibility of an enlarged clitoris and hermaphroditism. The postulate of a genetic basis of homosexuality and lesbianism has been prominent in recent research. And many lesbians' insistence on having been born lesbian reinforces such suspicions about genetic differences from heterosexual women. In addition, her anatomy cannot link her securely to 'woman', because unlike 'real' women, her female anatomy fails to destine her to be functionally a woman. That is, the lesbian's female body is not essentially connected with femininity and, moreover, is connected with functioning, in part, as a man in relation to women. She shares with members of the category 'man' a sexual desire for and love of women. That sexual desire for women removes her from the category 'woman'. And, as I will describe in the next chapter, lesbians were made imaginable during the late nineteenth century by constructing a type of person for whom gender deviance was a natural, if pathological, condition. That view continues to be partially constitutive of contemporary conceptions of lesbian identity. Thus, the very traits that Wittig took to be definitive of

---

[21] Judith Butler, *Gender Trouble: Feminism and the Subversion of Identity* (New York: Routledge, 1990), 17.
[22] Jacob Hale provides a useful and more complicated articulation of the features that are employed in deciding who fits the category 'woman' in 'Are Lesbians Women?' *Hypatia* 11 (1996): 94–121.
[23] Valerie Traub, 'The Psychomorphology of the Clitoris', *Gay and Lesbian Quarterly* 2 (1995): 81–113.

'man'—the enactment of masculine dominance over women, physically, psychologically, socially, and economically—are a 'natural' option for lesbians in a way that they are not an option for real (heterosexual) women. In short, lesbians are at best not-women—beings for whom the closest available category of sex/gender identity within a binary scheme is one that does not fit. The lesbian thus exits the category of 'woman', though without thereby entering the category 'man'.

Gender-deviant heterosexual women (i.e. women who resist patriarchal understandings of what it means to be a woman) do not similarly exit the category 'woman'. Gender deviance would result in not-woman status only if the content of the category 'woman' were fully exhausted by a description, such as Wittig's, of what it means to be a woman. I have been suggesting, on the contrary, that heterosexuality is one critical component of our cultural conception of the category 'woman'. Heterosexuality secures one's status as a real woman, which is to say, as having a body whose sex as female is above suspicion. Heterosexuality also guarantees a significant nonidentity between one's own and men's relation to women. The heterosexual woman will not have a sexual, romantic, marital, co-parenting relation to other women; she will have instead a *woman*'s relation to women. Thus even in her gender deviance, the heterosexual resister of patriarchally defined gender remains unambiguously a woman.

Because the lesbian stands outside the category 'woman', her experience of womanliness and its oppressive nature is not identical to that of the heterosexual feminist, who stands within the category 'woman', even if resistantly. Womanliness is not something the lesbian has the option of refusing or reconstructing for a better fit. It is, in our cultural understanding of what it means to be a lesbian, a fundamental impossibility for her. To be a not-woman is to be incapable of *being* fully a woman and of fitting within a binary sex/gender scheme. At most, the lesbian can be womanly only in the modes of being in drag and of passing. And if she experiences womanliness—the demand that she look like a woman, act like a woman—as oppressive, it is not because womanliness requires subordination to men (although this may also be her experience). It is instead because the demand that she be womanly is the demand that she pretend that the sex/gender 'woman' is a natural possibility for her and that she pass as a woman. As I will argue in Chapter 4, one of the central features of lesbian and gay subordination is the insistence that individuals present themselves as heterosexuals (and thus as clearly fitting into one of the sex/gender binaries) as a condition of access to the public sphere. Lesbians and gay men are thus pressured to closet the fact that they occupy a position between the categories 'man' and 'woman'.

From a lesbian perspective, then, the category 'woman' is oppressive because, within heterosexist societies, publicly appearing to belong in that category is compulsory for all anatomically female individuals. The category 'woman' is also oppressive because, within heterosexist societies, 'woman' and 'man' signify the only natural, normal, acceptable types of person; the middle position of the lesbian is thus constructed as the site of deviance, pathology, and moral depravity. Although feminist reconstructions of 'woman' may challenge gender norms, norms restricting woman-loving relations between women, and norms for acceptable female bodies, those reconstructions typically do not challenge the idea that the only natural, normal sex/genders are 'woman' and 'man'. On the contrary, they implicitly assume that 'woman' and 'man' exhaust the field of possible sorts of persons to be (even if it takes multiple categories of each to exhaust the taxonomy). The lesbian objection to being pressured to be a woman is not met by admissions that the category 'woman' is open to social construction and reconstruction. Nor is it met by the suggestion that there is no single category 'woman' but instead multiple categories of women. From a lesbian perspective, what has to be challenged is heterosexist society's demand that females be, or appear to be, women. For that demand denies the lesbian position. The lesbian position is one of being a not-woman. That position can be played out in multiple ways, for example, by insisting on being neither identifiably woman nor man, or by enacting femininity as a natural part of one's desire for women, or by enacting masculinity as a natural expression of one's sex/gender.

Failure to see the difference between feminist and lesbian relations to the category 'woman' may well result in mislocating lesbian politics and failing to see the potential friction between feminist and lesbian politics. I take the feminist critique of butch and femme lesbianism as a case in point. On that critique, both the lesbian appropriation of femininity by femmes and the lesbian appropriation of masculinity through butch sexual-social dominance repeat between women the power politics and misogyny that typifies male–female relations in a patriarchal society. Julia Penelope, for instance, argues that '[t]hose aspects of behavior and appearance labeled "femininity" in HP [heteropatriarchy] are dangerous for us. We still live *in* a heteropatriarchy and Lesbians who incorporate male ideas of appropriate female behaviors into their lives signal their acceptance of the HP version of reality'.[24] In particular, the feminine lesbian confirms heteropatriarchy's acceptance of the feminine woman and rejection of any trace of mannishness in women.

From a perspective concerned with undermining male–female dominance relations, there is no way of rendering politically harmless the appropriation of a role that requires sexual-social passivity and subordination, even if the appropriation is by a not-woman and even if she is not passive or subordinate primarily in relation to men. Here, the argument against femininity in lesbians directly parallels the argument against the masochist role in lesbian

---

[24] Julia Penelope, 'Heteropatriarchal Semantics and Lesbian Identity: The Ways a Lesbian Can Be', in *Call Me Lesbian: Lesbian Lives, Lesbian Theory* (Freedom, CA: Crossing Press, 1992), 78–97.

sadomasochism (s/m). The femme's and masochist's appeal to the voluntariness of their choices, the privacy of their practices, and the pleasure they derive from femininity and masochism, respectively, do not go all the way toward making what they do purely personal. Both femininity and female masochism acquire their meaning from what Penelope calls 'heteropatriachal semantics' as well as from the historical and material conditions of women's oppression. Those meanings cannot be dissolved at will.[25] To adopt either femininity or female masochism for oneself is to make use of a set of meanings produced through and sustained by men's oppression of women. It is thus to reveal one's personal failure to come to critical grips with the politics of women's position within patriarchy. Even if the femme's or masochist's personal choices are not political in the sense of publicly endorsing femininity or masochism in women, they are still political in the sense that they make use of public meanings which are tied to gender politics.

Nor can the appropriation of masculine dominance, aggression, and misogyny be rendered politically harmless. What the butch (as well as the sadist in lesbian s/m) confirms are the patriarchal equations of power with sexual dominance and superiority with masculinity. Janice Raymond's caustic remarks about lesbian s/m might equally express the feminist critique of butch-femme roles:

It is difficult to see what is so advanced or progressive about a position that locates 'desire', and that imprisons female sexual dynamism, vitality, and vigor, in old forms of sexual objectification, subordination, and violence, this time initiated by women and done with women's consent. The libertarians offer a supposed sexuality stripped naked of feminine taboo, but only able to dress itself in masculine garb. It is a male-constructed sexuality in drag.[26]

I have no intention of disagreeing with the claim that butch-femme role-playing runs contrary to feminist politics. What I do intend to take issue with is the assumption that feminist politics are necessarily lesbian politics. Judith Butler gives a quite different reading of the multiple appropriations of femininity and masculinity within the lesbian/gay community by butches, femmes, queens, dykes, and gaymale girls. It is a reading that I take to be closer to a lesbian perspective, even if farther from a feminist one. What the feminist critique omits is the fact that

[w]ithin lesbian contexts, the 'identification' with masculinity that appears as butch identity is not a simple assimilation of lesbianism back into the terms of heterosexuality. As one lesbian femme explained, she likes her boys to be girls . . . As a result, that masculinity, if that it can be called, is always brought into relief against a culturally

---

[25] For critical discussions of the meanings employed within s/m see especially Susan Leigh Star's 'Swastikas: The Street and the University', 131–6, and John Stoltenberg's 'Sadomasochism: Eroticized Violence, Eroticized Powerlessness', 124–30, in *Against Sadomasochism*.

[26] Janice G. Raymond, 'Putting the Politics Back into Lesbianism', *Women's Studies International Forum* 12 (1989): 149–56.

intelligible 'female body'. It is precisely this dissonant juxtaposition and the sexual tension that its transgression generates that constitute the object of desire.[27]

In Butler's view, it is also precisely this dissonant juxtaposition of masculinity and female body that enables the butch to enact masculinity in a way that *denaturalizes* the category 'man'. Heterosexist society assumes that masculinity is naturally united to the male body and desire for women. Similarly, it assumes that femininity is naturally united to the female body and desire for men. Butler argues, however, that the gender identities 'man' and 'woman' are not natural but the result of continuous gender performances. One can be a man, for example, only by continuously performing masculinity and desire for women through a male body. Heterosexual society sustains the illusion that the gender identities (heterosexual) man and (heterosexual) woman are distinctively natural by outlawing alternative performances. The butch lesbian gives an outlawed performance. She performs masculinity and desire for women through a female body. The butch gay man similarly gives an outlawed performance by performing masculinity and desire for men through a male body. Making visible the multiple locations of masculinity—on the heterosexual male body, the lesbian body, the gay man's body—helps create a condition in which either 'after a while, everyone starts to look like a drag queen'[28] or masculinity begins to seem equally natural wherever it appears. As a result, the categories 'woman' and 'man' cease to appear uniquely natural. Without such clearly natural or original gender identities, lesbians' subordinate status cannot be rationalized on the grounds that lesbians are unnatural, pathological beings.

Because challenging heterosexual dominance depends on deviant performances that reconfigure the elements of 'man' and 'woman', Butler rejects feminist attempts to outlaw butch and femme lesbian identities:

Lesbianism that defines itself in radical exclusion from heterosexuality deprives itself of the capacity to resignify the very heterosexual constructs by which it is partially and inevitably constituted. As a result, that lesbian strategy would consolidate compulsory heterosexuality in its oppressive forms.

The more insidious and effective strategy it seems is a thoroughgoing appropriation and redeployment of the categories of identity themselves . . .[29]

Terralee Bensinger gives a similar reading of butch-femme representations within lesbian pornography. Like Butler, she stresses the political significance

---

[27] Judith Butler, *Gender Trouble*, 123. For additional discussion of the creation of an apparently natural gender identity through repetitive gender performances see her 'Imitation and Gender Insubordination', in *Inside/Out: Lesbian Theories, Gay Theories*, ed. Diana Fuss (New York: Routledge, 1991), 13–31.

[28] Quote of the week from Allan Berube in 'City on a Hill', UCSC, 4 June, 1992, vol. 26 (30), 10. In 'Sexism' (*The Politics of Reality*), Marilyn Frye similarly comments that '[h]eterosexual critics of queers'' "role-playing" ought to look at themselves in the mirror on their way out for a night on the town to see who's in drag. The answer is, everybody is', 29.

[29] Butler, *Gender Trouble*, 128.

of displacing 'traditional heterosexual postures' of masculinity and femininity from their supposedly natural home on the heterosexual couple's bodies to the lesbian couple's bodies.[30]

The important thing here is that the reworking of these codes, within a lesbian context, de-naturalizes the illusion of a 'natural' heterosexuality (where such codes are 'appropriately' attached to female and male bodies in a sex/gender suture).[31]

In her view, however, the effectiveness of butch-femme representations depends not only on the displacement of masculinity and femininity on to nonheterosexual bodies, but also upon their shifting and ambivalent inscription on lesbian bodies. When elements of masculinity and femininity appear on the same body or shift back and forth between the bodies of the lesbian couple, gender is most fully destabilized and denaturalized.

One may, of course, doubt that performing masculinity and femininity on the lesbian body will have much political impact. When confined to the bedroom or public lesbian audiences, these performances cannot denaturalize gender for the larger cultural audience. Disrupting the larger culture's conviction that there are only two natural sex/genders, however, is what really matters politically. Even when made more broadly visible these performances may not have the desired effect. Lesbians are culturally conceived, in part, as types of persons from whom gender deviance is only to be expected. Thus, deviant performances may only confirm, rather than unsettle, the assumption that masculinity on a female body and femininity conjoined with desire for women are unnatural pathologies.

However, even if one doubts the political effectiveness of simply performing alternative masculinities and femininities, arguments like Butler's and Bensinger's are instructive on two counts. First, they suggest that from a specifically *lesbian* political point of view, there may be good reason to endorse butch-femme roles. At the very least, butch-femme roles need to be assessed in relation to the politics of lesbian and gay subordination. Second, from a specifically *feminist* political point of view, the reasons for endorsing butch-femme roles are not particularly persuasive. Lesbian politics and feminist politics are thus not guaranteed to overlap. Even if butch-femme lesbianism undermines belief in the naturalness of the gender binary 'man'/'woman' in relation to which lesbians are deemed unnatural and pathological, it does not follow from this that butch-femme lesbianism undermines patriarchy. The original feminist objection still stands. Butch lesbianism leaves in place the patriarchal equation of masculinity with power and dominance, while femme lesbianism leaves in place the patriarchal equation of femininity with weakness and subordination. Butler's, and perhaps also Bensinger's, political program would at best simply replace 'man'-based patriarchy (*male* power),

---

[30] Bensinger, 'Lesbian Pornography: The Re/Making of (a) Community', 84.
[31] Ibid.

with masculinity-based patriarchy (*masculine* power). Under masculinity-based patriarchy, anatomical females and males would have an equal opportunity to appropriate, with complete naturalness, masculine power over feminine individuals, who themselves could be either anatomically male or female.

What this feminist objection to lesbian efforts to denaturalize the sex/gender binary reveals is the fact that challenging lesbian and gay subordination and challenging women's oppression are not the same thing. The feminist political opposition to anyone's enacting conventional masculinity and femininity disables lesbians from effectively challenging the pathologizing of lesbian masculinity and (to a lesser extent) lesbian femininity. On the flip side, lesbians' insistence on the political value of their performing masculinity and femininity disables feminists from challenging masculine–feminine power relations. Neither side seems to see this. Both assume the *identity* of feminist politics and lesbian politics. This is simply a mistake. Lesbian and gay subordination and gender oppression are analytically distinct social systems, just as capitalism and patriarchy are distinct. Patriarchy can survive in a nonheterosexist society just as it can survive in a noncapitalist society. To the extent that butch-femme culture assigns greater power and privilege to masculine lesbians, that culture qualifies as a form of patriarchy. Similarly, when lesbians are subordinated to gay men within gay culture, patriarchy, without heterosexism, is also at work. Conversely, heterosexism can survive in a nonpatriarchal society. Heterosexism depends on treating masculine-male-heterosexual and feminine-female-heterosexual as the only natural and nondefective sex/genders. It does *not* depend on femininity and masculinity being defined and valued the way they are in patriarchal societies. Matriarchies could just as easily pathologize the middle position between the binary 'woman' and 'man'.[32]

Given this, one should expect that feminist politics and lesbian politics, though typically overlapping, may sometimes part company. Moreover, when those politics do conflict, there is no reason to expect that feminist lesbians will or should give priority to feminist politics. Being a woman (or better, being mistaken for a woman) and being oppressed as a woman are often not the most important facts in a lesbian's life. Being a lesbian and subordinated as a lesbian often matter more.

## II. Which Heterosexuality?

I said at the beginning that one main reason why lesbian issues tend to collapse into feminist issues is that the most well-developed model of heterosexuality available to lesbian feminist theorizing is one that takes heterosexuality to be both product and essential support of patriarchy. The

---

[32] Wittig makes a point similar to this in 'One is Not Born a Woman', in *The Straight Mind*, 10.

Radicalesbians, Monique Wittig, Charlotte Bunch, Adrienne Rich, and more recently Marilyn Frye[33] all take this view. On this feminist reading of hetero-sexuality, what defines heterosexuality is the requirement that women assume a dependent and subordinate relation to men. I have already argued that look-ing at heterosexuality this way results in claiming too much for lesbians. Lesbianism is mistakenly read as the quintessential form of feminist revolt. I intend to begin this section by expanding on this point that the political significance of institutionalized heterosexuality should not be interpreted solely in terms of the role heterosexuality plays in supporting male dom-inance. I will then turn to Raymond's and Hoagland's feminist attempts to avoid claiming too much for lesbians. Their strategy involves relocating the political problem in a particular *style* of 'heterosexualist' interaction rather than in heterosexuality *simpliciter*. On this view, the fact that lesbians (or heterosexual women, for that matter) are not in heterosexual relations with men does not mean that they are resisting gender oppression. To do that, they would need to avoid the style of interacting with men and women that one learns in a male-dominant culture. This strategy, I will argue, results in claim-ing too little for lesbians. It denies that there is anything intrinsically political about the fact that lesbians are not heterosexual and may resist cooperating in a social scheme that benefits heterosexuals at the expense of lesbians and gays. I will conclude with a quite different reading of heterosexuality, one that I take to be closer to a lesbian view if farther from a feminist one.

## Heterosexuality as Male Dominance

Heterosexuality, in Wittig's view, is a political and economic system of male dominance. The heterosexual social contract (to which only men have consented) stipulates that women belong to men. In particular, women's reproductive labor, including both child rearing and domestic chores, belongs to men by natural right much as a slave's labor belongs to his or her master by natural right. It is thus heterosexuality that enables men to appropriate women's labor and that supports a system of male dominance. In Wittig's view, lesbian refusal to be heterosexual challenges this system of male domin-ance, because being lesbian fundamentally means refusing to accept the 'economic, ideological and political power of men'.[34] Wittig's equation of lesbian resistance with feminist resistance is both obvious and explicit. She claims that to be a feminist is to fight for the disappearance of the sex-class 'woman' by refusing to participate in the heterosexual relations that created the sex-class 'woman' in the first place.[35] To be a feminist just *is* to be a lesbian.

In 'Lesbians in Revolt', Charlotte Bunch similarly equates heterosexuality

---

[33] Frye, 'Willful Virgin *or* Do You Have to Be a Lesbian to Be a Feminist?' in *Willful Virgin: Essays in Feminism* (Freedom, CA: Crossing Press, 1992), 124–37.

[34] Wittig, 'One is Not Born a Woman', 13.          [35] Ibid. 14.

with male control over women's labor; and like Wittig, she regards lesbianism as a political revolt against a system in which neither a woman nor her labor belong to herself. 'The lesbian . . . refuses to be a man's property, to submit to the unpaid labor system of housework and childcare. She rejects the nuclear family as the basic unit of production and consumption in capitalist society.'[36] In Bunch's view, commitment to heterosexuality is necessarily a commitment to supporting a male world, and thus a barrier to struggle against women's oppression. 'Being a lesbian means ending identification with, allegiance to, dependence on, and support of heterosexuality. It means ending your personal stake in the male world so that you join women individually and collectively in the struggle to end oppression.'[37]

At least two different objections might be raised to Wittig's and Bunch's implicit claim that one must be a lesbian to be a feminist. First, lesbianism only challenges male control of women in the family. But women's labor power has also been extensively controlled in the public sphere through male bosses, absence of maternity leave, sexual harassment, the job requirement of an 'appropriately' feminine appearance, insufficient availability of day care, sex segregation of women into lower paid jobs, and so on. As Ann Ferguson observes, enforced heterosexuality

may be one of the mechanisms [of male dominance], but it surely is not the single or sufficient one. Others, such as the control of female biological reproduction, male control of state and political power, and economic systems involving discrimination based on class and race, seem analytically distinct from coercive heterosexuality, yet are causes which support and perpetuate male dominance.[38]

Moreover, given both the decline of male power within the nuclear family and of the nuclear family itself, one might well claim that the public control of women's productive and reproductive labor is far more critical to the maintenance of patriarchy than the private control of women's labor within the nuclear family.

While this first objection focuses on the way that lesbianism may not be the only or even most fundamental means of resisting patriarchy, a second objection focuses on the fact that the kind of resistance being claimed for lesbians in fact belongs generally to feminists. As an empirical generalization about heterosexual relations, it is true that men continue to exercise control over women's private and public work lives. As Wittig might put it, it 'goes without saying' in the heterosexual social contract that women will assume primary responsibility for child rearing and domestic labor, that they will adjust their public work lives to the exigencies of their male partners, and that they will be at least partially economically dependent on their male partners' income. But

---

[36] Bunch, 'Lesbians in Revolt,' in *Passionate Politics*, 165.          [37] Ibid. 166.
[38] Ann Ferguson, 'Patriarchy, Sexual Identity, and the Sexual Revolution', in 'Viewpoint: On "Compulsory Heterosexuality and Lesbian Existence": Defining the Issues' by Ann Ferguson, Jacquelyn N. Zita, and Kathryn Pyne Addelson, *Signs* 7 (1981): 158–99, 170.

there are any number of ways of evading the terms of this contract without ceasing to be heterosexual. Thus, the claim that heterosexual relations are male-dominant is insufficient to support the claim that only lesbians are genuine resisters. Indeed, the heterosexual feminist who insists on a more equal partnership may resist patriarchy more effectively than many lesbians. As both Janice Raymond and Sarah Hoagland have argued, the importation of 'hetero-relations' into lesbian relationships enables patriarchal ways of thinking to be sustained within lesbian relationships themselves.[39]

### Heterosexualism v. Heterosexuality

Both Raymond and Hoagland avoid equating 'lesbian' with 'feminist' by distinguishing heterosexuality from 'hetero-relations' (Raymond) and 'heterosexualism' (Hoagland). Within their writing, 'heterosexuality' retains its customary referent to sexual object choice. 'Hetero-relations' and 'hetero-sexualism' refer to the patriarchal nature of relations in both the private and public spheres. According to Raymond, in a hetero-relational society, 'most of women's personal, social, political, professional, and economic relations are defined by the ideology that woman is for man'.[40] Hoagland similarly claims that heterosexualism 'is a particular economic, political, and emotional relationship between men and women: men must dominate women and women must subordinate themselves to men in any number of ways. As a result, men presume access to women while women remain riveted on men and are unable to sustain a community of women'.[41]

By distinguishing hetero-relations and heterosexualism from hetero-sexuality, Raymond and Hoagland avoid exaggerating the feminist element in lesbianism. Both recognize the potential failure of lesbians to disengage from heterosexualism. Lesbians themselves may be misogynistic and may engage in the same dominance-subordinance relations that typify heterosexualism. Thus, lesbian resistance to heterosexuality is not automatically a resistance to patriarchy. Because Raymond and Hoagland are sensitive to this fact, they are able to subject lesbian relations to feminist critique in a productive way. In addition, by recognizing that heterosexual women can redefine their relations to men in such a way that they both leave space for gyn/affectionate (i.e., woman loving) relations with women and refuse to participate in hetero-relations with men, Raymond avoids pitting lesbians against heterosexual women within the feminist community in a battle over who counts as a true feminist.

Their attempt, however, to avoid claiming too much for lesbianism comes at the cost of ultimately claiming too little for it. By putting the concept of hetero-relations or heterosexualism at the center of their lesbian-feminism, both effectively eliminate space for a *lesbian* theory. Within their work, the fact

---

[39] Hoagland, *Lesbian Ethics*.   [40] Raymond, *A Passion for Friends*, 11.
[41] Hoagland, *Lesbian Ethics*, 29.

that lesbians are not heterosexual and may resist their and gay men's subordination does not, in itself, have either political or conceptual significance. Whatever political significance lesbian personal lives may have is due entirely to the presence of or resistance to hetero-relations within those lives. The reduction of lesbian politics to feminist politics is quite obvious in Raymond's 'Putting the Politics back into Lesbianism'.[42] There, Raymond sharply criticizes lesbian lifestylers and sexual libertarians for failure to see that in advocating an anything-goes sexuality (including lesbian pornography and s/m) as the path to liberation, they are simply repeating the patriarchal image of woman as an essentially sexual being. Moreover, as I mentioned earlier, insofar as lesbian sex radicals advocate aggressive and violent forms of sexuality, they are simply putting a 'male-constructed sexuality in drag'.[43] What I want to underscore in Raymond's critique is that putting politics into lesbianism means putting *feminist* politics into lesbianism. She does not demand that lesbians put resistance to lesbian and gay subordination at the center of their lives. Thus, she does not ask whether or not lesbian s/m promotes *lesbian* politics.

One important consequence of equating lesbian with feminist politics in this way is that lesbians who have suffered the worst oppression, for example, the 1950s butches and femmes who risked repeated arrest and police harassment, often are the least politically interesting from a feminist point of view. Shane Phelan's criticism of Adrienne Rich for marginalizing real lesbians who resisted coercive pressure to be or behave like heterosexual women and for giving nonlesbians who resisted dependency on men pride of place on her lesbian continuum applies generally to those who equate lesbian politics with feminist politics:

. . . it becomes clear that the existence of these women [lesbians], those who have been targets of abuse for decades, is less interesting to lesbian feminists than the existence of women who never called themselves lesbians, never thought of themselves as such, and never faced the consequences of that. The sort of lesbian who laid the groundwork, built the urban subcultures, that allowed lesbians to find one another before feminism, is remembered primarily in the works of male historians. The relevant community is lesbian feminist, with the emphasis, curiously, on the feminist rather than the lesbian.[44]

From a feminist point of view whose political yardstick measures only distance from practices and institutions that oppress women, butches and femmes, lesbian sex radicals who promote pornography and s/m, lesbian mothers, and married lesbians all fail to measure up. All are vulnerable to the charge of appropriating for women and between women the very practices

[42] Raymond, 'Putting the Politics Back into Lesbianism'. See also her criticisms of lesbian s/m in the chapter 'Obstacles to Female Friendship', in *A Passion for Friends*, 149–202.

[43] Raymond, 'Putting the Politics Back into Lesbianism', 150.

[44] Phelan, *Identity Politics*, 69.

and institutions that have served so well to oppress women. Yet it is precisely these women, who insist on the reality and value of sex, romance, parenting, and marriage between women, who resist most strongly lesbian and gay subordination, including the reservation of the private sphere for male–female couples only. From a lesbian point of view whose political yardstick measures resistance to heterosexual privilege and the practices that compel lesbians and gays either to become heterosexual or closet their identities, butches and femmes, lesbian sex radicals, lesbian mothers, and married lesbians are neither politically uninteresting nor assimilationist.

Not only does the focus on heterosexualism rather than heterosexual dominance leave no space for understanding the inherently political nature of lesbianism, it also leaves no space for understanding the significance of specifically lesbian love. For instance, like Rich's notion of a lesbian continuum that includes both lesbians and heterosexual women, Raymond's 'use of the term *Gyn/affection* expresses a *continuum* of female friendship' that includes some (but not all) lesbian love as well as friendships between heterosexual women.[45] In Raymond's view, it is in Gyn/affection that women seize power from men and engage in a woman-identified act. Thus, it is gyn/affection that is politically significant. Specifically lesbian sexual and romantic attraction to women is left without any politically or conceptually interesting place to be. Raymond is by no means the first or only lesbian feminist to marginalize lesbian love in favor of a form of love between women that is more directly tied to feminist solidarity. Bunch, for example, claims that '[t]he lesbian, woman-identified-woman commits herself to women not only as an alternative to oppressive male–female relationships but primarily because she *loves* women'.[46] That this is not a particularized conception of love but rather feminist love of women as a class, becomes clear in the way she connects lesbian love with class solidarity: 'When women do give primary energies to other women, then it is possible to concentrate fully on building a movement for our liberation'.[47] In a more recent piece, Nett Hart similarly equates lesbian love with love of women as a class: 'We love women as a class and we love specific women. We embrace the concept that women can be loved, that women are inherently worthy of love'.[48] In both Bunch and Hart, there is a conceptual slide from 'love' in the sense of a sexual-romantic love of a particular woman to 'love' in the sense of valuing and respecting members of the category 'woman'. Although Raymond differs in being much more careful to keep the two types of love conceptually separated, all three prioritize love of women as a class. From a feminist point of view it is indeed the capacity to value members of the category 'woman' and to form strong primary bonds of friendship with many women that matters politically. But this is not lesbian

---

[45] Raymond, *A Passion for Friends*, 15.
[46] Bunch, 'Lesbians in Revolt', in *Passionate Politics*, 162.                    [47] Ibid.
[48] Nett Hart, 'Lesbian Desire as Social Action', in *Lesbian Philosophies and Cultures*, 295–303, 297.

love. Lesbians fall in love with, want to make love to, decide to set up a household with a *particular* other woman, not a class of women. It is for this particularized, sexualized love that lesbians are penalized in heterosexual society. Because of this, lesbian theory needs to move specifically lesbian love to the center of its political stage.

None of these remarks are intended to undercut either the value *for feminists* of work being done by lesbian feminists or the need to subject lesbian practice to feminist critique. They are meant to suggest that a full-blown lesbian-feminism cannot afford to interpret the political significance of institutionalized heterosexuality solely in terms of the role it plays in supporting male dominance.

*Heterosexual Dominance*

Although in patriarchal societies institutionalized heterosexuality enables what Gayle Rubin called the 'traffic in women', this is not the only possible function of organizing a society around the assumption that social actors are and ought to be heterosexually oriented.[49] Institutionalized heterosexuality also functions to insure reproduction by making the male–female reproductive unit fundamental to social structure, particularly, though not exclusively, to the structure of what might broadly be called the private sphere. (It is because the purpose of institutionalized heterosexuality is to sustain reproduction that threats to that system—for example, the education of women, or homosexuality—inevitably evoke in Anglo-American history some version of the race suicide argument.)

Institutionalized heterosexuality requires sex/gender dimorphism (i.e. people who fit the categories 'woman' and 'man') so that desire can be heterosexualized. It thus needs prohibitions against both category-crossing (e.g. against cross-dressing, effeminacy in men, mannishness in women) and against nonheterosexual desire.[50] As important as prohibitions are social institutions and practices that support sex/gender dimorphism and heterosexual desire—gendered rites of passage, a sexual division of labor, gendered dress, heterosexual erotica and pornography, heterosexualized humor, social activities that facilitate heterosexual coupling, and the like. The regulation of sexual desire through both prohibitions and support structures constitutes, however, only part of the institution of heterosexuality. Because institutionalized heterosexuality makes the male–female couple the locus of reproduction (including sexuality, child bearing and child rearing), the heterosexual family

---

[49] Gayle Rubin, 'The Traffic in Women', in *Toward and Anthropology of Women*, ed. Rayna Reiter (New York: Monthly Review Press, 1975).

[50] In societies like ours where it is primarily male desire that brings about male–female unions, the taboo on homosexuality is likely to be stronger. Similarly, where the gender labor of creating the appearance of marked gender dimorphism falls primarily on females, cross-dressing in women is likely to receive stricter sanctions.

occupies a keystone position in the social structure (a point that I will return to in Chapter 5). Central to institutionalized heterosexuality are, thus, the multiple practices that help heterosexuals to create families and that support the continuation of those families. These include dating services, match-makers, introductions to eligible partners, premarital counseling, marriage counseling, marriage and divorce laws, adoption services, reproductive technologies, family rates, family health care benefits, tax deductions for married couples, and so on.

What I am suggesting here is that it is a mistake to equate heterosexuality with the orientation of sexual desire and the taboo on lesbianism and homosexuality with a taboo on same-sex desire and sexual activity, as is popularly done. Heterosexuality is a way of organizing social life. In particular, it is a way of ensuring reproduction by organizing social life around the male–female couple and that couple's family. The heart of institutionalized heterosexuality is thus in the institution of the family itself.[51] This means that if one wants a complete set of the regulations that constitute the taboo on lesbianism and homosexuality, one needs to look at *all* of the practices that directly or indirectly insure that the family will be built around a male–female pair. The social and legal prohibition of same-sex sex is only the tip of the iceberg of the systematic heterosexualization of social life.

Institutionalized heterosexuality is a political system in which heterosexuals have and exercise power over nonheterosexuals. The underlying assumption is that normal social actors have a naturally given identity. They are naturally men or women, whose natural sexuality is heterosexual, and for whom the family based on a male–female pair is a natural social unit. When heterosexuality is taken to be *the* natural, nonpathological orientation, it comes to seem reasonable that the social, economic, and legal structure of any society will, and ought to, reflect this basic fact. So, for example, because it is taken for granted that men and women will be sexually interested in each other, children and adolescents are prepared for their experience of adult heterosexual desire. They are given (heterosexual) sex education, advice for attracting the opposite sex, norms for heterosexual behavior, and appropriate social occasions (such as dances or dating rituals) for enacting desire. Similarly, because it is taken for granted that men and women will bond in an intimate relationship, ultimately founding a family, social conventions, economic arrangements, and the legal structure are framed around this basic social fact. The heterosexual couple is represented linguistically (boyfriend–girlfriend, husband–wife) and is treated socially as a single unit (e.g. in joint invitations or in receiving joint gifts). It is legally licensed and legally supported through such entitlements as communal property, joint

---

[51] This helps to explain why it is relatively easy to garner toleration of lesbianism and homosexuality as private bedroom practices, while attempts to sanction lesbian and gay parenting and marriages meet with intense resistance.

custody or adoption of children, and the power to give proxy consent within the couple. The heterosexual couple is also recognized in the occupational structure, for example, in spousal health care benefits and restrictions on nepotism.

The sum total of all the social, economic, and legal arrangements that support the sexual and relational coupling of men with women constitutes heterosexual privilege. As I will argue in Chapter 4, it is privilege of a peculiar sort. What distinguishes lesbian and gay subordination from both racial and gender oppression is that systems that subordinate lesbians and gays *displace* gays and lesbians from both the public and private spheres. Institutionalized discrimination and the coercive force of the criminal law work to displace visible signs of lesbianism and homosexuality from the public sphere. An array of family-related policies, particularly barriers to same-sex marriage, adoption, and child custody, work to displace gays and lesbians from a protected private sphere. And at the extreme end, violence and 'therapeutic' treatment may be employed to eliminate lesbianism and homosexuality altogether.

## Conclusion

Unlike the heterosexual woman, including the heterosexual feminist, the lesbian experience of the institution of heterosexuality is of a system that pressures her to closet her desire for women and to appear publicly to be a member of the category 'woman'. In addition, unlike the heterosexual woman, the lesbian experience of the institution of heterosexuality is of a system that pathologizes the experience between lesbians of complete sexual fulfillment, of falling in love, of finding one's soulmate, of committing oneself, of marrying, of creating a home, and of starting a family. Unlike the heterosexual feminist, the lesbian's private sphere is not oppressive; it is unprotected.

Failure to see the difference between the heterosexual feminist's and the lesbian's relation to the institution of heterosexuality may well result in mislocating lesbian politics. From a feminist point of view, sexual interaction, romantic love, marriage, and the family are all danger zones because all have been distorted to serve male interests. It thus does not behoove feminist politics to begin by championing the importance of sexual interaction, romantic love, marriage, and the (couple-based) family. But it does behoove lesbian politics to start in precisely these places. As I will argue in Chapters 5 and 6, lesbians and gay men are not recognized as fully social beings because they are deemed unfit to enter the most basic and foundational social unit—the male–female couple and the family built on that couple. Thus, recognizing lesbians and gay men as social beings, and thus as individuals with socio-legal standing equal to that of heterosexuals, depends on the female–female and the male–male couple being recognized as a primary social unit. That in turn cannot be done without directly challenging the reservation of the primary structures of the private sphere for heterosexuals. Just as the heart of male privilege lies in the 'right' of access to women, so the heart of heterosexual privilege lies largely in the 'right' of access to sexual-romantic-marital-familial relationships. In Chapters 5 and 6, I will extend this argument for placing same-sex marriage and the family at the center of lesbian and gay politics.

# 3

# The Gender Closet

... it is first necessary to bring the lesbian subject out of the closet of feminist history.

(Sue-Ellen Case, 1993)[1]

In the previous chapter, I argued that lesbian-feminism of the 1980s wrongly placed resistance to patriarchy at the heart of what it means to be lesbian. The reduction of 'lesbian' to 'patriarchal resister' was a direct result of underestimating just how differently the category 'woman' oppresses heterosexual women versus lesbians. It was also a result of seriously underestimating just how differently institutionalized heterosexuality (what Rich called 'compulsory heterosexuality') oppresses heterosexual women versus lesbians. The consequence of this failure to acknowledge lesbian difference was, I argued, a mistaken identification of lesbian politics with feminist politics.

One might think inattention to specifically lesbian experience and politics is peculiar to 1980s feminism. After all, 1980s feminism had a penchant for thinking about 'Woman', rather than 'women', which invited exaggerated estimations both of the similarity between women's experiences and of the possibility of feminist political unity. It began by asking 'What do women share in common?' rather than 'How do women differ?' By contrast, 1990s feminism was above all marked by insistence that feminism become more inclusive by paying attention to differences between women, including differences in what it is politically most important for women of different races and classes to achieve. A suitably de-essentialized and difference-sensitive conception of 'women', rather than 'Woman', should enable us to center lesbians and lesbian politics within a feminist frame.

In this chapter I want to challenge the comfortable assumption that if only feminist theorizing begins from the right conception of 'woman' it would be adequate to the task of theorizing lesbians. Can one theorize about lesbians within any feminist frame that takes feminism to be fundamentally about women? This question would, of course, be a very odd one to raise about women of color, or poor women, or working class women, or Jewish women, or women of different nationalities. (At least it would be odd so long as we bracket their possible lesbianism.) But as I began to suggest in Chapter 2, at the center of lesbian difference is lesbians' questionable relation to the category 'woman' itself. For lesbians, the closest available category of sex/gender

[1] Sue-Ellen Case, 'Toward a Butch-Femme Aesthetic', in *The Lesbian and Gay Studies Reader*, ed. Henry Abelove, Michele Aina Barale, and David M. Halperin (New York: Routledge, 1993), 294–306, 295.

identity within a binary system is one that does not fit. This should raise concerns about the possibility of theorizing lesbians within a feminist frame. If one simply assumes that because lesbians are women they can of course be theorized within feminism, then neither the 'whether' nor the 'how' of doing this theorizing can be problematized. One need not work out what it is in the feminist frame and what it is about lesbians that enables the former to be applied to the latter. I am not sanguine about a 'yes' answer to my question: 'Can one theorize about lesbians within any feminist frame that takes feminism to be fundamentally about women?' For me, feminist theorizing about lesbians *is* a problem.

Consider: Even in the 1990s, outside of literature whose specific topic is lesbianism, lesbians typically do not make an appearance in feminist writings except via an occasional linguistic bow in their direction executed through the words 'lesbian', 'sexual orientation', or 'sexualities '. Race and class do not similarly remain systematically in the ghostly closet of referring terms. At the end of the 1990s, one might truthfully repeat Sue-Ellen Case's 1988 caustic observation about

the catechism of 'working-class-women-of-color' feminist theorists feel impelled to invoke at the outset of their research. What's wrong with this picture? It does not include the lesbian position. In fact, the isolation of the social dynamics of race and class successfully relegates sexual preference to an attendant position, so that even if the lesbian were to appear, she would be as a bridesmaid and never the bride.[2]

The problem is not just the lesbian's bridesmaid status. Her complete absence from the wedding may also go unnoticed.[3]

It is of course possible that the feminist frame *is* fully adequate to representing lesbians but, for various reasons, simply has not been adequately deployed to that end; thus the problem might simply be one of unrealized potential. *But*—and it is this 'but' that I intend to explore—it is also possible that the feminist frame itself operates in various ways to closet lesbians.

This may seem an unlikely possibility. The turn in feminism to an anti-essentialist, difference-sensitive frame promises to open whatever doors may formerly have been closed against lesbian inclusion. It is as a caution against automatic confidence in the power of a difference-sensitive feminist frame to represent lesbian difference that I intend this chapter. In section I, I probe the constructed concept of difference, examining both what difference has come to mean and the kind of socio-political analysis that enables the representation of difference. I argue that anti-essentialism has in fact worked *against* theorizing lesbian difference, because embedded in the conception of 'difference' is an assumed disanalogy between sexual orienta-

[2] Sue-Ellen Case, 'Toward a Butch-Femme Aesthetic', 294–306, 295.

[3] Consider e.g. Susan Moller Okin's excellently researched book, *Justice, Gender, and the Family* (New York: Basic Books, 1989), which completely omits the justice issues regarding the family that lesbians find themselves up against.

tion on the one hand, and race, class, and ethnicity on the other. In particular, differences in race, class, and ethnicity are taken to be important ones to recognize because they are major differences that oppositionally position some women to other women in a system of oppression. Differences in sexual orientation are not similarly taken as ones that oppositionally position heterosexual women and lesbians within a system of lesbian and gay subordination that is conceptually distinct from gender oppression. Thus, only race, class, and ethnic differences between lesbians, not lesbians' difference from heterosexual women, appear within the difference-sensitive feminist frame. In section II, I pursue the political boundaries around feminist representations of differences. There, using the 1980s lesbian feminist 'sex wars' as a case in point, I argue that feminist values and goals have worked against representing lesbian difference. In section III, I confront the underlying requirement of difference-sensitive feminism that lesbians be representable as different *women*. As I began to suggest in Chapter 2, in western culture, the lesbian as the bearer of a different, distinctive identity became imaginable largely by virtue of the late nineteenth century construction of a *nonbinary* sex/gender system in which the lesbian was positioned as the third sex; or, as Monique Wittig describes her, 'a not-woman, a not-man';[4] or as Judith Butler might describe her, as disruptively reconfiguring and redeploying the categories of sex.[5] If imagining the lesbian depends on imagining a position outside of 'woman' and 'man', then lesbian representation cannot be accomplished under the sign 'women'. Positioned in a line-up of womanly differences in race, class, nationality, religion, etc., *lesbian* difference cannot appear. In short, 'women' may operate as a lesbian closet.

## I. The Promise of Anti-essentialism

In 1980, Marilyn Frye charged women's studies with thoroughgoing heterosexism. She observed that

[l]ooking at women's studies from my Lesbian perspective and with my Lesbian feminist sensibility, what I see is that women's studies is heterosexual. The predominance of heterosexual perspectives, values, commitments, thought and vision is usually so complete and ubiquitous that it cannot be perceived, for lack of contrast.[6]

---

[4] Monique Wittig, 'One is not Born a Woman', in *The Straight Mind and Other Essays* (Boston: Beacon, 1992), 9–20.

[5] Judith Butler, *Gender Trouble: Feminism and the Subversion of Identity* (New York: Routledge, 1990). Havelock Ellis and Krafft-Ebing, Monique Wittig, and Judith Butler obviously differ substantially in their specific understandings of what it means for the lesbian to be outside the category 'woman'. In this chapter, however, I want to take seriously the significance of their agreeing that she is 'outside'.

[6] Marilyn Frye, 'A Lesbian's Perspective on Women's Studies, 1980', in *Willful Virgin: Essays in Feminism 1976–1992* (Freedom, CA: Crossing Press, 1992), 51–8, 51.

She urged lesbians to refrain from supporting women's studies. Feminist theorizing has dramatically changed since 1980.[7] In particular, feminist theorizing no longer makes the essentializing assumptions that 'woman' signifies a set of universal commonalities, that all women share a common oppression, and that a single feminist agenda will equally address all women's needs. In an effort to combat the racism, classism, and other biases built into earlier feminist theorizing, 'difference' has largely replaced 'woman' as the category of analysis. 'It would seem that dealing with the fact of differences is *the* project of women's studies today'.[8] Dealing with differences promises an inclusiveness that would address Marilyn Frye's charge of heterosexism in women's studies. It also promises to give a more positive reception to assertions of lesbian difference than Wittig received during the 1980s. Joan Nestle recollected that:

When Monique Wittig said at the Modern Languages Association Conference several years ago, 'I am not a woman, I am a Lesbian', there was a gasp from the audience, but the statement made sense to me. Of course I am a woman, but I belong to another geography as well, and the two worlds are complicated and unique.[9]

These promises of inclusion and receptivity to the thought that lesbians are not-women, however, warrant scrutiny.

## Lesbian Disappearance under 'Difference'

In her 1988 article on lesbian autobiography, Biddy Martin observes the potential political value for lesbians of focusing on lesbian difference from heterosexual women: 'Claims to difference conceived in terms of different identities have operated and continue to operate as interventions in facile assumptions of "sisterhood", assumptions that have tended to mask the operation of white, middle-class, heterosexual "womanhood" as the hidden but hegemonic referent'.[10] Thus, the production of lesbian autobiographical narratives 'may have strategic political value, given the continued, or perhaps renewed, invisibility of lesbians even in feminist work'.[11] Autobiographical collections, such as *The Lesbian Path*, *The Coming Out Stories*, and *The New Lesbians*, challenge the assumption that women's normal trajectory is 'toward adult heterosexuality, marriage, and motherhood'.[12] They also challenge the presumed continuity between biological sex, gender identity, and sexuality.[13] Since both assump-

---

[7] The specific change that Frye hoped for has not, however, come about. She asked that heterosexual feminists cease presenting heterosexuality as an inevitability to be 'coped with' and that they defend the rationality of their own choice to continue to be heterosexual.

[8] Christina Crosby, 'Dealing with Differences', in *Feminists Theorize the Political*, ed. Judith Butler and Joan W. Scott (New York: Routledge, 1992), 130–43, 131.

[9] Joan Nestle, 'Butch-Femme Relationships: Sexual Courage in the 1950s', in *A Restricted Country* (Ithaca, NY: Firebrand, 1987), 100–9, 106.

[10] Biddy Martin, 'Lesbian Identity and Autobiographical Difference[s]', in *The Lesbian and Gay Studies Reader*, 274–93, 275.     [11] Ibid.     [12] Ibid. 279.
[13] Ibid.

tions are often at work in feminist writing, lesbian autobiography helps to bring lesbian difference back into view.

Martin, however, is ultimately critical of lesbian anthologies like *The Coming Out Stories*. In her view, they do not instantiate a difference-sensitive feminism. What she means by 'sensitivity to difference' emerges in her critique of lesbian autobiographical anthologies and her proposed alternative for lesbian autobiographical writing. It is, paradoxically, a definition of 'difference' that implicitly excludes the representation of *lesbian* difference.

Published during the 1970s and 1980s, *The Coming Out Stories*, *The Lesbian Path*, and *The New Lesbians* narrate a lesbian identity heavily influenced by the emergence of lesbian-feminism, particularly its view of the lesbian as the truly woman-identified woman. 'Lesbianism, understood to be first and foremost about love for other women and for oneself as a woman, becomes a profoundly life-saving, self-loving, political resistance to patriarchal definitions and limitations in these narratives.'[14] In keeping with this portrayal of lesbians as *women*-identified women, 'sexual desire is often attenuated and appears as "love" in these narratives',[15] and the desirability of looking or acting like men or of engaging in butch-femme role-playing is denied.[16]

Martin criticizes these narratives, first, for representing as an essential, true, discovered identity what was in fact the constructed, historical product of feminism itself. As a result, the social and political currents underlying this particular lesbian identity remain obscured and uncriticizable. In her view, this essentializing, ahistorical, psychological approach to lesbian difference disqualifies these narratives from articulating a truly difference-sensitive perspective. Difference-sensitivity requires that the identity in whose name difference is claimed be subject to historical and political investigation in a way that opens a space for agency between the subject and her identity.

Second, she criticizes these narratives for ultimately failing to represent lesbian *difference*. How do they go wrong? One might think (as I do, but Martin in this article does not) that something has gone seriously wrong when lesbianism is de-sexualized. The woman-identified woman has no distinctive sexuality; one might say she has no sexuality at all. Hillary Allen, whom Martin quotes, makes the point particularly forcefully: 'In conventional terms, whatever is sexual about Political Lesbianism appears to be systematically attenuated: genitality will yield to an unspecified eroticism, eroticism to sensuality, sensuality to "primary emotional intensity", and emotional intensity to practical and political support'.[17] When feminist woman-loving replaces lesbian genital sexuality, lesbian identity disappears into feminist identity, and the *sexual* difference between heterosexual women and lesbians cannot be effectively represented. Moreover, when lesbian cross-dressing and

---

[14] Ibid. 280.  [15] Ibid.  [16] Ibid. 281.
[17] Hillary Allen, 'Political Lesbianism and Feminism—Space for a Sexual Politics?', qtd in Martin, 'Lesbian Identity', 280.

role-playing are denied, a distinctively lesbian relation to (and *outside of*) the binary gender categories 'man' and 'woman' disappears into a feminist relation to the gender category 'woman'. The woman-identified woman is incapable of either the femme's redeployment of femininity or the butch's gender-crossing. As a result, the *gender* difference between heterosexual women and lesbians cannot be effectively represented, indeed is repressed, under her image.

Although Martin does observe that lesbian specificity cannot be represented via a de-sexualized woman-identified woman, it becomes clear that she does not take this as the problem to be solved. On the contrary, she appears to endorse the equation of lesbianism with 'women's love for other women and for ourselves as women'.[18] Lesbian desire remains de-sexualized as the desire for connection with other women. In short, representing lesbians' difference from heterosexual women is *not*, in her account, critical to successfully representing lesbians within a difference-sensitive frame.

If 'difference' does not in part mean lesbian sexual and gender difference, what difference does matter in a difference-sensitive frame?—lesbians' difference from each other. In Martin's view—and she is not alone here—'difference-sensitivity' requires that any representation of women must recognize the boundaries imposed between women by race, class, ethnicity, and nationality. What Martin admires in the autobiographical anthologies *This Bridge Called My Back: Writings by Radical Women of Color* and, to a lesser extent, *Nice Jewish Girls*, is the way their narratives repeatedly insist that neither 'woman' nor 'lesbian' constitutes a unified category. Unity, rather than being the result of shared identity, is something that must be achieved without erasing differences between women or between lesbians.[19] Thus she does not object to the woman-identified woman because it erases lesbian differences from heterosexual women. She objects because it erases race, class, ethnic, and national differences between women and between lesbians by implying that a mere consciousness of being women (or lesbians) together is sufficient to produce unity among women. '[T]he feminist dream of a new world of women simply reproduces the demand that women of color (and women more generally) abandon their histories, the histories of their communities, their complex locations and selves, in the name of a unity that barely masks its white, middle-class cultural reference/referent.'[20]

Something is right and something is very wrong about this picture. It is surely right to deny that what being lesbian means to the course of one's life and to how one thinks about oneself can be distilled out from all other differences—in race, class, ethnicity, and nationality—and shared, in this pure form, by all lesbians. What Elizabeth Spelman calls 'tootsie roll metaphysics' or 'pop-bead metaphysics' is simply wrong.[21] It is not true that 'each part of

---

[18] Martin, 'Lesbian Identity', 284, also, 284, 287.
[19] Ibid. 283.                                                                                   [20] Ibid.
[21] Elizabeth V. Spelman, *Inessential Woman: Problems of Exclusion in Feminist Thought* (Boston: Beacon, 1988), 136.

my identity is separable from every other part, and the significance of each part is unaffected by the other parts'.[22] Nor does lesbian and gay subordination operate completely independently of gender, race, class, and ethnic oppressions. But it is surely equally wrong to *eliminate* the specificity of lesbian identity and lesbian and gay subordination from the picture. And this is exactly what has happened. The one difference that is not allowed to appear as a difference is the difference between lesbians and heterosexual women. The one structural and institutional barrier between women that is not allowed to appear is institutionalized heterosexual dominance. Because of that, rendering an account of lesbian specificity is not part of the project of constructing difference-sensitive lesbian narratives. What appears in the place of the woman-identified woman who figured in earlier lesbian autobiographies is, in effect, the difference-identified woman. In Martin's words, but intentionally echoing Cherrie Moraga, lesbianism is

a desire that transgresses the boundaries imposed by structures of race, class, ethnicity, nationality; it figures not as a desire that can efface or ignore the effects of those boundaries but as a provocation to take responsibility for them out of the desire for different kinds of connections.[23]

Almost immediately following this passage, it becomes clear that what really matters to lesbian autobiography is the portrayal of lesbian desire as the desire to connect across differences:

For a number of contributors, lesbian and not, the love of women, the pleasure in women's company, is said to sustain political analysis and struggle across divisions. This sense of a desire for connection, however partial and provisional, gives the pieces a particular force.[24]

'Lesbian' ceases to signify lesbians in their specific difference from heterosexual women. 'Lesbian' now signifies a kind of ideal (feminist) woman, *to whom* differences matter, but *whose own* difference does not. It is tempting at this point to paraphrase Martin's critique of lesbian-feminism quoted above: The difference-sensitive feminist dream of a new world of women negotiating unity across race, class, ethnic, and national differences simply reproduces the demand that lesbians abandon their histories, the histories of their communities, their complex locations and selves, in the name of an acknowledgement of difference.

I have spent a long time on Biddy Martin's article because it is an excellent piece of work in what I call the 'difference-sensitive feminist frame'. It is because this piece represents that frame so well, that it so usefully illustrates why the anti-essentialist move to difference has worked against, rather than for, representing lesbian difference.[25] Feminism has moved straight from

---

[22] Ibid.  [23] Martin, 'Lesbian Identity', 284.  [24] Ibid.
[25] In a more recent piece: 'Sexual Practice and Changing Lesbian Identities', in *Destabilizing Theory: Contemporary Feminist Debates*, ed. Michele Barrett and Anne Phillips (CA: Stanford University Press,

'There is no essential Woman identity' to 'There is no essential Lesbian identity'. In both cases, it is the appeal to race, class, ethnic, and national structures
that enables the anti-essentialist point to be made. Missing is a crucial inter-
mediate step: One reason why there is no essential Woman identity is because
institutionalized heterosexual dominance creates critical differences and
barriers between heterosexual and nonheterosexual women. Tarrying first
over the contrast between heterosexual and nonheterosexual women would
have made it clear why it makes sense, and why it is not necessarily essentializing, to speak categorically of 'lesbians' in the same way it makes sense to
speak categorically of 'black women' or 'women of color'. Because that did not
happen, invoking class, race, and other differences between lesbians has the
effect of causing lesbians to disappear. A similar invocation of differences
between black women does not have this effect. Because the general contours
of differently raced identities under a system of racial oppression have first
been delineated, investigating differences among black women is able to reveal
the *intersection* of race with other differences, such as class or nationality. In
the case of lesbians, however, given the absence of extensive socio-political
analyses of institutionalized lesbian and gay subordination and of the socially
constructed category 'lesbian', there is nothing lesbian for differences of race,
class, ethnicity, and nationality to intersect *with*.[26]

## II. The Promise of 'Gender and . . .' Analyses

The disappearance of lesbians under 'difference' is strikingly odd. After all,
difference-sensitive feminism is predicated on the assumption that gender is
not the sole determinant of woman's fate.[27] Although, historically, the first

---

1992) 93–119, Biddy Martin takes a quite different approach to lesbian difference. Sensitive to race and
class differences between lesbians as well as to the permeability of the lesbian-heterosexual opposition,
Martin also focuses on lesbians' difference from heterosexuals. In particular, she follows Butler in
understanding homosexual practices (particularly drag and butch-femme) as ones that reconfigure sex
and gender.

[26] An analogy may help clarify what I am looking for in looking for 'something lesbian'. Consider
the 'controlling images' of black women—the mammy, the matriarch, the Jezebel, and the welfare
mother—that I mentioned in Chapter 1. Without invoking an essentialized definition of 'woman', we
can say a lot about what makes these images gendered images, how they are connected across racial
lines to other gendered images, and how they function in a general pattern of women's subordination.
Similarly, without invoking an essentialized definition of 'black', we can say a lot about what makes
these images raced images, how they are connected across gender lines to other raced images, and how
they function in a general pattern of racial subordination. Consider now the sexual practice of butch-
femme relations. Feminists have commented (largely negatively) on the *gendered* character of butch-
femme relations and their similarity across sexuality lines to heterosexual gender relations. We could
also say why the preference of black butches for 'beautiful' white femmes is *raced* (this example is from
Martin, 'Sexual Practice'). But what is it about butch-femme that codes it as *lesbian*? If we can talk
meaningfully about the gendered and raced character of a practice without invoking essential definitions, then we should be able to talk equally meaningfully about the lesbian character of a practice. In
looking for 'something lesbian' I am looking for something to say about what might code a practice
lesbian other than the unhelpful fact that lesbians do it.

[27] bell hooks, *Feminist Theory: From Margin to Center* (Boston: South End Press, 1984), 14.

demand was that '[r]ace and class oppression . . . be recognized as feminist issues with as much relevance as sexism',[28] recognizing the subordination of lesbians and gay men seems a natural next step. Race and class constitute only two important factors with which gender must be integrated in a difference-sensitive analysis. The logical implication of any difference-sensitive feminism is that gender must also be integrated with the important factor of sexual orientation.

Elizabeth Spelman's construction of the difference-sensitive feminist frame brings the oddity of closeting lesbians under 'difference' into particularly clear view. She argues that the most fruitful and accurate way of performing integrated analyses is to begin thinking in terms of multiple genders (i.e. multiple kinds of women).[29] This has the advantage of short-circuiting the temptation to imagine that one's gender, or what it means to be a woman, is something that can be described independently of one's race, class, *or* one's sexual orientation. The image of different woman-genders also reminds us that feminism cannot be centrally about gender oppression unless it is at the same time centrally about racism, classism, and heterosexism.

Focusing on lesbians as a distinctive woman-gender produced at the intersection of gender and sexual orientation should have sparked reflection on *lesbian* difference in addition to the differences between lesbians. What I want to explore is the possibility that what Spelman calls the 'ampersand problem' (e.g. gender & race) may be a uniquely difficult problem when the ampersand conjoins gender with sexual orientation. In this section, I will examine feminist political motives for resisting the conjunction of 'woman' with 'sexual orientation'. In the following section, I will question whether lesbians can be represented as a *woman*-gender at all.

## Lesbian Disappearance under 'Gender'

Although largely antedating the emergence of difference-sensitive feminism, the sex wars over lesbian sadomasochism (s/m) illuminate some of the political motives for *not* representing lesbian sexual difference within a feminist frame.

In the 1980s, what came to be called the 'sex wars' constitute one of the few arenas in which lesbianism has been the explicit focus of feminist theorizing. The central bone of contention concerned which sexual practices should be construed as truly liberating for women.[30] Lesbian s/m occupied center stage in this debate. Because both opponents and proponents of lesbian s/m

---

[28] Ibid. 25.                                             [29] Spelman, 175.

[30] For helpful articles within this debate and summaries of that debate, see *Against Sadomasochism: A Radical Feminist Analysis*, ed. Robin Ruth Linden *et al.* (San Francisco: Frog in the Well, 1982); B. Ruby Rich, 'Feminism and Sexuality in the 1980s', *Feminist Studies* 12 (1986): 525–61; and Shane Phelan, 'Sadomasochism and the Meaning of Feminism', in *Identity Politics: Lesbian Feminism and the Limits of Community* (Philadelphia: Temple University Press, 1989), 99–134.

claimed to speak from a feminist point of view, and because both sides focused on the *gender* of lesbians as women in the context of rethinking lesbian *sexuality*, one might expect the entire debate to have been a concerted feminist attempt to work out the ampersand conjoining gender with sexual orientation. It was not. One of the most remarkable features of the debate is the way that *lesbian* sexuality continuously disappeared into *women's* sexuality.

Proponents of lesbian sadomasochism argued that, contrary to appearance, lesbian s/m does not conflict with feminist goals, because it substantially differs from heterosexual male-dominant, female-subordinate sexual relations which also eroticize violence. Because lesbians belong to the same sexual caste, lesbian s/m occurs outside of the larger frame of gender inegalitarian relations; and because the lesbian masochist consents to and controls the scene, she retains the right to determine what happens to her body. Moreover, lesbian s/m fantasies are clearly understood as just fantasies, and freedom to explore such fantasies and women's sexual pleasure is critical to women's liberation from repressive restrictions on women's sexuality. Finally, dominant-submissive s/m scripts enable women to explore safely their own feelings about power relations and, possibly also, to explore an inevitable feature of human relations.

Opponents responded with skepticism about the alleged disanalogy between inegalitarian heterosexual relations and lesbian sadomasochism. Lesbian s/m is a product of the larger, heterosexual culture which constructs sexuality as naturally sadomasochistic by eroticizing violence and humiliation.[31] The attraction to s/m is not natural but culturally produced; and lesbian sadomasochists, far from exploring a new, liberating sexuality, simply mirror the inegalitarian and sadomasochistic form that heterosexual relations take in a society where men are powerful and women powerless. To claim that, simply in virtue of its lesbian context, lesbian sadomasochism does not carry the connotations of male dominance over and violence against women is to indulge in the mistaken belief that the meaning of symbols and actions 'can be amputated from their historical and social context' and made to mean whatever one likes.[32] Rather, lesbian s/m fantasies endorse and perpetuate the values and systems of oppression that feminists are committed to undermining. Moreover, the masochist's claim to have given consent is suspect given

[31] Heterosexual sadomasochism, in Sally Roesch Wagner's words, 'is not a "kinky" deviation from normal heterosexual behavior. Rather, it is the defining quality of the power relationship between men and women. Sadism is the logical extension of behavior that arises out of male power. Self-will, dominance, unbridled anger and cold rationality: these qualities, bought at the expense of gentleness and concern for others, define the classic sadist as the "real" man. Selflessness, submission, lack of will, and unbridled emotionalist: these qualities demanded of women, to the detriment of concern for self and independence, portray the classic masochist'. (Sally Roesch Wagner, 'Pornography and the Sexual Revolution: The Backlash of Sadomasochism', in *Against Sadomasochism*, 23–44, 28.)

[32] Susan Leigh Star, 'Swastikas: The Street and the University', in *Against Sadomasochism*, 131–6, 133.

that '[f]or women, love is structured as masochism. For women, sex is structured as masochism. None of us escapes this message, not even lesbian feminists'.[33]

What I find interesting about these debates is that they proceed curiously unencumbered by the thought that *lesbianism* might complicate the analysis of s/m between women. Indeed, one could almost forget that lesbian sexuality is the issue. And for good reason. The entire debate takes place on the backdrop and avails itself of arguments used in debates about heterosexual women's sexuality. On the one hand, is the (hetero)sexual revolution of the 1970s with its revolt against sexual repression and advocacy of unrestricted sexual experimentation. On the other hand, is the anti-(heterosexual)pornography movement with its condemnation of (hetero)sexual objectification of and violence against women. At issue in both the larger pro- versus anti-sex debates and the smaller lesbian s/m debates is the disposition of *women's* sexuality, with heterosexual women's sexuality setting the terms of the debate.

Opponents assumed that lesbian s/m could be nothing but an imitation of the worst forms of heterosexuality. Proponents assumed that the value of s/m for lesbians could be nothing but the sexually liberating value it had for women. Neither side in the sex wars imagined that lesbianism had much to do with the issue.

Why should lesbianism have complicated the analysis of lesbian s/m? And why might that complication have been resisted?

## Imitation versus Solving Representational Problems

The idea that s/m (and butch-femme roles, pornography, dildos, etc.) gets into lesbian relations simply via imitation warrants scrutiny. Imitation implies that what lesbians find erotic in s/m, butch-femme roles, pornography, dildos, etc. is exactly what heterosexuals find erotic in these same things: violence, power differences, sexual objectification, male penetration. Hence, opponents concluded that lesbian s/m conflicts with feminist values. But why assume in the first place that s/m has no meaning for lesbians *beyond* what it does for heterosexuals? Given that the taboo on lesbian sexuality is itself a source of erotic charge, one might ask what connection s/m bears to the eroticism of the lesbian taboo. Does the attraction of s/m for lesbians lie not just in eroticized violence but more centrally in the power of s/m to represent the lesbian taboo? Moreover, given that 'lesbian' is a sexual identity, one might ask what connection s/m bears to the representation of lesbian identity. Does the attraction of s/m for lesbians lie in its power to represent lesbian difference from heterosexual women?

Ruby Rich has suggested that one result of feminism was that

---

[33] Wagner, 29.

[t]he lesbian moved from a position of outlaw to one of respectable citizen. Yet in the pre-Stonewall era prior to 1969, the lesbian was a far more criminal figure, her very sexuality criminalized in many laws, her desires unacceptable, and her clothing taboo (at least for the butch, who was the only visible lesbian in this period). . . . Thus, there was a very real sense of loss associated with the hard-won respectability: a loss of taboo and its eroticism.[34]

That respectability resulted partly from arguments to the effect that lesbians, from a feminist political point of view, are the truly woman-identified women. Partly, it resulted from lesbian feminists' cultivating (feminist) respectability by eschewing butch-femme roles, conducting egalitarian relations, and practicing nonpenetrative sex. Partly, it resulted from suggestions that lesbianism is natural to women, and heterosexuality the cultural product of compulsory heterosexuality.[35] Thus, Gayle Rubin could say of her experience of 1970s feminism that '[o]ne could luxuriate in the knowledge that not only was one not a slimy pervert, but one's sexuality was especially blessed on political grounds. As a result, I never quite understood the experience of being gay in the face of unrelenting contempt'.[36] But this blessing was mixed, and its price tag was the eroticism of the lesbian taboo. Reinvesting lesbianism with the eroticism of the taboo required importing tabooed practices into lesbianism. But where was a lesbian feminist to find a tabooed practice? In feminism itself—specifically, in the feminist prohibition of power structured sexual practices. Hence the particularly strong endorsement of s/m by lesbian feminists.[37]

Feminist theorizing, however, did more than render lesbian sexuality respectable. It eroded the distinction between lesbians and (feminist) hetero-

---

[34] Rich, 532.

[35] I am thinking here of Adrienne Rich's interpretation of Chodorow in 'Compulsory Heterosexuality and Lesbian Existence', in *The Signs Reader: Women, Gender and Scholarship*, ed. Elizabeth Abel and Emily K. Abel (Chicago: University of Chicago Press, 1983), 139–68.

[36] Gayle Rubin, 'The Leather Menace', qtd in Phelan, 103.

[37] This is a point Julia Creet stresses in 'Daughter of the Movement: The Psychodynamics of Lesbian S/M Fantasy', *Differences* 3 (1991): 135–59.

Some have argued that lesbian feminist advocacy of s/m, neo butch-femme, lesbian pornography, and public sex was a reaction to the sexually repressive prescriptivism of cultural feminism. See, e.g. Lillian Faderman, ch. 10 in *Odd Girls and Twilight Lovers* (New York: Penguin, 1992) and 'The Return of Butch and Femme: A Phenomenon of Lesbian Sexuality of the 1980s and l990s', *Journal of the History of Sexuality* 2 (1992): 578–96. This 'rebellion against repression' thesis, however, does not explain why it it was specifically *lesbians* who rebelled. Rich's and Creet's focus on the loss of the lesbian taboo does.

I do not mean to rule out alternative accounts of the lesbian-specific meaning of lesbian s/m, butch-femme, and lesbian pornography. The truth may be that *lesbian* feminist advocacy of these sexual forms was overdetermined. For instance, Judith Butler, and following her, Biddy Martin and Terallee Bensinger, have argued that the reconfigurations of masculinity and femininity in lesbian sexual practices denaturalizes gender and challenges the assumption of a natural gender binarism that underlies heterosexual society, and all too often feminist theory as well. See Butler, *Gender Trouble*, and 'Imitation and Gender Insubordination', in *Inside/Out*, ed. Diana Fuss (New York: Routledge, 1990), 13–31; Biddy Martin, 'Sexual Practice'; and Terralee Bensinger, 'Lesbian Pornography: The Re/Making of (a) Community', *Discourse* 15 (1992): 69–93.

sexual women, thereby undermining the possibility for *lesbian* representation. As we saw in the previous chapter, the Radicalesbians, Charlotte Bunch, and Adrienne Rich all offered de-sexualized and politicized readings of lesbianism as a matter of emotional commitment to women and resistance to patriarchally structured personal relations between men and women. The lesbian is the woman-identified woman. Thus, the mark of the lesbian ceases to be her sex/gender/sexuality outlaw status under institutionalized heterosexuality and becomes simply her gender outlaw status under patriarchy. Economically, socially, emotionally, and sexually she refuses to behave like a woman in relation to men. But even (careful) heterosexual women can claim this gender outlaw status. As a result, lesbian difference becomes unrepresentable under the gender sign 'woman-identified woman'.

Feminist reconstructions of the erotic exacerbated the problem by eroding the line between heterosexual women's and lesbians' erotic relations to women. Aimed at distinguishing *women*'s sexuality from men's, the new feminist eroticism stressed the deep satisfaction of acting on one's own needs for sharing and creativity, the importance of a passion for friends and shared work, and the quality of attention brought to both love and friendship.[38] On this conception of the erotic, heterosexual women and lesbians obviously can—and presumably *should* in so far as they are woman-identified—have *the same* erotic relations to women. The new feminist eroticism also equated heterosexuality with the male-identified; and it oppositionally positioned heterosexuality not against homosexuality, but against *women*'s egalitarian, passionate, attentive, 'erotic' relations. Thus, the contrast between heterosexuality and homosexuality, which is crucial to thinking about lesbian difference, disappeared from view.

Barred from using her desire for women to represent lesbian difference, how could a lesbian feminist represent lesbian difference and the difference of lesbian eroticism?—by deploying male-identified heterosexual forms in lesbian feminist sexual practices. She could then claim that what distinguishes the lesbian is her power to appropriate seemingly male-identified sexual forms and use them for woman-identified purposes—something heterosexual women cannot do.

The problem created for lesbian representation by the woman-identified woman and her nonsexual eroticism interestingly echoes the problem created for lesbian representation during the first decades of the twentieth century by the Victorian image of romantic friendships. In 'The Mythic Mannish Lesbian', Esther Newton argues that Radclyffe Hall uses the mannish lesbian Stephen Gordon as the protagonist in *The Well of Loneliness* for the purpose

[38] I am thinking particularly of Audre Lorde 'Uses of the Erotic: the Erotic as Power', in *Sister Outsider: Essays and Speeches by Audre Lorde* (Trumansburg, NY: Crossing Press, 1984), 53–9; Janice G. Raymond, *A Passion for Friends: Toward a Philosophy of Female Affection* (Boston: Beacon, 1986); and Sarah Lucia Hoagland, *Lesbian Ethics: Toward New Value* (Palo Alto, CA: Institute of Lesbian Studies, 1988).

of representing lesbian sexuality, and that she could not have achieved this aim by using a less mannish figure.[39] As Newton points out, Victorian wisdom held that women are not sexual beings. Thus, the first generation of New Women in the late nineteenth century who sought out romantic friendships with other women rather than marrying lacked a conceptual framework to envision their relations as sexual ones. '[W]hat "pure" women did with each other, no matter how good it felt, could not be conceived as sexual within the terms of the nineteenth century romantic discourse'.[40] Unlike the first generation, who equated liberation with autonomy from family, the second generation of New Women, which included Radclyffe Hall, equated liberation with sexual freedom. But how was a lesbian to represent her sexuality given the construction of romantic friendships between women as asexual and the attribution of sexual desire only to men?—by deploying *masculine* gender images within her relation to women. Thus, Newton concludes that

Hall and many other feminists like her embraced, sometimes with ambivalence, the image of the mannish lesbian and the discourse of the sexologists about inversion primarily because they desperately wanted to break out of the asexual model of romantic friendship.[41]

Mannishness in the early 1900s and male-identified sexual forms in the 1970s and 1980s can, then, both be read as lesbian representational strategies, aimed at solving different problems of lesbian representation. For Radclyffe Hall, the problem was how to represent lesbian *sexuality* in a world that equated 'sexual' with 'male'. For lesbian feminists, the problem was how to represent *lesbian* sexuality in a world of erotic woman-bonding that includes both heterosexual women and lesbians.

The point of these observations is threefold. First, in the sex war debates, gender operated as a lesbian closet despite the debate's focus on lesbian sexual practice. Cast as a debate over *women*'s sexuality, the arguments rendered invisible the problems posed by feminism for lesbian eroticism and lesbian representation. Second, feminist political investment in distinguishing *women*'s sexuality from men's motivated the denial of sexual differences between heterosexual women and lesbians. 'Heterosexuality' came to refer not to a sexual orientation, but to a particular dominant-submissive style of sexual interaction between men and women. Third, the distinctively lesbian deployment (even, or especially, within feminism) of masculinity and male-identified sexual forms suggests that any conjunction of 'sexual orientation' with 'woman' will be an uneasy one. As I will argue in the next section, lesbian slippage between 'woman' and 'man' suggests that the lesbian is not just another woman-gender.

[39] Esther Newton, 'The Mythic Mannish Lesbian: Radclyffe Hall and the New Woman', *Signs* 9 (1984): 557–75.

[40] Ibid. 561.                                                                       [41] Ibid. 560.

## III.  The Dangers of Gender

I have argued that both the 1980s notion of the lesbian as the woman-identified woman and the 1990s attempt to avoid essentialism by attending exclusively to differences between lesbians obscures the difference between heterosexual women and lesbians. As a result, theorizing that takes as its subject the woman-identified woman or the differences between lesbians is unlikely to represent lesbian difference effectively. If theorizing about lesbians is to be possible within a feminist frame, then we need to bring them into this frame as *lesbians*, and not as women-identified women or as so differentiated by race, class, and ethnicity that they lack any specificity of their own. But what does bringing them in as lesbians mean?

If lesbian difference is to be brought into view, it would seem that we would need to begin by defining what it means to be lesbian, what distinguishes being lesbian from being heterosexual, and who does and does not count as a lesbian. This, however, is a highly problematic approach, as many have noted. To begin with, there does not appear to be any viable way of defining 'lesbian' that simultaneously allows us to do lesbian history while avoiding a falsely ahistorical and essentializing description of lesbian identity. As has often been noted, the terms 'lesbianism' and 'heterosexuality' are inventions of late nineteenth century sexologists. The content of those terms, as we presently understand them, is largely (though not exclusively) the product of medical theorizing begun by sexologists and revised and elaborated by subsequent psychoanalytic theorizing through the 1960s. Given this, some have argued that the very notion of a sexual orientation is a recent invention and that lesbians and homosexuals simply do not exist prior to the late nineteenth century.[42] Others have argued that there were in fact culturally available concepts of sexual attraction between women prior to the late nineteenth century (e.g. the tribade and the female husband), but that these concepts differ enough from contemporary understandings of lesbianism to make it unwise and inaccurate to use the term 'lesbian' for these earlier relationships.[43] In short, if we try to define lesbian difference by relying on our historically specific understanding of lesbianism, we will find ourselves either denying that it is possible to do lesbian history at all or we will end up doing a lesbian history that obscures important historical differences in how women's intimate interactions with each other were conceived.

In response to this problem, some have suggested that 'lesbian' be interpreted as a cluster concept. That is, 'lesbian' does not have any one meaning but refers to a variety of relationships between women that have existed in different time periods and different cultures.[44] This strategy, however, does

---

[42] David M. Halperin, 'Is There a History of Sexuality?' in *The Lesbian and Gay Studies Reader*, 416–31.

[43] Judith Halberstam, *Female Masculinity* (Durham, NC: Duke University Press, 1998).

[44] Claudia Card takes this approach in *Lesbian Choices* (New York: Columbia University Press, 1995).

not solve the basic problem that *any* attempt to describe what 'lesbian' refers to will inevitably have to rely on twentieth-century, western understandings of the term. Consider, in order to decide which relationships to include under the cluster concept 'lesbian', we have to begin from some sense of the range of characteristics that are and are not relevant to being a lesbian. What, for example, are we to do with passionate, but quite possibly asexual, friendships between women in the nineteenth century? If we include them because they involve woman-bonding, it looks as though we are relying on a distinctly feminist notion of what it means to be a lesbian. If we exclude them because they are asexual, it looks as though we are relying on a distinctly twentieth-century psychological notion of lesbianism as a sexual orientation. In either case, contemporary conceptions of what it means to be a lesbian are being used to construct the cluster concept which is then applied to historical periods that may not share our conception of what the salient features of relationships between women are.

Attempting to define lesbian difference is problematic for other reasons as well. Those who self-identify as lesbian often do not agree on what it means to be a lesbian. Because what it means to be a lesbian is contested, no one definition of lesbianism is likely to capture the multiple subjective experiences and interpretations of being a lesbian. To make matters worse, disagreement about what it means to be a lesbian has often had a strongly normative tone. This is because any definition of lesbianism lends itself to being used against those who self-identify as lesbian but who do not fit the proposed definition. 'You are not a *real* lesbian, because you do not do ____, or you do do ____'. Because the project of specifying lesbian difference looks like the project of deciding which people count as real lesbians and which do not, and thus who may speak for lesbians and who may not, the project of defining difference may seem an unwise one to embark.

Both objections to defining lesbian difference are serious ones. But caution needs to be taken in what we infer from them. It would be a mistake to infer that specifying lesbian difference is uniquely problematic. It is not. Exactly the same worries could be raised about any attempt to specify women's difference from men, or blacks' difference from whites. First, like 'lesbian', 'woman' is a historically variable, social construct. Were we to take seriously the social constructedness of gender, we in fact should raise the same sort of questions about who belongs in women's history as are often raised about who belongs in lesbian history. Do male *berdache* belong? Do male to female transsexuals? That telling women's history is typically not taken to be problematic may say more about the frequency with which 'woman' is uncritically equated with 'female' than about any transhistorical uniformity in the concept 'woman'. But if taking seriously the social constructedness of 'woman' would not motivate us (as I think it would not) to give up doing women's history or to think that specifying women's difference from men was a hopeless project, then the constructedness of 'lesbian' should not motivate us to reach those conclusions either. In Chapter 1, I suggested one specific reason why we should not give up doing lesbian history even if there were no lesbians, as we understand the category, in other time periods or cultures. Our main interest in telling a lesbian and gay history may be a political one, for example, to show how parochial our contemporary attitudes toward same-sex sexual activity are. For that purpose, it is useful to use our contemporary definitions of lesbianism and homosexuality. I called these 'fictional essences' to underscore the fact that we need not take ourselves to be making any claim about who *really* is, from some transhistorical perspective, a lesbian.

Second, just as the specification of lesbian difference has sometimes been used to judge who is a real lesbian entitled to speak about lesbian experience, so the specification of women's difference from men has sometimes been used to judge who counts as a real woman and thus who is entitled to speak for women. Male to female transsexuals, for example, have often been excluded from women's and lesbians' spaces on the grounds that they are not real women. If the normative misuses to which a specification of sex/gender differences can be put would not motivate us (as I think they would not) to give up drawing sex/gender distinctions, then the normative misuses to which specifications of sexual orientation differences can be put should not motivate us to give up drawing sexual orientation distinctions. It is also important to keep in mind the difference between asking: 'Who is a real lesbian?' and 'Who represents the lesbian?'. 'Who is a real lesbian?' is a normatively loaded question, any particular answer to which is likely to be contested by at least some of those who identify as lesbian. 'Who represents the lesbian?' is not similarly normatively loaded. The latter question simply asks us to specify those broadly shared cultural understandings of lesbian difference that make it possible for us to 'read' some persons more easily than others as lesbian. Through what images does the lesbian become most imaginable? What images invite a lesbian reading? Those images, I want to suggest, are neither simply images of same-sex sexuality nor images of gender deviance, though they may include both. The lesbian becomes most imaginable via images that make salient her position outside the sex/gender binary 'woman' and 'man'.

## The Third Sex

Martha Vicinus, for example, opens her essay on the history of lesbianism with the image of Rosa Bonheur, a woman who dressed like a man and lived with a woman and who wrote her sister in 1884: 'It amuses me to see how puzzled the people are. They wonder to which sex I belong. The ladies especially lose themselves in conjectures about "the little old man who looks so lively" '.[45] Vicinus introduces Bonheur in order to pose the problem of doing

[45] Martha Vicinus, ' "They Wonder To Which Sex I Belong": The Historical Roots of the Modern Lesbian Identity', in *The Lesbian and Gay Studies Reader*, 432–52, 432.

lesbian history. We know nothing of Bonheur's sexuality, only that she enjoyed her gender ambiguity and her passionate friendship with the more feminine Nathalie Micas. What is there about Bonheur that represents the lesbian and invites us to see her as a lesbian? On the one hand, there is her passionate friendship and devotion to another woman. She is one among many women in the second half of the nineteenth century who sustained a long-term, emotionally intense relation to another woman. But why choose Bonheur rather than Micas to pose the problem of doing lesbian history? Why ask whether the *cross-dressed* Bonheur is a lesbian as though she, but not Micas, were an especially tantalizing candidate?

Bonheur is one among many cross-dressing women who lived with, married, or had sexual affairs with women. In the eighteenth century, there are Mary East who passed as James How and had a wife for thirty-five years, the ladies of Llangollen who lived together and attired themselves in a cross between men's and women's styles, and Catherine Margaretha Linck who passed as a man and was executed when her wife revealed that Linck was a woman.[46] In the nineteenth century, there are Bonheur, and Louisa Lumsden who though not crossed-dressed was the husband of Constance Maynard in their Boston marriage. In the twentieth century there are Gertrude Stein, clad in a large overcoat, Greek sandals, loose skirts, and cropped hair, married to the more feminine Alice B. Toklas; the tie and top hat sporting George Sand; and Radclyffe Hall passing as John and her fictional creation, mannish Stephen Gordon, whose lover was the feminine Mary. There are the butch lesbians of the 1940s and 1950s with their femme cohorts and more contemporary varieties of masculine and feminine lesbians.

Who among these women have the most power to represent, make imaginable, the lesbian—the feminine women (the wives) or the cross-dressed women (the husbands)? It would seem to be the latter. Bonheur, Gertrude Stein, Stephen Gordon, and butches figure the lesbian in ways their more feminine counterparts cannot. In their power to generate the question 'To which sex does s/he belong?', they invite a reading of them as lesbians.

I am not here suggesting that the mannish lesbian, the butch, is a real lesbian in ways the feminine lesbian, the femme, is not. On the contrary, to take mannishness itself as the marker of the lesbian is to read literally what is merely symbolic.[47] It is to fail to see that mannishness figures the lesbian only because, and only so long as, it successfully raises the question: 'To which sex

---

[46] All mentioned by Vicinus. The history of cross-dressed women is also discussed by Lillian Faderman in *Surpassing the Love of Men: Romantic Friendship and Love between Women from the Renaissance to the Present* (New York: Morrow, 1981); and by Marjorie Garber in *Vested Interests: Cross-Dressing and Cultural Anxiety (New York: HarperPerennial, 1993).*

[47] An analogy may clarify the point. Suppose I present you with a picture of a person seated, reading in a library full of books and a picture of a person walking through a cornfield at dawn. I ask, 'Which image more powerfully represents the scholar?' The library picture does. To infer from this that people in cornfields cannot be scholars or that everyone in libraries is a scholar would be a mistake—a mistake made possible by taking literally a symbolic image of the scholar.

does s/he belong?' The more vigorously one attempts to read the cross-dressed or mannish female for signs that she is unambiguously a woman, the less powerful become cross-dressing and mannishness as symbols for the lesbian. Similarly, the more vigorously one attempts to read femme lesbian sexuality for sex/gender ambiguity, the more powerfully femme sexuality figures the lesbian.[48]

A similar point might be made about same-sex sexuality. Since the mid twentieth century, sexual object choice rather than gender deviance has been the primary cultural marker of lesbianism and homosexuality. But images of same-sex sexual attraction and activity, like images of mannishness, figure the lesbian only because, and only so long as, they successfully raise the question 'To which sex does s/he belong?' For a variety of reasons, same-sex sexuality may fail to raise that question. The more vigorously same-sex desire is recast as a phase or a product of situational factors, such as confinement to same-sex prisons, the less power does that desire have to represent an exit from the category 'woman' and from the unity of femaleness and femininity with heterosexual orientation. Similarly, the more vigorously same-sex desire is recast as desire for an individual *person* rather than desire for a woman, or as desire by an individual person rather than by a female, the less power does that desire have to represent lesbians' sex/gender difference from women. In Celia Kitzinger's study of lesbian identity, for example, some lesbians argued that they are just *persons* who happen to desire women sexually. Their sexuality is a private, personal matter, constituting 'only a small and relatively insignificant part of the "whole person" '.[49] In this construction, sex takes place between people, and same-sex activity does not mark one out as different, a lesbian. The affirmation of same-sex desire can coexist with a denial of lesbian difference only because same-sex desire does not by itself represent lesbian difference any more than gender deviance by itself represents lesbian difference.[50] As I suggested in the previous chapter, lesbians become imaginable by culturally constructing a kind of person who violates the unity of female anatomy, heterosexual desire, and gender behavior in a way that positions them outside the sex/gender binary of 'woman' and 'man'.

If it is not just same-sex desire (or gender deviance), but an ambiguous

---

[48] Developing both Judith Butler's notion of 'the logic of inversion', where what first appeared feminine in the femme inverts into the masculine (Butler, 'Imitation and Gender Insubordination') and Joan Nestle's descriptions of femme sexual power (Nestle, *A Restricted Country*), Biddy Martin reads femme (and butch) sexuality as resisting categorization into the unambiguously feminine (or masculine). Martin, 'Sexual Practice'.

[49] Celia Kitzinger, *The Social Construction of Lesbianism* (London: Sage, 1987), 111.

[50] Significantly, those same women adopted anti-feminist stances, particularly toward what they perceived as the unfeminine appearance of feminists. As one woman observes of feminist lesbians, 'Once they have "become lesbians" they are relieved to think they will never again have to wear pretty clothes or curl their hair. Nonsense!' (Kitzinger, 142). They secure their status as people, rather than lesbians, by presenting themselves as possessors of an unambiguously womanly femininity. My guess is that they would equally resist being read as femmes, that is, as possessors of an ambiguously womanly identity.

relation to the categories 'woman' and 'man' that most powerfully represents the lesbian, then the most common objection to the woman-identified woman—namely that this image *de-sexualizes* lesbians—may be somewhat misplaced. The elision of lesbian difference may result less from desexualizing lesbian desire than from the firm insistence that lesbians are unambiguously *women*. The feminist stress on lesbians' authentic womanhood has much the same effect as Kitzinger's subjects' stress on lesbians' personhood, namely, the erasure of lesbian difference. Rosa Bonheur's sex/gender ambiguity disappears under the categories 'person' and 'woman'.[51]

The power of sex/gender ambiguity to represent the lesbian dates from Carl von Westphal's case study of the congenital invert published in 1869. Westphal's case brought the lesbian as a distinct medical category of person-ality type into being and inaugurated an explosion of psychiatric studies of the invert, the third sex, the woman with a touch of the hermaphrodite, the male soul trapped in a female body, the unsexed, the semi-women. Havelock Ellis and Richard von Krafft-Ebing, who were two of Westphal's more famous disciples, and others officialized lesbian and homosexual difference. But as the above list of referring terms suggests, and as Foucault warns,

[w]e must not forget that the psychological, psychiatric, medical category of homo-sexuality was constituted from the moment it was characterized . . . less by a type of sexual relations than by a certain quality of sexual sensibility, a certain way of invert-ing the masculine and the feminine in oneself. Homosexuality appeared as one of the forms of sexuality when it was transposed from the practice of sodomy onto a kind of interior androgyny, a hermaphrodism of the soul.[52]

Havelock Ellis, for example, describes the sexually inverted woman as some-one in whom some trace of masculinity or boyishness is to be found. She elic-its, often subtly, the thought, 'she ought to have been a man'. She has a masculine straightforwardness and sense of honor, wears male attire when practicable, has a penchant for cigarettes and cigars, is a good whistler (male inverts cannot whistle), likes athletics but not needlework, is aggressive (sometimes committing violent crimes like men), and may be both muscular and hairy.[53] Though obviously intrigued by lesbian sexual desire, Ellis makes sexual desire take a backseat to gender inversion. Indeed, sex and desire between women do not differentiate the invert from either the 'normal' woman or the 'class of women' to whom the sexual invert is attracted. Normal women may sexually interact when segregated from men in prisons, convents,

---

[51] I deliberately use 'sex/gender' here. Lesbian gender ambiguity—her openness to readings as masculine and feminine—is intimately connected with lesbian sex ambiguity (i.e. to questions about whether she is 'really' female at all and to suspicions about her anatomy). While I do not endorse biol-ogizing lesbianism, I do want to claim that reading a person as lesbian involves reading her as ambigu-ously gendered *and* ambiguously sexed.

[52] Michel Foucault, *The History of Sexuality, vol. I: An Introduction* (New York: Vintage, 1990), 43.

[53] Havelock Ellis, *Studies in the Psychology of Sex, vol. II: Sexual Inversion* (Philadelphia: F. A. Davis, 1928). See especially ch. IV.

girls' and women's schools, or harems; and, in Ellis's view, pubescent girls normally experience attractions to other girls. The class of women to whom inverts are attracted, though not quite normal, he thought, are typically 'womanly' and not true inverts.

Krafft-Ebing, though not equating lesbianism with inverted gender style, did equate the most degenerate forms of lesbianism with an inverted gender style. In his view, lesbianism took four increasingly degenerate forms: psychical hermaphroditism, or what we might now call bisexuality; homo-sexuality, or sexual desire oriented toward the same sex; viraginity, where lesbian desire is coupled with a preference for the masculine role; and gynandry, or 'men-women', in which the body itself appears masculine (she 'possesses of the feminine qualities only the genital organs').[54] In describing viraginity, Krafft-Ebing focuses on the women's tomboyish childhood, their preference for playing with soldiers, and their inclination for male garments, science, smoking, drinking, and imagining themselves men in relation to women. 'The masculine soul, heaving in the female bosom', he remarks, 'finds pleasure in the pursuit of manly sports and in manifestations of courage and bravado'.[55] He adds that '[u]ranism may nearly always be suspected in females wearing their hair short or who dress in the fashion of men, or pursue the sports and pastimes of their male acquaintances . . .'.[56]

In his descriptions of lesbianism, Krafft-Ebing, unlike Ellis, appears on the surface to conceptualize lesbian sexual desire independently of gender-images, since gender-crossing characterizes only the more degenerative stages. But this is only a surface appearance. In an effort to explain same-sex desire, Krafft-Ebing posits a psycho-sexual cerebral center which would normally develop homologous to the 'sexual glands' but which in lesbians develops contrary to them. The result is a masculine psycho-sexual center in a feminine brain.[57] Thus, even if some lesbians are not masculine in character, they are nevertheless not fully women.

## The Instability of Lesbian Representation

In returning to the sexological literature on lesbians, my aim is not to endorse its particular pathologizing, biologizing, and masculinizing descriptions. My point instead is that the *lesbian* became and remains conceivable, representable, in virtue of the creation of a new category of individuals who were *outside* of the sex/gender categories 'woman' and 'man'. If she has a sex or gender, it is neither female nor male. As I read the sexologists, the lesbian is not constituted by her mannishness, but more fundamentally by her externality to binary sex/gender categories. Hirschfeld's image of the male soul

---

[54] Richard von Krafft-Ebing, *Psychopathia Sexualis: A Medico-Forensic Study* (New York: Pioneer Publication, 1947), 399, 336.

[55] Ibid. 300.          [56] Ibid. 398.          [57] Ibid. 348–49.

trapped in a female body, Ellis's image of the boyish woman, and Krafft-Ebing's image of the masculine psycho-sexual center in a feminine brain are multiple efforts to represent the possibility of being someone who is not-woman, not-man.

It is no surprise that in the wake of sexology's particular strategy for representing the not-woman, not-man, cross-dressing became the vehicle for articulating lesbian personhood. In 1920s Paris, for instance, cigarette smoking, cropped hair, monocle wearing, top hats and tails signaled lesbian 'sexual difference *within*'.[58] Nor is it surprising that Radclyffe Hall chose mannish Stephen Gordon rather than womanly Mary to represent the lesbian. But as Marjorie Garber points out, gender-crossing strategies of lesbian representation are inherently unstable because they are perpetually open to being appropriated by and for heterosexual women. Smoking, which both Ellis and Krafft-Ebing associated with lesbianism was, by the 1940s taken over by heterosexual women.[59] And '[l]esbian styles of the 20s—men's formal dress, top hats and tails—popularized onstage by entertainers like Marlene Dietrich and Judy Garland, became high fashion statements, menswear for women re-sexualized as straight (as well as gay) style'. According to Newton, Radclyffe Hall's own cross-dressing and the cross-dressed figure of Stephen Gordon represented not only the lesbian inner self but also 'the New Woman's rebellion against the male order', and was thus open to appropriation by heterosexual feminists who had their own interests in gender-deviant representational strategies.[60] Butch lesbian style of the 1940s and 1950s also proved unstable. In a toned-down form, lesbian butch style became *the* feminist style and the symbol for the authentic, non-male-identified woman.[61] Contemporary marketing strategies contribute to the instability of lesbian representation. Danae Clark, for example, argues that advertisers are now employing dual marketing strategies that offer to lesbian consumers styles and images that are coded lesbian but that heterosexual consumers will not detect.[62]

Cross-dressing, however, is not the only possible representational strategy. Monique Wittig argued that lesbians are not-women, not-men, because they, unlike members of the category 'woman', are economically and socially independent of men.[63] She figures lesbians' position outside the binary gender system by means of their economic and social relations, not their cross-dressing. But like earlier lesbian representational strategies, this one also proved unstable. Wittig's symbol of the lesbian becomes in later feminist work the symbol of the (straight) feminist, the liberated woman. This instability of lesbian representation is exactly what one would expect given the social construction of gender itself.

---

[58] Garber, 155.        [59] Ibid. 155–7.        [60] Newton, 570.
[61] Faderman, 'The Return of Butch and Femme'.
[62] Danae Clark, 'Commodity Lesbianism', in *The Lesbian and Gay Studies Reader*, 186–201.
[63] Monique Wittig, 'One is Not Born a Woman', in *The Straight Mind*, 20.

## The Disappearance of the Lesbian under the De-essentialized Woman

We are now in a position to see why the de-essentializing of the category 'woman' might endanger lesbian representation. So long as 'woman' remains substantively filled in, lesbians can representationally position themselves outside of that category, although those representations will have to continually shift to accommodate shifts in the meaning of 'woman'. The de-essentialist, difference-sensitive turn in feminism presents a vastly new and more difficult challenge for lesbian representation. If 'woman' has no essential meaning, but there are, instead, multiple and open-ended ways that women can be, how does one go about representing oneself *outside* 'woman' rather than *differently inside* 'woman'? After all, it seems that not only is being the sort of person who sexually desires women one of the ways a woman can be, but so is being mannish, butch, using a dildo, engaging in s/m, marrying a woman, and so on.

Judith Butler's particular de-essentializing strategy helps pose the problem in an acute form. 'Woman', in her view, is something one can never fully *be*, because there are no natural women. The illusion of a natural binarism of gender categories into 'woman' and 'man' is the result of repetitive (and panicked) performances of a unity between body, gender, and (heterosexual) desire. One consequence of this view is that neither masculinity nor femininity naturally belong to a particular sex. The illusion that femininity belongs to women in a way masculinity does not is simply the result of the compulsoriness of that particular gender performance for women. But it is open to women to perform otherwise. The mannish lesbian is, on this reading, neither imitating a man (since there is no real or natural man to imitate) nor necessarily being unwomanly. '[I]n acting in a masculine way, *she changes the very meaning of what it is to be a woman*; indeed, she expands the meaning of what it means to be a woman to include a cultural possibility that it previously excluded'.[64]

Once 'woman' is denaturalized and opened up in this way, the lesbian may well find herself in a hopeless representational position. *Nothing* she does may count as positioning her outside of the category 'woman'. *Everything* she does may be read simply as expanding the meaning of 'woman'. What was originally intended within feminism as a move away from a totalizing conception of 'woman' that was incapable of admitting differences between women, now becomes totalizing in a quite different way. Although virtually any self-representation may be permitted within the category 'woman', and the meaning of 'woman' remains perpetually open to contestation, the one thing that may not be possible is self-representation *outside* of that category.

Butler herself does not come to this conclusion. In her view, 'the effect of

---

[64] Judith Butler, 'Gendering the Body: Beauvoir's Philosophical Contribution', in *Women, Knowledge, and Reality: Explorations in Feminist Philosophy*, ed. Ann Garry and Marilyn Pearsall (Boston: Unwin Hyman, 1989), 253–62, 260 (my emphasis).

this carnival of gender [that becomes possible when the meanings of 'masculine' and 'feminine' become fluid] can be conceptualized in one of two ways, either as an internal expansion of existing gender categories or as a proliferation of gender itself beyond the usual two'.[65] That is, the denaturalization of 'woman' and 'man' could facilitate lesbian representation by underscoring the plausibility of constructing a third (or fourth, etc.) sex. Rather than being perpetually accused of being a woman who imitates men, the lesbian could claim to be a distinct gender.

However, the imperative driving difference-sensitive feminism—to acknowledge differences between women and to frame a nonexclusionary feminist agenda—militates against this latter option. If feminists are to theorize the lesbian and include lesbian rights among feminist political goals, the lesbian must first be brought under the sign 'woman'. There, she may contest the meaning of woman. What she may not do is announce her defection from the category 'woman'. If this is in fact, as I think it is, the compulsory effect of a difference-sensitive feminist frame, then gender will operate within feminism as a lesbian closet. The lesbian becomes the lesbian *woman*. This means that we must read her sexuality as constituting only an accidental difference. She is essentially a woman. Stripped of the monstrous image of the third sex—not-woman, not-man—lesbian sexuality becomes just sex, a woman's sexuality, and as such simply a set of acts or practices that cannot challenge the binarism of gender. In addition, having subsumed the lesbian under 'women', it would seem that we must read heterosexism as a set of penalties addressed to the lesbian for her failure to conform to an essentializing cultural definition of 'woman'. Within this feminist frame, we may not read heterosexism as addressed to her failure to be a woman of any sort at all.

## Conclusion

I have argued, in section I, that feminist theorizing has failed to capture lesbian difference because it has not begun with a full-blown theory of lesbian and gay subordination fully parallel to race and class oppression. In order to theorize the lesbian within a feminist frame we would need an analysis of the distinctive social, legal, and ideological position of the lesbian under institutionalized heterosexuality. This would mean, among other factors, examining the ways that heterosexuals and nonheterosexuals constitute opposing political classes. Under theorizing lesbian and gay subordination resulted in feminist constructions of lesbian identity that served more to obscure lesbian difference than to illuminate it—first, the woman-identified woman, then more recently, the difference-identified woman.

In section II, I suggested that the problem runs deeper than under theoriz-

---

[65] Butler, 253–62, 260.

ing. The feminist goals of emancipating women's sexuality from patriarchy and of specifying a distinctive (nongenital) women's eroticism necessitated blurring the distinction between lesbian and heterosexual women's sexuality. Thus, feminist political commitments may motivate suppressing lesbian difference.

In section III, I argued that the problem runs deeper yet. Even if the ampersand between gender and sexual orientation were fully articulated, gender may continue operating as a lesbian closet. Lesbian difference was originally made conceivable and representable through the image of the third sex, the not-woman, not-man. To place lesbians within the category 'woman' (or 'women') is, then, in a real sense not to see lesbians, but only women with a different sexuality. My point here is directly parallel to Marjorie Garber's critique of feminist readings of transvestites like Michael/Dorothy in *Tootsie*. To see him/her as just a man dressed in women's clothes (and so, for example, to criticize him for posturing as a better woman than 'real' women are) is to fail to see the cross-dresser. Within a world populated solely by men and women, the cross-dresser *as a cross-dresser* disappears. 'This tendency to erase the third term, to appropriate the cross-dresser "as" one of the two sexes, is,' Garber notes,

emblematic of a fairly consistent critical desire to look away from the transvestite as transvestite, not to see cross-dressing except as male or female manque . . . . And this tendency might be called an *underestimation* of the object.[66]

To appropriate the lesbian as a woman similarly underestimates the lesbian.

Can one theorize the lesbian within a feminist frame? This, I think, depends on whether 'woman' delimits the feminist frame. If feminism is about women, then lesbians cannot adequately be theorized within that frame.[67] If, instead, feminism is about women *and* the open space of possibilities between the binary 'woman'/'man', then lesbians can be theorized within a feminist frame. But the cost of opening the feminist frame this way is quite high. With the lesbian not-woman enter the gay man, the heterosexual and gay male transvestite, the male-to-female transsexual, the male lesbian and the like— this time *not* as men or imitation women, but as the third term between gender binaries. In an opened frame, these male bodies could no longer be constructed as the Other to women. They would be fully feminist subjects. Also enter the female-to-male transsexual and the varieties of female masculinity, including female husbands and stone butches, described by Judith Halberstam—this time not as imitation men, but as the third term between gender binaries.[68] In an opened frame, these female bodies could no

---

[66] Garber, 10.

[67] To be sure, lesbians are mistaken for women and oppressed as women. And as a 'not-woman', the lesbian is conceptually linked to 'woman'. Thus, quite a lot, even if not everything, can be said about lesbians within a feminist frame.

[68] Judith Halberstam, *Female Masculinity*.

longer be constructed as women. They would be nonwomanly feminist subjects. I suspect that this transformation of males and nonimitatively masculine females into feminist subjects is a move many feminists would reject. If so, the lesbian will remain not only outside 'woman' but outside feminism.

# 4
# The Shape of Lesbian and Gay Subordination

In introducing this book, I offered two very general reasons for treating lesbian and gay subordination as a separate axis of oppression. First, getting a fix on the most fundamental contours of lesbian and gay subordination is essential if one is to have any hope of accurately picking out and describing the distinctively heterosexist dimensions of social experiences and practices. Just as outlining the structure of race, class, and gender oppression has been critical to social critique of particular racist, sexist, and classist practices, so outlining the structure of lesbian and gay subordination is a critical first step to more informed and well-targeted social criticism of heterosexist practices. In the previous chapter, I argued that lesbians disappear from view even in difference-sensitive feminism because one crucial preliminary question was not addressed: What *is* the structure of lesbian and gay subordination? A feminist method aimed at uncovering the intersections of different systems of oppression cannot hope to bring lesbians from the margin to the center unless this question is first answered.

Second, it seems to me pragmatically necessary to assume that lesbian and gay subordination is a separate axis. Making this assumption helps feminists guard against the danger of theorizing from a heterosexual viewpoint without noticing that they are doing so. If one has neither a model in mind of what lesbian and gay subordination typically looks like nor a deep appreciation of how differently lesbians and gays experience subordination, heterosexual bias in theorizing will be hard to avoid.

But it is not simply feminism that needs an analysis of the general structure of lesbian and gay subordination. An effective lesbian and gay politics needs it. Because lesbianism and homosexuality are distinctively sexual identities, it is tempting to assume without question that the center of lesbian and gay politics should be opposition to sexual regulations. In addition, because combating racial and gender discrimination are so central to our understanding of what civil rights are all about, it is tempting to assume without question that advocating anti-discrimination laws that protect gays and lesbians against the *material* costs of subordination—lost income, opportunity, authority, and status—are also at the center of lesbian and gay politics. I think these assumptions need to be questioned. Because any system of subordination will deprive the subordinated of important liberties and social goods, we need to begin an investigation of lesbian and gay subordination by asking *which* liberties and *which* social goods are most centrally involved. And we need to be open to the possibility that the answer will not be 'sexual liberty' or 'the material benefits of equal opportunity'.

I will be arguing that lesbian and gay subordination differs substantially in form from gender and racial oppression. In particular, lesbian and gay subordination does not materialize in a disadvantaged *place* that would sharply reduce the access of lesbians and gay men as a group to basic social goods like income, wealth, education, employment, and authoritative social positions. Instead, lesbian and gay subordination consists in the systematic *dis*placement of gay men and lesbians to the outside of civil society so that gay men and lesbians have no legitimized place, not even a disadvantaged one. Lesbians and gays are displaced from civil society's public sphere via the requirement that all citizens adopt at least the appearance of a heterosexual identity as a condition of access to the public sphere. Thus, gays and lesbians must adopt a pseudonymous heterosexual identity in order to gain full access to the public sphere.[1] This, in effect, displaces gay and lesbian *identities* from the public sphere. Lesbians and gays are also displaced from civil society's private sphere—namely, the sphere of marriage and family—via the bar on same-sex marriage and legal restrictions on adoption and child custody. Finally, gays and lesbians are displaced from civil society's future via legal, psychiatric, educational, and familial practices, such as anti-gay educational policies, whose aim is to prevent future generations of lesbian and gay people. As a result, the basic social goods denied to gays and lesbians are, above all, entitlement to represent one's identity publicly, access to a legitimate and protected private sphere, and control over the character of future generations.

Because the desirability of placing marriage and family at the center of lesbian and gay politics is contested by lesbians and gays themselves, I will wait to address lesbians' and gay's displacement from the private sphere until Chapters 5 and 6. In this chapter, I will concentrate on lesbians' and gays' displacement from the public sphere and from our social future. Since the concept of displacement differs substantially from the concept of oppression used in race and gender critiques, I will begin in section I by explaining why I think that the method of documenting oppression that is standardly used in gender and race critiques is ineffective in the case of lesbian and gay subordination. I will then turn to examining lesbian and gay displacement from the public sphere and our social future in sections II and III, ending in section IV with a response to the claim that displacing lesbians and gays is justified because their conduct is immoral.

---

[1] My notion of a pseudonymous heterosexual identity owes a great deal to James Woods's notion of a 'counterfeit identity' in his book with Jay H. Lucas, *The Corporate Closet: The Professional Lives of Gay Men in America* (New York: Free Press, 1993). Woods uses 'counterfeit identity' for gay men who actively manage their public identity in order to pass as heterosexual.

## I. The Problem of Nonlocated Subjects

The language of 'gay and lesbian rights', following as it does on the heels of the civil and women's rights movements, suggests that there is a natural analogy, between the political position of gay men and lesbians on the one hand, and of women and racial minorities on the other. Analogies are not hard to find. Gay men and lesbians face a formidable array of discriminatory policies and practices that limit their liberty and opportunity. Legally, gays and lesbians in the United States are in much the same position as racial minorities and women prior to the civil rights act—unprotected against informal discrimination and subject to differential treatment under the law.

Any developed analogy between the political position of gay men and lesbians and that of racial minorities and women, however, would have to go substantially beyond attending to formal and informal discriminatory policies. Over the past several decades, feminists and race theorists have developed analyses of gender and racial injustice as matters not merely of inequity, but of oppression. That is, sexism and racism are systematically built into the ways that we, as a society, live and think. Implicated in gender oppression, for instance, are gender socialization, the gender structure of the family, the unpaid and devalued status of domestic-reproductive labor, inferiorizing stereotypes of women, the conceptual distinction between public and private spheres, the cultural normalization of violence toward women, and the feminization of poverty. To understand gender oppression is to understand the *place* of women in socio-economic structures and practices, the disadvantaging *effects* of occupying that place, and the factors that systematically keep women *in place*. For example, the private sphere, urban ghettoes, pink-collar jobs, sex industry work, positions of welfare dependency, and the poverty zone are all places disproportionately inhabited by women.

A central difficulty in developing the notion of lesbian and gay subordination is that lesbians and gay men, unlike women and racial minorities, do not appear to be located in any particular social structural places. Consider the significance of the popular lesbian and gay slogan: 'We are everywhere'. Designed to challenge the disclaimer: 'I don't know anyone who is gay or lesbian', the slogan draws attention to two key features of gay and lesbian existence. First, gay men and lesbians do not occupy any specific socio-economic position. Although they constitute a social group, this does not translate into a statistical concentration in any particular socio-economic location. Second, it is possible to be unaware that gay men and lesbians are everywhere because the closet, coupled with the presumption that social actors are heterosexual, allows gay men and lesbians to circumvent the discriminatory practices designed to enable heterosexuals to avoid knowing any lesbians or gay men. These are not profound observations, but they have an important implication. Theorizing about sexual orientation subordination cannot be modeled on theorizing about gender and racial oppression. In particular, it cannot use the same method for documenting the existence of oppression.

Marxist, liberal, and socialist feminisms, for instance, share the basic assumption that persons cleanly and unambiguously sort into either the identity category 'woman' or the identity category 'man' and that who has which identity is readily identifiable by others. The identities 'woman' and 'man' are written on bodies and thus are socially visible. As a result, persons who *are* women will be socially treated *as* women, and persons who *are* men will be socially treated *as* men.[2] The fact that women typically cannot evade being identified as women, and thus cannot evade being treated as women, makes it possible to adopt a general methodological strategy to documenting a gender-based form of oppression. The strategy is to ask where, as a result of being treated *as* women, persons who *are* women end up being located in the economic, familial, welfare bureaucratic, educational, military, and other social institutions and structures. Asking where women are located reveals the fact that women are disproportionately concentrated in pink-collar jobs, in paid domestic service, in wife–mother roles, and in welfare dependency positions. An argument can then be constructed showing that these are disadvantaging positions and that there is no fact about women that justifies women's disproportionate concentration in such disadvantaging places. Gender, then, arguably makes a difference to the lives of women that it ought not to make.

Marxist and socialist feminism rely heavily on the fact that persons who are women and persons who are men occupy different locations in a gender-structured labor system.[3] In particular, women do both unpaid sexual-reproductive-domestic labor and (under)paid productive labor that exploits their womanly capacities and characteristics. Analyses of women's labor reveals the difference gender makes to one's vulnerability to exploitation, impoverishment, and commodification (e.g. of one's sex-affective capacities), all of which

[2] This is not to say that persons who are women will only be treated as women. Those persons will also have a race, a class status, an age, and an ethnicity, all of which, insofar as they are publicly visible markers of identity, will determine how they are treated. I also do not mean to suggest that being treated 'as a woman' amounts to some one thing. Again, race, class, ethnicity, and age will shape the concrete form that being treated 'as a woman' takes. Nor do I mean to suggest that for all persons who are women, gender is the primary determinate of how they are treated. Race and known lesbianism, homosexuality, or bisexuality can have powerful consequences for how persons are treated that are largely independent of gender.

[3] See e.g. Ann Ferguson, 'On Conceiving Motherhood and Sexuality: A Feminist Materialist Approach', in *Mothering: Essays in Feminist Theory*, ed. Joyce Trebilcot (Totowa: Rowman & Allanheld, 1983) 153–82; Alison M. Jaggar, *Feminist Politics and Human Nature* (Totowa: Rowman & Allanheld, 1983); Nancy Fraser, 'Women, Welfare, and the Politics of Need Interpretation', in *Unruly Practices, Power, Discourse, and Gender in Contemporary Social Theory* (Minneapolis: University of Minnesota Press, 1989), 144–60; Heidi Hartmann, 'The Unhappy Marriage of Marxism and Feminism: Toward a More Progressive Union', in *Feminist Frameworks*, 2nd edn, ed. Alison M. Jaggar and Paula S. Rothenberg (New York: McGraw-Hill, 1984), 172–89; Shulamith Firestone, *The Dialectic of Sex: The Case for Feminist Revolution* (New York: Morrow, 1970); Zillah Eisenstein, ed. *Capitalist Patriarchy and the Case for Socialist Feminism* (New York: Monthly Review Press, 1979); Nancy Chodorow, *The Reproduction of Mothering: Psychoanalysis and the Sociology of Gender* (Berkeley: University of California Press, 1978), 173–90.

are, from a Marxist viewpoint, characteristics of unjust social systems. The Marxist-socialist case for gender oppression thus uses a 'place and numbers' approach: There are identifiable places in the division of labor which large numbers of women disproportionately occupy, and which thus are reasonably regarded as women's places. Those women's places can be critiqued from a Marxist-socialist viewpoint as wrongful or wrong-imposing places.

Liberal feminism similarly employs a 'place and numbers' approach. Liberal feminism relies heavily on the fact that women and men occupy different locations in a gendered opportunity structure.[4] In particular, women confront formal, informal, and structural barriers (e.g. the gendered structure of the family) to securing social goods that men do not face. Analyses of those barriers reveal the difference gender makes to one's opportunity for educational and economic attainment, physical security, independence from patriarchal or welfare bureaucratic authority, and the like. The liberal case for gender oppression thus depends on a 'place and numbers' approach. There are identifiable places in the opportunity structure which large numbers of women disproportionately occupy, and which thus are reasonably regarded as women's places. Those women's places can be critiqued from a liberal viewpoint as wrongful regardless of who occupies them or as unfairly distributing social goods and opportunities on the irrelevant basis of gender, or both.[5]

A 'place and numbers' approach is not similarly useful for analyzing lesbian and gay subordination, because persons do not unambiguously and visibly sort into the identity categories 'heterosexual' and 'homosexual'. Sexual orientation is not connected to any visible bodily marker. And because sexual orientation is variously determined by appeal to acts, desires, fantasies, demeanor, or some combination, there may be so much slippage and overlap between 'heterosexual' and 'homosexual' that no clean distinction between the two groups is possible.[6] Even supposing two clearly distinct sorts of persons—homosexual and heterosexual—homosexuals are not readily identifiable. The social presumption that persons are heterosexual unless there is clear evidence

---

[4] See e.g. Barbara F. Reskin and Heidi I. Hartmann, ed. *Women's Work, Men's Work: Sex Segregation on the Job* (Washington, DC: National Academy Press, 1986); Betty Friedan, *The Feminine Mystique* (New York: Norton, 1963); Alison M. Jaggar, *Feminist Politics and Human Nature* (Totowa: Rowman & Allanheld, 1983); Susan Moller Okin, *Justice, Gender and the Family* (New York: Basic Books, 1989); Ruth Sidel, *Women and Children Last* (New York: Viking, 1986); Jane English, ed. *Sex Equality* (New York: Prentice Hall, 1977); Zillah R. Eisenstein, *The Radical Future of Liberal Feminism* (New York: Longman, 1981); Sylvia Ann Hewlett, *A Lesser Life: The Myth of Women's Liberation in America* (New York: Morrow, 1986).

[5] The approach used in Susan Moller Okin's *Justice, Gender, and the Family* (1989) exemplifies the liberal approach to gender oppression. For her, the wife–mothering place in the family is in itself a wrongfully disadvantaging place. In addition, because women are the ones typically occupying that place, the wife–mother role unfairly limits *women's* opportunities.

[6] Judith Butler, 'Imitation and Gender Insubordination', in *Inside/Out: Lesbian Theories, Gay Theories*, ed. Diana Fuss (New York: Routledge, 1991), 13–31; Eve Kosofsky Sedgwick, *Epistemology of the Closet* (Berkeley: University of California Press, 1990), 182–212; Janet E. Halley, 'The Construction of Heterosexuality', in *Fear of a Queer Planet: Queer Politics and Social Theory*, ed. Michael Warner (Minneapolis: University of Minnesota Press, 1993), 82–102.

to the contrary helps to conceal gay men and lesbians. Sexual identity can also be deliberately concealed. As a result, persons who *are* lesbian or gay often evade being socially treated *as* lesbian or gay persons. Instead, they are treated as members of the social group 'heterosexual'. From the point of view of public perception of identity, the social group 'heterosexual' is in fact a default group composed of persons who are heterosexual and persons who are not but whose deviance is not publicly identifiable.[7]

In the absence of large numbers of obviously gay or lesbian persons, there is little point to creating 'gay places' or 'lesbian places' in the socio-economic structure. Even were there such places, gay men and lesbians would not be located primarily in those places. Via the presumption of heterosexuality and the active closeting of lesbian or gay identity, lesbians and gay men move into heterosexual places in employment, the military, and the family.[8] As a result, the 'place and numbers' approach that proved useful in revealing gender-based and race-based forms of oppression fails to reveal an analogous lesbian and gay subordination.

Consider, for example, how the invisibility of gay men and lesbians handicaps a Marxist or socialist analysis. Persons who are gay or lesbian do not do any distinctive kind of labor. There is no lesbian work comparable to women's work, and only a few occupations (e.g. hairdresser or clothes designer) are stereotyped as gay jobs. One might, of course, argue that being outside the labor system, and thus economically marginalized, is itself a place to which gays and lesbians are assigned. It is true that those identified as gay or lesbian may well be denied or fired from jobs in the paid workforce and prevented from participating in the creation, care, and education of children. The attempt to remove or exclude gay men and lesbians completely from paid productive labor and the labor of reproducing the next generation *is* important in understanding lesbian and gay subordination.[9] However, unlike social groups whose members are readily identifiable, gays and lesbians evade statistical concentration in a marginalizing place. Thus, sexual orientation does not make the kind of difference to one's material conditions that, by contrast, gender and race do. Lesbian and gay subordination does not materialize.

Lesbian and gay invisibility similarly handicaps traditional liberal analyses. Neither formal law nor informal discriminatory policies and practices have the necessary consequence of systematically preventing persons who are gay or lesbian from exercising their liberties or having access to opportunities. Consider, for example, the substantially different impact of the military policy

---

[7] Janet E. Halley, 'The Construction of Heterosexuality', in *Fear of a Queer Planet*, 85–6.

[8] By 'moving into the family' I have a number of factors in mind. Gays and lesbians can avoid being expelled from their native family by closeting their homosexuality or lesbianism; they can be heterosexually married, creating conventional families of their own; and they can create gay and lesbian families, protecting those families from intervention by closeting them.

[9] Iris Marion Young argues that marginalization—having one's labor refused because of one's group membership—is one face that oppression takes. See Iris Marion Young, *Justice and the Politics of Difference* (Princeton: Princeton University Press, 1990), 53–5.

barring women from combat and its policy of barring gay men and lesbians from military service. The former effectively bars women from combat. The latter does not effectively bar persons who are gay or lesbian from service; it only bars the identifiably gay or lesbian. Provided that they pass as heterosexual, gay men and lesbians will occupy virtually the same location in the opportunity structure as heterosexuals. Once again, sexual orientation subordination does not materialize.

Organizations on the religious right have capitalized on this fact (with help from the gay rights movement itself, which has found it strategically useful to underscore gay and lesbian economic clout). As part of their argument against covering lesbians and gay men under anti-discrimination laws, they have pointed to the dissimilarity between the material conditions of racial minorities on the one hand, and gay men and lesbians on the other.[10] Arguments assuming that a social group could not be a target of systematic injustice if that group enjoys a reasonable level of material well-being employ precisely the conception of group-based injustice that feminists and race theorists have relied on. Group-based injustice, on this view, occurs when large numbers of a particular social group are disproportionately clustered in opportunity-limiting and highly exploitable places. Because this is not true of gays and lesbians, the religious right, echoing Justice White in the *Bowers v. Hardwick* decision, has tended to find gay and lesbian minority rights claims to be facetious claims for special rights.[11] Leftist counterarguments that point to the systematic disadvantaging of those *publicly identified* as gay or lesbian miss the mark, since the situation of uncloseted gays and lesbians is not necessarily representative of gays and lesbians as a group. Many gay men and lesbians protect themselves against being disadvantaged by concealing their lesbian or gay identity and by adopting a pseudonymous heterosexual identity. Even those who do not deliberately try to pass as straight are routinely treated as heterosexuals, since the social presumption is that persons are heterosexual unless proven otherwise.

Locked into a conception of group-based injustice whose measure is access to socio-economic goods, both the right and the left ignore the closet. The right underscores the absence of high numbers of gay men and lesbians who have been disadvantaged, ignoring the compulsory closeting and presumption of heterosexuality that makes liberty and access to opportunity possible.

---

[10] The video 'Gay Rights, Special Rights', produced by the Traditional Values Coalition, takes just this tack. According to the spokesperson for TVC, 30,000 copies were distributed between July and December 1993, 500 to congress members and the rest to church groups, civic associations, reporters, and local PTAs. See *Village Voice*, 14 Dec. 1993, 23. The same sort of argument was also used during the publicity surrounding Colorado's Amendment 2 (which barred the state from enacting any future anti-discrimination policy).

[11] 'Against a background in which many US states have criminalized sodomy and still do, to claim that a right to engage in such conduct is "deeply rooted in this Nation's history and tradition" or "implicit in the concept of ordered liberty" is, at best, facetious'. *Bowers v. Hardwick*, 478 U.S. 186 (1986), 194.

The left underscores the deprivations of liberty and opportunity suffered by those identified as gay or lesbian, ignoring the way the closet and the presumption of heterosexuality protects gays and lesbians as a group from suffering those consequences.

Because of the difference between gender and racial oppression on the one hand, and lesbian and gay subordination on the other, a different methodological approach to understanding lesbian and gay subordination is needed. Rather than focusing on the *disadvantaging effects* of being treated as a lesbian or gay man, it will be more productive to focus on the *displacement* of homosexuality and lesbianism to the outside of civil society. What deserves particular attention are the ways that: (1) in heterosexual society all citizens are required to adopt a real or pseudonymous heterosexual identity as a condition of access to the public sphere, and (2) heterosexual society gets reproduced generationally through legal, psychiatric, educational, and familial practices whose aim is to prevent future generations of lesbian and gay people.

## II. Displacing Lesbian and Gay Identities from the Public Sphere

If we ask: 'How are gay and lesbian identities displaced from the public sphere?' the most obvious answer is 'by penalizing those who fail to closet their identities'. Thus, discriminatory treatment in employment, housing, military service, and so on is likely to be what first comes to mind. Although I will turn, later, to examining the way that discriminatory policies in the United States military, employment practices, and court decisions have worked to displace gay and lesbian identities (if not the persons themselves) from the public sphere, I want to begin by examining how we as a culture think about same-sex *sexuality*. The pressure to closet lesbian and gay identities in the public sphere is ultimately rooted in a particular way of thinking about homosexuality and lesbianism. Homosexuality and lesbianism are equated with sexual acts, especially with sodomy, in a way that heterosexuality is not similarly reduced to a set of sexual acts. As a result, we as a culture think that it is reasonable not to mention homosexuality and lesbianism in the public sphere, either because the acts are too morally abhorrent to bear public mention or, more neutrally, because sex is a private matter that belongs in the bedroom, not in public spaces. Oscar Wilde's famous description of homosexuality as the 'love that dare not speak its name' reflects a long history of referring to sodomy as the 'unmentionable crime'. But even in a more sexually liberalized era, homosexuality continues to be publicly unmentionable because it is equated with private sexual activity.

An examination of the majority and minority opinions in the notorious United States Supreme Court case of *Bowers v. Hardwick* that upheld Georgia's anti-sodomy law provides one clear window into the cultural equation of homosexuality and lesbianism with private activity. In examining the court's reasoning about sodomy in *Bowers v. Hardwick*, my interest is not in critiquing laws restricting private, consensual sexual activity between adults. Nor is my interest in arguing that sodomy laws in the United States should be overturned because they violate a constitutional right to privacy. On the contrary, what I want to suggest is that preoccupation with protecting gay and lesbian private sexual activity misses a more central political problem—the privatization of all things lesbian or gay through their equation with sexual acts.

## The Privatization of Lesbianism and Homosexuality

The privatization of all things lesbian and gay is rooted in a long history of regarding sodomy as a distinctively unmentionable crime. Prior to the secularization of sodomy prohibitions in the sixteenth century, 'sodomy had been defined in strictly ecclesiastical terms as one of the gravest sins against divine law whose name alone proved such an affront to God that it was often named only as the unnamable': *inter Christianos non nominandum*.[12] Throughout the seventeenth century, sodomy continued to be referred to within British law as the crime that among Christians is not to be mentioned. And a century later, Blackstone uses this same (non)description in his *Commentaries on the Laws of England*, remarking:

I will not act so disagreeable a part, to my readers as well as myself, as to dwell any longer upon a subject, the very mention of which is a disgrace to human nature. It will be more eligible to imitate in this respect the delicacy of our English law, which treats it, in its very indictments, as a crime not fit to be named; '*peccatum illud horribile, inter christianos non nominandum*'.[13]

Even after the removal of sodomy from the roster of capital crimes in 1861 and its reincorporation in 1885 under a British statute prohibiting gross indecency between men, sodomy continued to be publicly regarded as the unspeakable crime—this time not because of its grave sinfulness but because of its grave violation of standards of decency.[14] In the United States, some state statutes still refuse to name what they prohibit, instead referring with vague decency to 'crimes against nature'.[15] As recently as 1986, in his concurring opinion in *Hardwick*, Justice Burger recalled the words of Blackstone, pronouncing sodomy 'a heinous act "the very mention of which is a disgrace to human nature", and "a crime not fit to be named" '.[16]

---

[12] Ed Cohen, 'Legislating the Norm: From Sodomy to Gross Indecency', in *Displacing Homophobia: Gay Male Perspectives in Literature and Culture*, ed. Ronald R. Butters, John M. Clum, and Michael Moon (Durham NC: Duke University Press, 1989), 169–207, 169, 173.

[13] William Blackstone, Esq., *Commentary on the Laws of England*, 8th edn (Oxford: Clarendon Press, 1778). 4, 215

[14] Cohen, 188.

[15] Massachusetts General Legislature, ch. 272, §34 (1986); Tennessee Code Ann. §39-2-612 (1980); Florida Statute, §800.02 (1987); Mississippi Code of 1972, secs 97-29-59.

[16] *Bowers v. Hardwick*, 194.

In short, the history of laws prohibiting sodomy and acts of gross indecency between men is also a history of imposing a linguistic taboo on publicly naming and describing both the specific sex act of sodomy and an amorphous class of same-sex interactions ('gross indecency' or 'homosexual conduct'). Thus, it is the history of laws that not only render privately performed sex a matter of public concern but that also *privatize* would be public acts of linguistic representation. That dual history ultimately has the dual effect of undercutting the claim of gay men and lesbians to have a private sphere where their sexual, affiliational, and familial relations are protected from public intrusion *and* of denying them any entitlement to represent themselves in the public sphere as lesbians and gay men. It is, in brief, a history of denying to gay men and lesbians both a private sphere and a public sphere.

Sodomy laws are often criticized for having the first effect. They criminalize some persons' private, consensual sexual activity. They thus appear both discriminatory and a violation of the right to privacy. The second effect—that is, the way that the very language of sodomy laws and legal reasoning about sodomy assumes that homosexuality and lesbianism should not be publicly represented—is rarely remarked. But it is important. Sodomy laws and legal reasoning about sodomy reflect a general cultural assumption that homosexuality and lesbianism are and ought to be nonpublic. This removal of homosexuality and lesbianism from the public sphere and their linguistic seclusion in 'the love that dare not speak its name' are central to lesbian and gay subordination.

The assumption that homosexuality and lesbianism belong, if anywhere, behind closed doors dominated both majority and minority opinions in *Bowers v. Hardwick*. In an insightful assessment of the majority and minority opinions in *Hardwick*, Robert L. Caserio observes

> [w]hat is unsettling is that both sides cannot permit to homosexuals a space of appearance in the public realm. While the Court majority justifies supervising—and even eliminating—homosexual privacy, and while the Court minority defends homosexual privacy, both sides agree that homosexuality is only a private matter. This exclusive identification of homosexuality with privacy guarantees that the judges, at their worst, will equate homosexuality with sodomitical sexual intimacies . . .; and at their best, with emotional intimacies relevant only to the private sphere. Hence for both sides, homosexuality has no public, no *political*, existence. . . . So the arguments of both sides of the Court maintain a long ideological tradition: that homosexual life, whether supervised or not, is and should be a closeted life.[17]

What Caserio draws attention to here is the double meaning of 'private'. 'Private' refers ambiguously to: (a) what is done in the private sphere behind closed doors, away from public view, and often away from public knowledge, and (b) what is beyond the reach of legitimate governmental control whether

---

[17] Robert L. Caserio, 'Supreme Court Discourse vs. Homosexual Fiction', in *Displacing Homophobia*, 255–89, 261–2.

done behind closed doors or not. Although disagreeing over whether sodomy is private with respect to legal regulation, both majority and dissenting opinions in *Hardwick* agree that homosexuality (and not just sodomy) is an inherently private, behind-closed-doors practice. Both equate homosexuality with sexual activity, and in particular, with sexual activity that is completely disconnected from life in the public sphere. Neither contextualizes homosexual sodomy within the broad set of acts by which one might enact a sexual identity, where that set includes not only private sex acts but also public choices of domestic partner, co-parent, political group affiliations, dress, styles of interaction with others of the same and opposite sex, and self-representation as the bearer of a particular sexual identity.[18] As a result, the connection between the demand to be let alone to conduct one's sex life as a homosexual, and the demand to be let alone to enter the public sphere as a homosexual cannot be made.

In the majority opinion, the privatization of homosexuality occurs via the rhetorical strategy of equating homosexuality with sodomy. Justice White's majority opinion and Justice Burger's concurring opinion repeatedly substitute the terms 'homosexual conduct', 'homosexual activity', 'homosexual practices', and 'homosexuality' for the term 'homosexual sodomy'.[19] 'Homosexual conduct', 'homosexual activities', 'homosexual practices' and 'homosexuality' are not, in fact, equivalent expressions for 'homosexual sodomy'. 'Homosexual conduct, activities, or practices' refers broadly to any activity that seems to presuppose same-sex desires or a gay or lesbian identity. The military, for example, classifies the attempt to marry someone of the same sex as homosexual conduct.[20] One central effect of rhetorically substituting 'homosexual conduct' for 'homosexual sodomy' is to suggest that homosexual conduct and homosexual sodomy are one and the same thing.[21] Enacting a homosexual identity in one's conduct and practices is thus reduced to nothing but performing acts of sodomy. Reduced to mere sex (indeed to a single kind of sex act), homosexuality appears utterly out of place in and irrelevant to the public sphere, including work, social interaction, education, the media, and the military.

Moreover, reduced to mere sex, homosexual conduct ceases to include gay and lesbian marriages, parenting, and procreative choices. Thus, for Justice White, *homosexual* sodomy not only has no connection to *heterosexual* family, marriage, or procreation; it has no connection to *homosexual* families,

---

[18] Justice White implicitly contextualizes heterosexual sex acts within a broad set of acts by which heterosexual identity might be enacted. It is, in his view, specifically homosexual activity that has no connection with marriage, the family, and procreation. Heterosexual sexual activity, one is left to assume, does have this connection to more public marital and familial statuses.

[19] *Bowers v. Hardwick*, 186, 189, 191, 195, 196.

[20] Code of Federal Regulations 32 (1993) Pt. 41, App. A.

[21] For an interesting discussion of the confusion of act and identity in White's majority opinion see Janet E. Halley, 'Reasoning About Sodomy: Act and Identity In and After *Bowers v. Hardwick*', *Virginia Law Review* 79 (1993): 1721–80.

marriages, or procreative choices, since these are not recognized as possible forms of homosexual conduct. Marriage, the family, and procreation are, however, very much part of the public sphere (i.e. the sphere of activities not confined behind closed doors away from public view). Their public aspects include public celebrations of marriages, anniversaries, and births, baby showers, maternity leave policies, spousal health benefits, family-oriented public entertainment, public aid to families with dependent children, tax breaks for married persons, joint invitations to couples, entitlement to give proxy consent, family planning clinics, artificial insemination services, and adoption services. Claiming 'no connection between family, marriage, or procreation on the one hand and homosexual activity on the other'[22] thus displaces homosexuality from the public sphere.

Justice Blackmun, although disagreeing that the state may legitimately regulate sodomy, did not challenge the assumption that homosexuality concerns only a person's private, intimate life behind closed doors. The broad 'right to be let alone' that he identifies at the outset of his dissent, turns out to be, when applied to homosexual sodomy, a much narrower right to be let alone with respect to intimate, 'intensely private',[23] physical, sexual associations that take place within one's own home. Because Blackmun, like Justice White, equates homosexuality with mere sex, he contextualizes homosexual sodomy with other (private) sex acts—heterosexual sexual activity between unmarried persons, heterosexual sodomy between married persons,[24] and the (private) viewing of obscene materials.[25] He does not contextualize sodomy among potentially public ways of enacting an identity, way of life,[26] or in his words, 'self-definition'.

In sum, both court opinions privatize homosexuality by misdescribing homosexuality as a matter of mere sexual intimacies. By depicting homosexuality as inherently private, occurring behind closed doors, the unmentionability of lesbian and gay identity in the public sphere is made to seem natural and normal. In other words, court rhetoric served to legitimize a central feature of lesbian and gay subordination, namely, the reservation of the public sphere for heterosexuals only.[27]

The unmentionability of homosexuality and lesbianism in the *public*

---

[22] *Bowers v. Hardwick*, 191.

[23] Ibid. 213.                                        [24] Ibid. 210, fn. 4.

[25] The analogy between Harwick's case and *Stanley v. Georgia*, 394 U.S. 557 (1969), which concerned private consumption of pornography in one's own home, is central to Justice Blackmun's argument.

[26] That is, instead of relying on *Stanley v. Georgia*, he might have relied more heavily on *Wisconsin v. Yoder*, which protected individuals' right to be let alone to choose 'a way of life that [may be] odd or even erratic but interferes with no interests of others' [*Wisconsin v. Yoder*, 406 U.S. 205 (1972), 224), qtd Blackmun. In *Wisconsin* the Court upheld the Amish's right to decide against extended formal schooling for their children.

[27] This is not to say that securing a right to privacy with respect to gay and lesbian sexual activities is unimportant. It is, however, to say that the rhetoric of privacy arguments can do as much to sustain sexual orientation subordination as to intervene in it.

sphere effectively displaces gay and lesbian identities to the outside of civil society. By contrast, unlike this love that 'dare not speak its name', heterosexuality is the love whose name is continually spoken in the everyday routines and institutions of public social life. Heterosexuals move about in the public sphere as heterosexuals, and that identity is by no means a private matter. Public social interaction and the structure of public institutions are pervaded with the assumption that public actors are heterosexual and with opportunities to represent themselves as such. Humor, formal and informal dress codes, corporate benefits policies, 'scripts' for everyday conversation about personal life, public display of family pictures, and so on presuppose that public persons are heterosexual. They also enable individuals to publicly represent themselves as heterosexuals.[28]

This double standard for heterosexual versus homosexual self-representation is based on the assumption that heterosexuality is and ought to be constitutive of what it means to be a public actor. The equation of a public actor with a heterosexual actor is in part sustained by regarding homosexual identity as a private, behind-closed-doors matter, as White and Blackmun did. It is also sustained by requiring that gay men and lesbians adopt a pseudonymous heterosexual identity as a condition of access to the public sphere. That requirement is enforced through discriminatory practices and policies that penalize individuals for publicly representing themselves as gay or lesbian.

### Prohibiting the Public Representation of Identity

Because gay and lesbian self-representations, not the persons themselves, are removed from the public sphere, gay and lesbian exclusion from the public sphere is disanalogous to that of women and racial minorities. Historically, the public sphere has been the privileged domain of men and whites. That privilege was (is) maintained by laws, policies, and practices limiting women's and racial minorities' access to the public sphere, and by penalizing overly public women and racial minorities (e.g. through rape and lynching[29]). Significantly, making the public sphere the privileged domain of men and whites requires discriminating on the basis of status (i.e. discriminating

---

[28] James Woods gives a thorough account of the heterosexualization of corporate life in *The Corporate Closet*.

[29] 'Women have been raped by men, most often by gangs of men, for many of the same reasons that blacks were lynched by gangs of whites: as a group punishment for being uppity, for getting out of line, for failing to recognize "one's place", for assuming sexual freedoms. . . .' Susan Brownmiller, *Against Our Will: Men, Women, and Rape* (New York: Simon & Schuster, 1976), 281. 'Laws were formulated primarily to exclude black men from adult male prerogatives in the public sphere, and lynching meshed with these legal mechanisms of exclusion': Jacquelyn Dowd Hall, ' "The Mind that Burns in Each Body": Women, Rape, and Racial Violence', in *Race, Class, and Gender*, ed. Margaret L. Andersen and Patricia Hill Collins (Belmont: Wadsworth, 1992), 397–412, 400. Hall notes that lynching increased following the period of reconstruction after the US Civil War, and rapes increased during the antifeminist backlash. These occurrences suggest a correlation between lynching and rape on the one hand, and increased public activity on the other.

against persons who *are* women, and persons who *are* racial minorities). By contrast, making the public sphere the privileged domain of heterosexuals does not. The presence of persons who are gay or lesbian need not contaminate the heteronormativity of public space provided that homosexuality and lesbianism, as identities, remain private matters, and provided that, in public, gay men and lesbians adopt pseudonymous heterosexual identities.

As I suggested in section I, this disanalogy is significant. Although gender and racial justice, in the form of equal access to the public sphere, can reasonably be pursued through policies prohibiting discrimination on the basis of status, sexuality justice cannot. Status-based policies that affirm that public actors may *be* lesbian or gay fail to address the basic mechanism by which gay men and lesbians have been denied equal access to the public sphere, namely, the effective denial through laws, policies, and public practices that public actors may *represent* themselves as lesbians or gay men.

The distinction between status and conduct is not clearly and explicitly presupposed by policies prohibiting discrimination on the basis of race or sex status. On the contrary, restricting distinctively raced or gendered conduct seems *prima facie* to be a form of race or sex status discrimination. Nor has the distinction between *having* a particular status and making one's status *known* to others been presupposed by sex and race anti-discrimination policies. On the contrary, one obvious effect of anti-discrimination policies is the visible increase in the number of persons who are racial minorities and/or women.

By contrast, both the status-conduct and the having-making known distinctions have been central to US policies that supposedly do not discriminate on the basis of sexual orientation status. For example, US military policy concerning gay and lesbian service members has in the past implicitly invoked, and now explicitly invokes, a distinction between status and conduct. That distinction is supposedly critical to framing a policy that does not discriminate on the basis of who one *is* yet still grants the military authority to regulate what its members *do*. In reality, the distinction is critical to controlling the identities that are allowed to appear in the military's public space.

Prior to 1994, US military policy prohibited not only sexual activity between persons of the same sex, but also making one's homosexuality known.[30] Publicly stating 'I am a lesbian' warranted discharge no less than did private lesbian sexual acts. In discussing the proposed new policy, revealingly dubbed 'don't ask, don't tell', the Senate Armed Services Committee chairman, Sam Nunn, affirmed that avowing one's homosexuality or lesbianism *is* conduct and ought to be prohibited.[31] Although the policy that actually went

---

[30] One of the bases for separation was the fact that '[t]he member has stated that he or she is a homosexual or bisexual . . .'. Code of Federal Regulations 32 (1993) Pt. 41, App. A, pt 1, H.1.c.2.

[31] Pat Towell, 'Nunn Offers a Compromise: "Don't Ask/Don't Tell" '. 51 *Congressional Quarterly Weekly Report*, 1993, 1240.

into effect in 1994 does not make self-identifying statements automatic grounds for dismissal, it does make them grounds for starting an investigation, 'and once such an investigation is started, the service member would have to prove that he had not engaged in homosexual acts'.[32] In controlling public identity, not just sexual acts, both old and new policies in effect require that the persons who are to be exempted from status-discrimination adopt a pseudonymous heterosexual identity.[33]

US courts have also invoked the status-conduct distinction to the same end of controlling public identity. In *Norton v. Macy*,[34] the District of Columbia Circuit Court denied that sexual orientation was rationally related to the efficiency of the civil service. Norton, a budget analyst, was discharged from the National Aeronautics and Space Administration for immoral conduct and for 'possessing personality traits which render[ed] him "unsuitable for further Government employment" ',[35] after confessing, in what even the court deemed a dubiously legal police interrogation, to previous homosexual experiences.[36] The court ruled that employees could not be dismissed simply for being gay or lesbian. Some particularized and substantiated evidence of a connection between the employee's homosexuality and the efficiency of the service needed to be shown. But the court also emphasized that the plaintiff was 'an extremely infrequent offender, who neither openly flaunts nor carelessly displays his unorthodox sexual conduct in public',[37] implying that he might reasonably have been dismissed for refusing to appear heterosexual in public space.

In a subsequent case, *Singer v. United States Civil Service Commission*,[38] the court came to just that conclusion. John F. Singer, a clerk typist for the Seattle Office of the Equal Employment Opportunity Commission, was fired by the Civil Service Commission for 'flaunting' and 'broadcasting' his homosexuality and for receiving 'wide-spread publicity in this respect in at least two states'.[39] The Commission noted that Singer had kissed a male in front of the building elevator and in the company cafeteria, had applied with another man for a marriage license, had 'homosexual advertisements' on the windows of his car,

---

[32] Michael R. Gordon, 'Pentagon spells out rules for ousting homosexuals'. *New York Times*, 23 Dec. 1993, AI, A14.

[33] Revealingly, General Norman Schwarzkopf testified that 'homosexuals have served in the past and done a great job serving their country, and I feel they can in the future' but 'it's *open* homosexuality in a unit that causes this breakdown in unit cohesion'. Qtd in Anne B. Goldstein, 'Reasoning about Homosexuality: A Commentary on Janet Halley's "Reasoning about Sodomy: Act and Identity In and After *Bowers v. Hardwick*" '. *Virginia Law Review* 79 (1993): 1721–804, 1803 (my emphasis).

[34] *Norton v. Macy* 417 F.2d, 1161 (1969).            [35] Ibid. 1162.

[36] Clifford Norton was apprehended by a Morals Squad after he picked up a man, drove him once around Lafayette Square and dropped him off again. The Morals Squad interrogated Norton for two hours, and a NASA security chief interrogated him for an additional three, before Norton finally conceded that he had some prior homosexual experiences. However, he denied that he was homosexual and denied that on this night he had done anything more than invite the man he picked up in for a drink.            [37] Ibid. 1167.

[38] *Singer v. United States Civil Service Commission*, 530 F.2d, 247 (1976).

[39] Ibid. 250 (quoting Civil Service Commission letter to Singer).

was on the Board of Directors of the Seattle Gay Alliance, showed by his 'dress and demeanor' that he intended to continue his homosexual activity, and had received television, newspaper, radio, and magazine publicity.[40] The Commission denied that Singer was discharged because of his status. Instead, it claimed that Singer's 'repeated flaunting and advocacy of a controversial lifestyle'[41] would undermine public confidence in, and thus the efficiency of, the Civil Service. The court agreed. Noting that '[t]he problem is to arrive at the proper balance between the interests of the employee, as a citizen, and the interest of the Government, as an employer',[42] the court proceeded to stress that what distinguished *Singer* from *Norton* was that Singer had not, as Norton had, kept his homosexuality private.[43] In publicly occupying a discredited identity, Singer brought discredit on his employer.

What both the US military in its new policy and the courts in *Norton* and *Singer* acknowledge is that public actors may *be* gay or lesbian. What they may not do is make those identities known by *representing* themselves as lesbian or gay. Instead, both military policy and government employment practice in effect require lesbians and gays to adopt pseudonymous heterosexual identities in their public lives. As a result, status-based nondiscrimination policies fail to remedy lesbian and gay subordination precisely because they affirm, rather than contest, the reasonableness of treating gay and lesbian identities as discreditable and discrediting, and as identities that persons can have no strong interest in publicizing.

Briefly considering what the gender analog to status-conduct distinguishing policies would look like brings into sharper focus their oppressive character. Imagine, for example, a military service policy that, while claiming not to discriminate against persons who *are* women, proceeded to ban all conduct that made women publicly identifiable *as* women. Women would be subject to discharge both for engaging in womanly activities (say, joining the National Organization for Women or wearing women's clothing) and for making the self-identifying statement: 'I am a woman'. Avowing their womanhood and/or flaunting or carelessly displaying their unorthodox gender in public would constitute a breach of acceptable military conduct.[44] While not discriminating on one level (one may *be* a woman), this fictional policy clearly discriminates on another. It would burden women with the task of managing their public identities so that they appear to be men. And it would prohibit women from doing what men may do, namely, represent themselves as having the identities that they do have.[45]

---

[40]  Ibid. 249 (summarizing Commission letter to Singer).                [41]  Ibid. 251.
[42]  Ibid. 252.                                                                        [43]  Ibid. 255.
[44]  Although some women would find it easier than others to conceal their gender and adopt a pseudonymously male identity (just as some gay men and lesbians find it easier than others to adopt a pseudonymous heterosexual identity), the status-conduct distinction would permit the military or any other institution that adopted such a policy to claim that it was not discriminating against persons who *are* women, but only against womanly conduct.
[45]  The example is not entirely fictional. While claiming not to discriminate against persons because

*Restricting Speech versus Restricting Who may Speak*

Within a US legal framework, it is tempting to think that what is wrong with these restrictions on public self-representation is that they violate first amendment rights to freedom of speech and association. Preoccupation with protecting gay and lesbian freedom of speech, however, misses the more central political problem. Silencing public representations of one's lesbian or gay identity does not simply impose limits on what gays and lesbians can say that are not similarly imposed on heterosexuals. More fundamentally, penalizing gays and lesbians for making clear that they are gay or lesbian enforces the view that only heterosexuals (real or merely apparent) may speak at all. To see this, it will be useful to look at court cases where first amendment protections became an issue. Again, as in the earlier discussion of legal reasoning about sodomy, my interest is not in evaluating court interpretations of the first amendment. On the contrary, the point is that legal appeals to a right to free speech fail to reach the deeper issue—the limitation on *who* may speak, not just on *what* may be said.

In *benShalom v. Secretary of the Army*, the District Court invoked the first amendment to protect self-identifying speech.[46] Miriam benShalom, a member of the army reserves, was discharged on the grounds that she evidenced homosexual tendencies, desires, or interests. She had in fact acknowledged on several occasions that she was lesbian. The District Court argued that the Army could not dismiss a service member for simply declaring her lesbianism because this violated soldiers' first amendment rights 'to meet with homosexuals and discuss current problems or advocate changes in status quo' and 'to receive information and ideas about homosexuality'.[47] In their critical take on *benShalom*, the editors of the *Harvard Law Review* argue that 'regulations that penalize individuals who state that they are gay or lesbian . . . burden the right to express dissenting views on sexuality and sex roles, and, as such, contravene the first amendment's goal of preserving a multiplicity of world views and attitudes'.[48]

One might think that this is why the Sixth Circuit Court of Appeals erred in *Rowland v. Mad River Local School District*.[49] Marjorie Rowland, a high school counselor, disclosed her bisexuality to several fellow school employees and was subsequently asked to resign. When she refused, she was suspended, then transferred to a position with no student contact, and then not rehired

they are women or black, employers may penalize employees for not exhibiting sufficiently masculine or white traits. The disanalogy between gay men and lesbians on the one hand, and women and blacks on the other is perhaps best understood as one of degree.

[46] *benShalom v. Secretary of the Army*, 489 F. Supp. 964 (1980).

[47] Ibid. 967.

[48] Editors of the Harvard Law Review, *Sexual Orientation and the Law* (Cambridge: Harvard University Press, 1989), 63.

[49] *Rowland v. Mad River Local School District*, 730 F.2d, 444 (1984).

after her contract expired. Relying on the *Connick* test,[50] the Court deemed Rowland's disclosure merely personal, not the public speech of a citizen speaking on a matter of public concern and debate. It thus refused to grant first amendment protections to her disclosure.

Both Judge Edwards, dissenting from the Sixth Circuit Court's majority opinion, and Justice Brennan, dissenting from the denial of certiorari,[51] took issue with this classification of Rowland's identity-statement as merely personal. The Circuit Court had argued that '[t]here was absolutely no evidence of any public concern in the community or at Stebbins High with the issue of bisexuality among school personnel when she began speaking to others about her own sexual preference'.[52] Taking a larger view of the public, both Judge Edwards[53] and Justice Brennan[54] argued that public debate about the rights of homosexuals was in fact currently ongoing (even if not at Stebbins High), and thus '[t]he fact of petitioner's bisexuality, once spoken, necessarily and ineluctably involved her in that debate'.[55]

However tempting invoking first amendment protections in this way may be, there is something odd about classifying representations of one's identity as *either* public (debatable) or private (merely personal) speech. Consider, first, the fictional gender policy. Is discharging a person for stating: 'I am a woman' best criticized as a violation of rights to speech, expression, and association? Is one's gender, like one's political views, simply a possible subject of speech or basis of association? Or is it instead constitutive of being a speaker? In our social world, gender is such a fundamental social category that it is the first thing people want to know about the persons with whom they interact, and '[t]he pressure on each of us to guess or determine the sex of everybody else both generates and is exhibited in a great pressure on each of us to *inform* everybody all the time of our sex'.[56] Furthermore, in our social world the psychological process of becoming gendered is part of the process of becoming a self, a subject, an 'I'. In short, speakers enter into the world of speech and expression as gendered subjects. Thus, gender is better viewed as a feature of being a speaker rather than simply something one might wish to express to others. To prohibit a particular gendered self-representation in the public world is, then, to do much more than restrict what a speaker may say or with whom she may associate. It is to deny that a particular subject may speak at

---

[50] *Connick v. Myers*, 461 U.S. 138 (1983). In *Connick* the Court held that 'when a public employee speaks not as a citizen upon matters of public concern, but instead as an employee upon matters only of personal interest, absent the most unusual circumstances, a federal court is not the appropriate forum in which to review the wisdom of a personnel decision taken by a public agency allegedly in reaction to the employee's behavior'. (103 S.Ct. at 1690, qtd in Rowland at 449).

[51] *Rowland v. Mad River Local School District, Montgomery County, Ohio*, 470 U.S. 1009.

[52] *Rowland*, 730 F.2d, 449.                                     [53] Ibid. 452–3.

[54] *Rowland*, 470 U.S. 1012.                                     [55] Ibid.

[56] Marilyn Frye, 'Sexism', in *The Politics of Reality: Essays in Feminist Theory* (Freedom, CA: Crossing Press, 1983), 17–40, 17, 23. Frye argues that sex-marking and sex-identification are basic to, and a condition of the intelligibility of, our interactions.

all. Under the fictional gender policy, women may not speak. Only men, real and pseudonymous, may.

Like gender, sexuality is a fundamentally constitutive feature of our social world and of the persons who inhabit it. For better or worse, we have inherited a view of sexuality as something that, like gender, pervades the entire personality and orients persons in the social world. That is, we assume that everyone necessarily has a determinable sexual orientation as part of their basic psychological makeup. Just as there are no persons who lack a gender (either man or woman), there are no persons who lack a sexual orientation (either heterosexual, lesbian, gay, or bisexual). Thus persons enter the adult world of speech and expression as sexual subjects, even if we may not know exactly what sexual orientation a particular person has, just as we may not always know which gender a particular person is. Unlike gender, however, the pressure to find out others' sexual orientation and to make one's own sexual orientation known is relieved, for heterosexuals at least, by the presumption that everyone is heterosexual unless there is clear evidence to the contrary. That presumed heterosexuality, however, is better viewed as a presumption about what kind of speakers there are rather than a presumption about what speakers might wish to express. As in the case of gender, prohibiting lesbian, gay, and bisexual self-representation in the public world not only restricts the content of speech, but more importantly denies that lesbian, gay, or bisexual subjects may speak at all. Only heterosexuals, real and pseudonymous, may.

The upshot of the court's decision in *Rowland* was precisely to deny that a bisexual subject may speak. Although denying that Rowland could be penalized simply for her status as a bisexual, it affirmed that it was permissible for the school to discipline her for making statements about her sexual preference.[57] In a social context like ours, where speakers' heterosexuality is presumed, this amounts to ruling that employers may penalize their employees for refusing to speak as (presumed) heterosexual subjects.

In short, the first amendment protects speech, guaranteeing that some things *may be said*. It does not protect speakers, guaranteeing that some sorts of speakers *may do the saying*. When Marjorie Rowland announced 'I am a bisexual', she specified who was doing the saying. However unfortunate the consequences, the court majority was right not to equate, as Judge Edwards and Justice Brennan did, her statement 'I am a bisexual' with the expression of an opinion about sexuality. To secure openly gay and lesbian persons' access to the public sphere by equating self-identifying statements with expressions of opinion errs by mistaking the question of *who* may speak for the question of *what* may be said.

In addition, securing access to the public sphere under the first amendment implies that openly gay men and lesbians have entitlement only to *politicized*

---

[57] *Rowland v. Mad River*, 730 F.2d, 450.

publicity and only to the public sphere of *political* debate. It implies, that is, that they have no claim to being mentionable—to being public—*except* under social conditions that make their mention a political, public, and debated subject. This was, in essence, both the Sixth Circuit's majority view and that of Judge Edwards and Justice Brennan. Their disagreement centered on the question of whether or not bisexuality was in fact a subject of political debate, and thus whether or not Rowland's self-identifying statement qualified for first amendment protection. No one questioned the broader implications of interpreting the entitlement to publicly identify oneself as a first amendment entitlement, and thus of protecting self-identifications *only on condition* that they occur as part of a larger public debate. But when the formally equal first amendment entitlement of *all* persons to identify their sexuality in the public arena is put into play in a heteronormative social world, the result will be *de facto* inequality between heterosexuals' and nonheterosexuals' entitlement to utter self-identifying statements. To say that the social world is heteronormative is to say that the social world is structured on the presumption that it is both natural and normal for persons to be heterosexual. The heteronormativity of the social world guarantees that heterosexuals will have broad access, *as* heterosexuals, to all public spaces and all social life that takes place beyond the closed doors of their homes—streets, workplaces, schools, and entertainment. Thus, heterosexuals need not rely on first amendment protections to guarantee the acceptable publicizing of heterosexual identity. They need not prove that 'I am a heterosexual' is part of a public debate in order to secure their public self-identifications. Thus, in fact, the access of heterosexuals to the public sphere is not conditional, nor is the public to which they are guaranteed access limited to a sphere of political debate.

Finally, entering the public only under the aegis of free speech, openly gay, lesbian, and bisexual persons enter public space as *debatable* speakers. If, to proclaim one's homosexuality is itself equivalent to stating a political opinion, then that same proclamation will also necessarily and ineluctably be an invitation to having one's deviance from heterosexual norms challenged and debated by others. Once publicly proclaimed, there will be no social immunity from public scrutiny and public criticism. By contrast, the heteronormativity of public life outside the private home guarantees that heterosexual self-representation will be immunized against public scrutiny and challenge. Put simply, heterosexuals may claim that their heterosexual lives of dating, flirting, marriage, and procreating are their 'private' business—not open for debate— while simultaneously enacting those 'private' lives in public space. The liberty to conduct one's private life in this public *nonpoliticized* space is precisely what gay men and lesbians do not have. In *Rowland*, the court affirmed that they do not have this liberty.

In sum, neither status-based anti-discrimination policies nor first amendment protections of speech adequately guarantee gay men and lesbians that they may 'dare speak their names'. Because public, self-identifying statements may be deemed conduct rather than integrally connected to status, status-based policies may simply entitle individuals to *be* lesbian or gay in public space, but not to *represent* themselves as lesbian or gay in public space. Because the first amendment only protects speech on matters of public concern, it protects gay men's and lesbians' self-identifying statements only when they are part of a public debate about homosexual rights. Self-identifications, like Marjorie Rowland's, uttered in confidence or as part of everyday personal conversation in public space escape first amendment protection. Thus, the first amendment entitles lesbians and gay men to enter *arguments* about their sexuality; it does not entitle them to be lesbian or gay *speakers* regardless of the subject of conversation.

There is, of course, merit in using whatever legal tools are available, including anti-discrimination and free speech protections, to secure more equal liberties for lesbians and gay men. In doing so, however, it is important not to lose sight of the fact that the central liberty at stake is the liberty to represent oneself as gay or lesbian in the public sphere. At the center of lesbian and gay subordination is the requirement that everyone occupy a (real or pseudony-mous) heterosexual identity as a condition of access to the public sphere.

## III. Preventing Future Generations of Gay and Lesbian Persons

I turn now to the displacement of lesbians and gays from our social future. I will begin with some historical remarks about the psychiatric distinction between true and situational homosexuality. Then I will turn to considering how this distinction has affected psychiatric, legal, educational, and familial practices whose aim is to prevent future generations of lesbians and gays.

From the first emergence of sexual inversion in psychiatric taxonomies of the late nineteenth century, the distinctions between congenital and acquired homosexuality, between homosexuality as a personality type and mere same-sex behavior, and between cross-genderization and same-sex sexual activity were central to understandings of the forms that homosexuality and lesbian-ism could take. Recall that for the early twentieth-century sexologists, Havelock Ellis and Richard von Krafft-Ebing, both of whom played a central role in establishing and defining sexual inversion as a psychiatric condition, true inverts came by their homosexuality congenitally; and their distinguish-ing feature was not the orientation of their desire, but their cross-genderiza-tion, that is, their apparent constitution as a unique personality type—the third sex. True congenital inversion was contrasted with acquired situational inversion. Situational factors were thought to be capable of turning true heterosexuals into persons who, though not significantly cross-gendered, sexually desired others of the same sex. Those situational factors included childhood masturbation, confinement to same-sex environments in prisons, convents, and boarding schools, participation in the women's movement, and the seductive advances of true inverts. While congenital inversion was, perhaps, incorrigible, acquired inversion was, on this view, both curable and preventable by manipulating situational factors and inculcating proper sexual habits.

The true versus acquired distinction affected and continues to affect US policy concerning gay men and lesbians. During World War II, for example, psychiatrists became increasingly involved in setting military policy. Motivated partly by psychiatric insistence on the difference between true homosexuality and mere same-sex conduct, and partly by the practical need to retain military personnel, the military attempted to distinguish 'true' from 'salvageable' homosexuals.[58] Current US military policy continues to distinguish between true and situational homosexuals, with the burden of proof falling on those charged with same-sex conduct to demonstrate that they are truly heterosexuals.[59]

In the 1990s, the search for a gay gene continued the tradition of equating true homosexuality with a congenital condition. Arguments for gay-tolerant policies based on the claim that gay men and lesbians are 'born that way' fall squarely in line with early twentieth-century arguments, most notably by Magnus Hirschfeld and his Scientific-Humanitarian Committee, for social acceptance of the congenital invert. Given, however, a pervasive cultural distinction between true and situational homosexuals, arguments advocating toleration of those who cannot help being homosexual are doomed from the outset to be ineffective against a broad band of social policies whose aim is not so much the differential treatment of truly and incorrigibly gay and lesbian persons as the prevention of new gay and lesbian persons.

In an essay ironically titled 'How to Bring Your Kids up Gay', Eve Sedgwick argues that increasing tolerance of adult gay persons has gone hand-in-hand with the attempt to prevent new gay persons from coming into being.[61] She notes that in the same year that the American Psychiatric Association (APA) depathologized homosexuality, it added a new category—Gender Identity Disorder of Childhood—to its *Diagnostic and Statistical Manual*'s roster of pathological conditions.[62] Boys become susceptible to this diagnosis if, in addition to expressing distress about being a boy, they display a 'preoccupation with female stereotypical activities as manifested by a preference for either cross-dressing or simulating female attire, or by a compelling desire to participate in the games and pastimes of girls'.[63] The revised edition, DSM-III-R, adds, '. . . and rejection of male

---

[58] Allan Berube, *Coming Out Under Fire: A History of Gay Men and Women in World War II* (New York: Plume, 1990), 136–8.

[59] Code of Federal Regulations 32 (1993) Pt 41, App. A, pt l, H.1.c.1.

[60] John Lauritsen and David Thorstad, *The Early Homosexual Rights Movement, 1864–1935* (New York: Times Change Press, 1974).

[61] Eve Kosofsky Sedgwick, 'How to Bring Your Kids up Gay', in *Fear of a Queer Planet*, 69.

[62] APA, *Diagnostic and Statistical Manual of Mental Disorders*, (DSM-III), 3rd edn. (Washington, DC: APA, 1980). (The APA de-pathologized homosexuality in 1973, although DSM-III was not published until 1980).　　　　　　　　[63] Ibid. 266.

stereotypical toys, games, and activities'.[64] Similarly, girls become susceptible to this diagnosis if, in addition to expressing distress about being a girl, they show a 'persistent marked aversion to normative feminine clothing and insistence on wearing stereotypical masculine clothing, e.g., boys' underwear and other accessories'.[65] Harkening back to sexologists' equation of true inversion, not with same-sex desire, but with cross-genderization, this new disorder appears to be as much about the early detection and prevention of homosexuality as about control of gender deviance. The message of DSM-III, in Sedgwick's view, is that while *adult* homosexuals deserve dignified treatment at the hands of psychiatric professionals, psychiatrists may (and perhaps ought to) intervene in the lives of proto-gay *children* to prevent new gay persons from coming into being.[66]

Gay preventative measures have been framed not only as matters of gender health, but matters also of parental rights and duties. One of the psychiatrists Sedgwick critiques, for example, invokes the theory of parental dominion to justify parental intervention in proto-gay children's lives. He remarks, 'the rights of parents to oversee the development of children is a long-established principle. Who is to dictate that parents may not try to raise their children in a manner that maximizes the possibility of a heterosexual outcome?'[67] Others construe intervention as obligatory. In her article advocating gay access to surrogacy, Sharon Elizabeth Rush, moves swiftly from sanctioning adult homosexuality to condemning the creation of new gay persons:

Many heterosexual parents may be quite tolerant and accepting of homosexuality, and many homosexual parents may be quite proud to be homosexual. Nevertheless, given the social reprobation that at present attaches to being homosexual in the United States, and given the love and affection that most parents feel toward their children, I find it unbelievable that any parents—heterosexual or homosexual—would teach their children to be homosexual. Responsible and loving parents who were given a choice, in my opinion, simply would not choose to subject their child to the pain and isolation that inevitably attach to being a member of a socially disdained group.[68]

However legitimated—whether on grounds of psychological health, parental rights, or parental obligation—the goal of preventing children from turning out gay underlies policies that restrict gay and lesbian parenting, employment in child care, early education, and child service organizations

[64] APA, *Diagnostic and Statistical Manual* (DSM-III-R) 3rd rev. edn. (Washington, DC: APA, 1987), 73.

[65] Ibid.

[66] Dignified treatment of gay men and lesbians within psychiatry has not, of course, always been the norm. Efforts to 'cure' gay men and lesbians reached their peak during the 1950s and 1960s. For an autobiographical account, see Martin Duberman, *Cures: A Gay Man's Odyssey* (New York: Dutton, 1992).

[67] Sedgewick, 78.

[68] Sharon Elizabeth Rush, 'Breaking with Tradition: Surrogacy and Gay Fathers', in *Kindred Matters: Rethinking the Philosophy of the Family*, ed. Diana Tietjens Meyers, Kenneth Kipnis, and Cornelius F. Murphy (Ithaca, NY: Cornell University Press, 1993), 102–42, l02, ll9.

(e.g. the Boy Scouts of America), as well as policies that restrict the sexual content of school curricula.

For instance, one of the University of Missouri's principal reasons for refusing to recognize the student group Gay Lib was that '[w]hat happens to a latent or potential homosexual from the standpoint of his environment can cause him to become or not to become a homosexual'.[69] In the University's and dissenting Judge Regan's view, the University had a responsibility to protect potential homosexuals from becoming overt homosexuals.[70] And that, in their view, meant protecting them from being influenced by their fellow (overtly) gay and lesbian students.

The goal of preventing new gay and lesbian persons also figured centrally in the court ruling on the 1988 New Hampshire adoption law that 'prohibits any person who is homosexual from adopting any person, from being licensed as a member of a foster family, and from running day care centers'.[71] That law also prohibited heterosexuals from adopting children if there were adult lesbians or gays living or visiting for long periods in their households. When asked for a judicial opinion on the constitutionality of this law, the New Hampshire Supreme Court ignored any criteria of fitness to parent other than capacity to raise children to be heterosexual. In its view, 'the legislature can rationally act on the theory that a role model can influence the child's developing sexual identity',[72] and thus can legitimately regard gay and lesbian persons as unfit for adoptive and foster parenting. Although New Hampshire repealed its ban on gay and lesbian adoption and foster parenting in 1999, Florida continues to have a similar ban. In 1999, the child welfare agencies in both Arkansas and Utah instituted policies barring lesbians and gays from fostering children or adopting foster children; and bills were introduced in Texas and Oklahoma to prevent gays and lesbians from adopting children from state agencies.

Similar worries about the possibility of creating new generations of gay and lesbian persons surface in custody cases. Gay and lesbian parents may be subjected to special visitation restrictions designed to prevent their children from exposure to gay 'lifestyles'; for example, the child may not be taken to gay and lesbian gatherings or churches, visit overnight, or visit while a same-sex partner or other 'known homosexuals' are present; and the parent may be required to end a same-sex relationship or not live with his or her partner.[73]

Gay prevention also underlies attempts to outlaw the 'promotion' of homosexuality in schools. In 1988, Britain passed Clause 28 of the Local

---

[69] *Gay Lib v. University of Missouri*, 558 F.2d, 848, 852 (1977) (summarizing the Board of Curators of the University of Missouri's resolution).          [70] Ibid. 859.

[71] Qtd. *Opinion of the Justices*, Supreme Court of New Hampshire, 530 A.2d, 21, 23 (N.H. 1987).

[72] Ibid. 25.

[73] Editors of the Harvard Law Review, 122–3. Sylvia A. Law, 'Homosexuality and the Social Meaning of Gender', *Wisconsin Law Review* 1988 (1988): 187–235, 191; Lynn D. Wardle, 'The Potential Impact of Homosexual Parenting on Children', *University of Illinois Law Review* 1997 (1997): 833–99, 880.

Government Act which stipulated that 'A local authority shall not—(a) intentionally promote homosexuality or publish material with the intention of promoting homosexuality; (b) promote the teaching in any maintained school of the acceptability of homosexuality as a pretended family relationship'.[74] In a similar vein, a 1992 Oregon ballot measure would have amended the state constitution to prohibit the use of state facilities to 'promote, encourage, or facilitate homosexuality'. It would also have required that the Oregon Department of Higher Education and the public schools 'assist in setting a standard for Oregon's youth that recognizes homosexuality . . . as abnormal, wrong, unnatural and perverse and that these behaviors are to be discouraged and avoided'.[75] Both 'no promo homo' policies, as legal theorist Nan Hunter calls them, were antedated by the (failed) 1978 California Briggs Initiative under which any school employee could be fired for 'advocating, soliciting, imposing, encouraging or promoting of private or public homosexual activity directed at, or likely to come to the attention of schoolchildren and/or other employees'.[76]

Heterosexual control over standards of child mental health, over blood, adoptive, and foster parenting, and over the socialization of children in public institutions facilitates the reproduction of heterosexual society. It ensures that adult gay men and lesbians will have little say in what kinds of persons future generations will be. And even if it is not possible to make proto-gay children turn out heterosexual, gay preventative socialization practices can go some way toward ensuring that the next generation of gay men and lesbians will accept as reasonable both the requirement of adopting a pseudonymous heterosexual identity as a condition of access to the public sphere and their exclusion from any socially legitimated, 'nonpretended' private sphere of marriage, parenting, and family life. Public commitment to gay prevention also legitimates the continued punitive expulsion of older gay and lesbian children from their own families and the termination of the emotional and material support that families provide for children.

It is tempting to respond to these various gay preventative strategies by arguing that pathologizing gender deviance in childhood makes little sense in a psychiatric scheme that depathologizes homosexuality; that in point of fact the children of gay men and lesbians are just as likely to grow up heterosexual as are the children of heterosexuals; and that 'no promo homo' policies involve censorship and the legal underwriting of one set of moral values. Although having a place, such arguments miss the more central issue. That issue

---

[74] Quoted in Jeffrey Weeks, 'Pretended Family Relationships', in *Against Nature: Essays on History, Sexuality, and Identity* (Concord, MA: Paul & Company, 1991), 137. Weeks also provides a socio-historical analysis of why the family became a focus of British legal attention.

[75] Timothy Egan, 'Oregon Measure Asks State to Repress Homosexuality', *New York Times*, 16 Aug. 1992, A34.

[76] California Proposition 6, §3(b)(2) (1978). Qtd in Nan D. Hunter, 'Identity, Speech, and Equality', *Virginia Law Review* 79 (1993): 1695–720, 1703. She gives a detailed account of the full range of 'no promo homo' policies.

concerns whether heterosexuals as a social group may legitimately claim for themselves exclusive entitlement to determine the character of future generations.

## IV. Subordination, Morality, and Social Authority

My argument for the liberty to enact one's sexual identity in the public sphere and the liberty to influence the character of future generations may well seem question-begging. Requiring some individuals to refrain from flaunting their identity in public and disabling them from influencing children might be justified. If so, depriving lesbians and gay men of these two basic liberties does not amount to subordination. Opponents of lesbian and gay rights take exactly this view. They assert that so-called lesbian and gay subordination is not analogous to race or gender oppression. Women and racial minorities are not, as a group, engaging in morally objectionable conduct. Lesbians and gay men are. Whatever social penalties or barriers lesbians and gay men face are not imposed on them simply because of their status as is the case in race and gender oppression. On the contrary, the status 'lesbian' or 'homosexual' is integrally connected to (is, indeed, defined by) a particular sexual conduct. It is that sexual conduct that discriminatory policies aim to exclude from the public sphere and from influencing children. As John Finnis has observed, gay rights proponents themselves typically do not see anti-discrimination protections as narrowly focused on prohibiting discrimination against those who are believed to have same-sex desires. 'Instead . . . , "gay rights" movements interpret the phrase [outlawing discrimination based on sexual orientation] as extending full legal protection to *public* activities intended specifically to promote, procure and facilitate homosexual *conduct*.'[77] So, for example, full-fledged nondiscrimination policies are seen as protecting lesbian and gay student groups, 'flaunting' behavior like Singer's, and being uncloseted in the military.

But if same-sex conduct is morally objectionable, and if the state has legitimate authority to control the moral climate of the public sphere and to protect children from immoral influences, then it is also legitimate for the state to refuse to protect lesbians and gay men against discrimination and to install policies protecting children from their influence. Thus showing that lesbians and gay men are not allowed free access to the public sphere *as* lesbians and gay men and that they face barriers to influencing the character of the next generation is insufficient to establish that lesbians and gays are subordinated. One would, in addition, have to argue either that lesbian and gay sexual behavior is morally acceptable; or one would have to argue that laws based on morality are not legitimate.

---

[77] John Finnis, 'Law, Morality, and Sexual Orientation', *Notre Dame Journal of Law, Ethics and Public Policy* 9 (1995): 11–39, 16.

In fact, I think one can go a long way (if not the entire way) toward showing that gay men and lesbians are subordinated without engaging either the moral question ('Is same-sex sexual activity morally acceptable or morally wrong?') or the political question ('Is the state entitled to frame laws based on moral beliefs?'). Opposition to lesbian and gay rights often begins from the reduction of lesbianism and homosexuality to a set of sex acts. Once this reduction is made, it becomes fairly easy to argue that promoting a kind of sexual activity (whether morally objectionable or not) is often inappropriate in the public sphere, for example, at work. It also becomes fairly easy to argue that promoting a kind of sexual activity (whether morally objectionable or not) in front of children is typically inappropriate. As I suggested earlier, however, this reduction of lesbianism and homosexuality to sex acts is simply a mistake. We do not similarly reduce heterosexuality to sex acts. Heterosexuality is a complex phenomena including dress styles, modes of nonsexual interaction with the opposite sex and same sex, flirting, dating, romantic attachments, marital and parenting relations, and so on. Heterosexuality is displayed and 'promoted' in the way we segregate bathrooms by sex, on ballroom dance floors, in dinner seating arrangements, at proms, in lingerie advertisements, at wedding ceremonies, in the display of family photos, and so on.

Taking heterosexuality as the model for what it means to have a sexual orientation brings into view the fact that sexual orientations are not merely orientations of sexual activity and desires. They are, more broadly, ways of being oriented in the *social world*. Policies geared toward protecting children from the immoralities of homosexuality and lesbianism are not narrowly aimed at protecting children against being influenced to engage in particular sexual acts. They are more broadly aimed at preventing children from adopting a general orientation in the social world from whose vantage point they might find it reasonable to prize a picture of, sit next to, dance with, date, have a crush on, or dream of marrying someone of the same sex. It is a vantage point from which social events, literature, film, dress styles, teasing, and jokes premised on the presumption of heterosexuality appear uninteresting or uninviting. Discriminatory policies confronted by lesbian and gay adults have the similarly broad aim of controlling the visibility of a way of being oriented in the social world.

If what is being controlled is not the doing and promotion of sexual acts but instead a general orientation in the social world, then justifying that control will require moral arguments that go well beyond showing what is wrong with particular sexual acts. It will also require a more extensive political argument showing why the state may legitimately control not just particular immoral acts but an entire way of being oriented in the social world. In short, once we cease falsely reducing lesbianism and homosexuality to sexual acts, it becomes much less clear that controlling lesbianism and homosexuality could be justifiable. As I suggested earlier, the net effect of permitting discrimination against lesbians and gays is to displace the identities 'lesbian' and 'gay' from the public sphere and to permit only the identity 'heterosexual' to appear. I also suggested that sexual orientation is basic to identity in the same way that gender is; one cannot be a public actor and not have *some* (assumed) sexual orientation or *some* (assumed) gender. Thus, displacing gay and lesbian identities from the public sphere looks like displacing a type of person (not just the sexual acts of some persons) from civil society.

The immorality culturally attached to lesbianism and homosexuality is in fact not narrowly attached to sexual acts. It is attached to *being* the sort of person who is oriented in the social world as a lesbian or gay man. With the medical elaboration in the late nineteenth century of a special kind of person, the homosexual, sodomy shifted from being simply a forbidden act, like abortion or adultery, to being one among many indicators of an underlying psycho-sexual personality structure.[78] Subsequent psychiatric accounts of the homosexual as perverted, psychopathological, sexually voracious, and emotionally unstable opened the doors for the invention of a type of person for whom moral depravity is constitutive of his or her nature. Immorality came to reside in *who* the homosexual or lesbian is, not just in what he or she does.

The image of gay men and lesbians as morally depraved fully flowered in the McCarthy era's programs to purge the military and civil service of all 'sexual perverts'. Gay men and lesbians were, by their very nature, a threat to national security, an inherently subversive element in society, and 'generally unsuitable' for government employment.[79] They were declared to be so by an executive order, which ordered their dismissal from all branches of government service.[80] Evidence, however thin, of mere homosexual *tendencies*, even in the complete absence of evidence of actual sexual activity, was sufficient grounds for dismissal.[81] And in 1952, Congress officially closed the national borders to immigrants with 'psychopathic personalities', (i.e. gay men and lesbians).[82]

This equation, consolidated in the 1950s, of homosexuality and lesbianism with immorality produced both an equation of *being* gay or lesbian with committing immoral acts as well as a concomitant presumption that whatever it is that heterosexuals are doing (even if that includes same-sex conduct) is

[78] e.g. the collection of essays in *Forms of Desire*. Michel Foucault has perhaps become most well known for articulating the thesis that the homosexual is a social construction. *The History of Sexuality, vol. 1: An Introduction* (New York: Vintage-Random House, 1990).

[79] Senate Subcommittee for the Commission on Expenditure in the Executive Departments, *Employment of Homosexuals and Other Sex Perverts in Government*, 81st Cong., 2nd sess., 1950, S. Doc. 24, 3.

[80] President, Executive Order 10,450. Federal Register. 182489 (1953).

[81] Lillian Faderman, *Odd Girls and Twilight Lovers: A History of Lesbian Life in Twentieth Century America* (New York: Penguin, 1992), 142–4.

[82] Public Law 414, 82nd Cong., sess. (1952), *Immigration and Nationality Act*. For an historical account of the McCarthy era purge of homosexuals, see Allan Berube, *Coming Out Under Fire*.

probably morally innocent. As a result, normative judgments about same-sex conduct are not in fact just about conduct. They are instead mediated by distinctions between homosexual predator and heterosexual prey, the corrupt homosexual and the corrupted heterosexual, the (homo) sexual 'addict' and the heterosexual performer of occasional same-sex acts.

In *Morrison v. State Board of Education*, for example, judicial discussion of Morrison's same-sex activity was mediated by assumptions about who Morrison was.[83] When Marc Morrison's week-long sexual relationship with a fellow teacher, Fred Schneringer, came to light, the California State Board of Education charged Morrison with immoral and unprofessional conduct, and revoked his licenses to teach secondary school and exceptional children. The court argued that the Board's interpretation of 'immoral conduct' was overly broad, unconnected to considerations of employees' fitness to teach, and threatened 'arbitrarily [to] impair the right of the individual to live his private life, apart from his job, as he deems fit'.[84] Moreover, there was no evidence that Morrison had sought improper relations with students, had failed to convey to them correct principles of morality, or that his relationship with co-workers had been affected by the incident. In short, there was no evidence of his unfitness to teach.[85] However, the facts that the court chose to especially highlight in *Morrison* did not concern Morrison's work performance. Rather, the court highlighted facts that indicated that Morrison was not really a homosexual, even if he had engaged in same-sex sex. The court repeatedly stressed the 'limited' nature of Morrison's homosexual relationship and observed that Morrison and Schneringer were suffering severe emotional stress at the time, that Morrison had suggested women whom Schneringer might date, that with the exception of the Schneringer incident Morrison had not had any 'homosexual urges' in a dozen years, and that there was no evidence of 'abnormal activities or desires' since that incident.[86] Here, the court seems less interested in ascertaining whether Morrison's private conduct affected his public work performance than in ascertaining *who* Morrison really is. Is he really a homosexual, that is, a morally suspect kind of person, whose fitness to teach might reasonably be doubted? Or is he more innocently just a heterosexual performer of homosexual acts?

Because *being* gay or lesbian is equated with immorality, the normative status of the identities 'gay' and 'lesbian' ends up *preceding* and infecting the normative status of their acts. What makes same-sex touching, kissing, handholding, knee-squeezing, cohabitation, and marriage wrong is neither so much their same-sexedness nor their likely eventuation in sodomy. Rather, it is their being done by a kind of person, that is, their being *homosexual* or *lesbian* acts—not just their same-sexedness. This is perhaps nowhere more clearly evident than in military policy itself. Army regulations exempt from

---

[83] California 461 P.2d, 375 (1969).    [84] Ibid. 394.
[85] Ibid. 392.    [86] Ibid. 377–8.

automatic discharge soldiers who have engaged in same-sex sex but who can prove that same-sex sexuality was a departure from customary behavior, is unlikely to recur, and is undesired.[87] As Judge Norris so nicely summarized Army policy in *Watkins v. U.S. Army*:

> If a straight soldier and a gay soldier of the same sex engage in homosexual acts because they are drunk, immature or curious, the straight soldier may remain in the Army while the gay soldier is automatically terminated. In short, the regulations do not penalize soldiers for engaging in [same-sex] acts; they penalize soldiers who have engaged in [same-sex] acts only when the Army decides that those soldiers are actually gay.[88]

The distinction between an act of same-sex sex (which can be done by either heterosexuals or nonheterosexuals) and a specifically *homosexual* act (which can only be done by homosexuals) is here out in the open. It is also out in the open in New Hampshire's former statute against gay and lesbian adoption, which distinguishes between true homosexuals and those who have engaged in same-sex sex but can claim a heterosexual identity.[89] The distinction between same-sex act and distinctively homosexual act operated more covertly in *Hardwick*. In Justice White's view, 'the issue presented is whether the Federal Constitution confers a fundamental right upon *homosexuals* to engage in sodomy'.[90] This framing of the question not only ignores the facially neutral character of Georgia's sodomy statute, more importantly, it ignores the fact that Georgia's statute concerns acts, not identities. That statute prohibits same-sex sodomy regardless of whether the doer is homosexual or heterosexual. Having shifted the focus from acts to identities, Justice White concludes that *homosexuals* have no right to engage in sodomy, leaving open the possibility that *heterosexuals* do (regardless of the sex of their partner in sodomy).[91]

The point of these examples is to call into question arguments that justify penalizing or restricting gays and lesbians on the grounds that gays and lesbians are engaged in immoral *conduct*. If normative judgments about same-sex conduct depend on first ascertaining *who* is engaged in that conduct (a heterosexual or nonheterosexual), then it is not simply conduct that is being regulated when gays and lesbians are penalized or restricted. It is gays and lesbians as a type of person.

The point of these examples is also to highlight the way that equating *being* a homosexual with immorality produces a novel civic status: the citizen-deviant. Because all things gay or lesbian are routinely coupled, in legal and lay imaginations, with sodomy, child molestation, solicitation, promiscuity or

---

[87] Lauritsen and Thorstad, *The Early Homosexual Rights Movement, 1864–1935*.

[88] *Watkins v. U.S. Army*, 699, 715 (1989) (Judge Norris, concurring). For clarity, I have substituted 'same-sex' for 'homosexual' in the original text..

[89] *Opinion of the Justices* 530 A.2d at 24.          [90] *Bowers v. Hardwick*, 186 (my emphasis).

[91] See Halley, 'Reasoning about Sodomy'.

some other category of immorality, nothing one does *as* a gay man or lesbian is untainted by the specter of immorality. Everything one does becomes an act of promoting immorality. And every gay-positive statement metamorphoses into an endorsement of immorality.

Constructed as citizen-deviants, gay men and lesbians occupy a shadowy territory neither fully outside nor fully inside civil society. Unlike the criminally insane, whose inability to tell right from wrong disqualifies them from civic status, gay men and lesbians formally possess civic status. But unlike heterosexual citizens, whose relation to immorality is presumed to be merely contingent (they might or might not engage in immoral activity), gay men and lesbians are presumed to be inherently implicated in immoral activity. Constituted as undesirable citizen-deviants, gay men and lesbians manage to contribute to production and reproduction and to fulfill their civic duties as 'reverse malingers'—persons who falsify their status not in order to escape from civic burdens but in order to accept them.[92]

This citizen-deviant status gives discriminatory policies against gay men and lesbians a distinctive flavor. While racial and gender discrimination are largely predicated on *inferiorizing* stereotypes, sexuality discrimination is largely predicated on *immoralizing* stereotypes whose ultimate suggestion is not that gay men and lesbians are *incompetent*, but that they are *untrustworthy* members of civil society. Socially constituted as beings whose very nature it is to commit crimes against nature, God, and state, gay men and lesbians, insofar as they publicly claim those identities, speak under a pall of guilt. Unlike their presumed innocent and civic-minded heterosexual counterparts, they cannot represent themselves as gay men or lesbians without undermining their standing in the public sphere. That includes their standing to challenge conventional moral and legal norms. Heterosexuals have, for example, been extremely successful in decriminalizing heterosexual crimes against nature—the use of birth control, abortion, adultery, and heterosexual sodomy. Heterosexuals have also been reasonably successful in pluralizing acceptable family arrangements—divorce, single-parenting, egalitarian gender arrangements, separate husband and wife domiciles. As presumed trustworthy members of civil society, heterosexuals have the standing to claim that they simply have different moral opinions about the permissibility of 'alternative' sexual and familial practices and to request that law and social practices recognize differences of opinion. As presumed untrustworthy members, lesbians' and gay men's expression of different, disagreeing moral opinions is continuously vulnerable to being reconstituted as a promotion of immorality. In short, defined as citizen-deviants, gay men and lesbians are

---

[92] 'Reverse malinger' was the military's inventive label during World War II for gay men and lesbians who presented themselves as heterosexuals in order to do military service. See Berube, *Coming Out Under Fire*, 20. The military may discharge servicemen not only for being homosexual but also for 'fraudulent enlistment' if they did not originally declare their homosexuality.

denied equal standing to participate in legal, social, and moral debates, including, most importantly, debates over the place of gay and lesbian identity in the public and private spheres.

## Conclusion

In this chapter, I have aimed to establish the following points. First, lesbian and gay subordination is not best understood as a matter of confining persons who are gay or lesbian to subordinate, disadvantaging, exploitable places within sexuality structured public and private hierarchies. Thus specific measures, such as anti-discrimination protection for gay men and lesbians, should not be seen as primarily aimed at remedying systematic inequities in their material conditions and access to opportunities. Second, lesbian and gay subordination is better understood as a matter of displacing gay and lesbian identities to the outside of civil society, and thus denying a place for gay and lesbian identities within both public and private spheres. Third, gay and lesbian identities are displaced from workplaces, streets, the military, markets, schools, and other public spaces by requiring gay men and lesbians to adopt pseudonymous heterosexual identities as a condition of access to those public spaces. Displacing gay and lesbian identities from the public sphere in this way amounts to reserving the public sphere for heterosexuals only. Fourth, gay and lesbian identities are displaced from our social future via legal, educational, psychiatric, and familial practices that are aimed at insuring the heterosexuality of future generations. The institutionalization of gay preventative and heterosexual productive measures amounts to reserving for heterosexuals only exclusive entitlement to determine the character of future generations.

Throughout, I have implicitly been suggesting that in order to see what is subordinating, or oppressive, about lesbians' and gays' social experience, we need to think more imaginatively and broadly about what counts as a basic liberty or a basic social good. Because it is possible to closet one's identity, gays and lesbians can largely evade the deprivation of civil liberties, such as the right to vote, and the reduction of access to basic goods, such as income and status, which have characterized gender and race oppression. If we use a conventional list of civil liberties and basic goods to assess gays' and lesbians' social position, that position does not appear to be a pervasively and systematically subordinating one. If however, the liberty to enter the public sphere without first closeting one's identity and the liberty to influence the character of future generations are basic liberties of citizens, then it is possible to make a case that lesbians and gays are systematically denied two important, basic liberties. In the next two chapters, I will be arguing that, in respect to marriage and the family, the most important liberty to secure for lesbians and gays is equal definitional authority to say what counts as a marriage or a family.

# 5

# Defending Marriage

On 21 September 1996, President Clinton signed into law the Defense of Marriage Act (DOMA). That Act did two things. It amended the Full Faith and Credit Clause so that states that do not already expressly prohibit same-sex marriages would not be required to honor same-sex marriages performed in other states. Second, it 'defended' marriage by defining marriage for federal purposes as involving one man and one woman.

The immediate impetus behind the Defense of Marriage Act was the Hawaii Supreme Court's ruling in *Baehr v. Lewin* that a same-sex marriage bar would be deemed an unconstitutional form of sex discrimination unless the state could demonstrate a compelling interest served by prohibiting same-sex marriage. Although the Hawaii case received a great deal of notoriety, court suits for the right of gays and lesbians to marry are not new. They date from the 1970s. Previous suits, however, invariably stumbled on courts' insistence that marriage is by definition between a man and a woman. If same-sex marriage is definitionally impossible, then gays and lesbians are not being denied a fundamental right to marry when same-sex unions are not legally recognized. In addition, the 1986 Supreme Court ruling in *Bowers v. Hardwick*, affirming the constitutionality of anti-sodomy laws, have made arguments for same-sex marriage even more difficult. Courts have assumed that sodomy is the act that defines the class 'homosexual'. And if it is constitutional to prohibit sodomy, it must similarly be constitutional to impose additional restrictions on members of this class—such as prohibiting same-sex marriage. Thus, equal protection arguments that marriage bars discriminate against gays and lesbians have been unsuccessful. What distinguished the Hawaii case was the court's unwillingness to use definitional arguments to rule out same-sex marriage and its willingness to consider a different equal protection argument, namely, that same-sex marriage bars discriminate on the basis of sex.

Although it might seem that the Hawaii Supreme Court was moving in an obviously correct direction, while Congress, in passing the Defense of Marriage Act, was not, the topic of same-sex marriage rights has in fact been controversial among lesbians and gays. Because the right to same-sex marriage is so controversial, that right is not, at first blush, a promising candidate for the center of lesbian and gay politics. However, I intend to argue that that is exactly where the right to same-sex marriage belongs. The argument will span this and the following chapter. Although it might seem most natural to begin by responding to objections to same-sex marriage, especially the forceful and multi-pronged attack mounted by lesbian feminists, I will defer discussion of lesbian feminist critiques until Chapter 6. Before we can fully assess any particular critique of same-sex marriage, we need to know whether the marriage bar is simply one restriction among many that gays and lesbians face or whether it plays an especially central role in sustaining lesbian and gay oppression. If the latter is true, then much stronger arguments will be needed for not pursuing the right to marry within a lesbian and gay politics. In this chapter, I intend to argue that same-sex marriage bars do play an especially central role in displacing gays and lesbians to the outside of civil society. In particular, being fit for marriage is intimately bound up with our cultural conception of what it means to be a citizen. This is because marriage is culturally conceived as playing a uniquely foundational role in sustaining civil society. As a result, only those who are fit to enter marital and family life deserve full civic status. Bars on same-sex marriage encode and enforce the view that lesbians and gays are inessential citizens because they are unable to participate in the foundational social institution. Marriage bars thus play a critical role in displacing gays and lesbians.

At first glance, it might seem that formal considerations of justice alone provide a sufficient reason for endorsing same-sex marriage rights. Consider that, under American jurisprudence, the right to marry is generally assumed to be part of a more basic right to privacy. Appealing to tradition, particularly religious tradition, seems an inadequate basis in a liberal society for limiting same-sex couples' right to privacy. Historically, such appeals have been used to justify not only same-sex marriage bars, but also bars to interracial marriage. And just as anti-miscegenation laws constitute a form of racial discrimination, so too same-sex marriage bars seem to constitute a form of sexual orientation discrimination. Thus, on grounds of formal equality alone, one might reject bars on same-sex marriage.

In addition, the most obvious reasons in favor of same-sex marriage rights are practical. Marriage gives access to a set of material benefits—dental and health insurance, income tax breaks, and spousal social security and pension benefits. Marriage also provides spouses with legal protection against third parties' (e.g. grandparents and sperm donors) claims to child custody and visitation rights as well as rights to give proxy consent and to inherit. Marriage also facilitates partnerships by giving spouses immigration preference and a right to conjugal visits. Here too, formal considerations of justice suggest that it is wrong to deny same-sex couples the rights and benefits of marriage that heterosexual couples enjoy.

However, gay and lesbian opponents of same-sex marriage rights are, I think, correct *not* to accept these sorts of arguments as sufficient and to insist that some persuasive positive moral argument is necessary. In particular, they are right not to accept considerations of formal equality as sufficient reasons to give political priority to securing marriage rights. The problem with arguments appealing to formal equality is that they are aimed narrowly at answering the question of *who* should have marriage rights given that some do. They do not fully answer equally important questions about whether *anyone* should have this right or about *how important* this right is. Claudia Card helpfully brings out this point in her article against same-sex marriage.[1] She invites us to imagine a world in which white men are permitted to own slaves, but white women are not. On grounds of formal equality, one might argue that it is unjust to deprive white women of a right that white men have. Yet the right to own slaves is not a right anyone should have. What is needed in the case of marriage, then, is a positive moral argument for the value of *any one* having a right to marry. In addition, we need a positive moral argument for *how import-ant* that right is if it is a legitimate right. By themselves, arguments appealing to formal equality do not tell us this. There may in fact be moral reasons for not giving political priority to securing this right. Some have argued that distributing benefits, such as health insurance, through marriage is itself unjust. Others have argued that marriage has historically been oppressive to women and that to seek same-sex marriage rights amounts to endorsing a sexist institution. Yet others have argued that gay men and lesbians should resist normalizing institutions like marriage and should instead continue creating multiple new forms of intimate and familial arrangements. Finally, even if seeking same-sex marriage rights were entirely unobjectionable, it might still be true that other political goals, such as securing coverage under anti-discrimination laws, might intervene more directly in the system of heterosexual domination and thus deserve higher priority.

Thus, because we need to know why formal equality with respect to marriage rights is worth pursuing and how much priority those rights should be given, we need to ask what positive moral arguments there might be. Examining the positive moral argument for marriage rights matters for a second reason as well. The moral significance of extending rights is to a large extent a function of the sorts of arguments that get culturally circulated in the process of extending rights. Take, for example, anti-discrimination laws protecting women. While the laws themselves contributed to greater equality, the culturally circulated arguments against sex discrimination have arguably had a greater impact. They have helped to produce a cultural world in which critical reflection on gender roles, on the assumption that biology is destiny, and on power relations between women and men regularly takes place. Quite different arguments supporting anti-discrimination laws *could* have gained cultural prominence. In 1792, Mary Wollstonecraft, for example, argued for women's right to education on the grounds that better education would better fit women for their roles as children's educators and their husband's compan-ion.[2] And she argued for women's employment opportunities so that women would be able to support their families in the event of their husband's death.

---

[1] Claudia Card, 'Against Marriage and Motherhood', *Hypatia* 11 (1996): 1–23.
[2] Mary Wollstonecraft, *A Vindication of the Rights of Woman* (New York: Norton, 1967).

Culturally contextualized within these sorts of arguments, anti-discrimination laws would not have had the same moral significance. They would be viewed as supporting a system of separate gender roles for men and women rather than as constituting a challenge to that system.

It is especially because it matters *which* arguments get culturally circulated that I think the positive arguments for same-sex marriage rights warrant careful scrutiny. In what follows, I will focus on three different arguments. The first argument links marriage rights to a normative ideal of long-term, monogamous, sexually faithful intimacy and defends marriage rights on the basis of the value of that ideal. The second argument presses the connection between homophobia and sexism, stressing the way that securing same-sex marriage rights might reduce sexism. This is the sort of argument that the Hawaii Supreme Court relied on. The third argument, and the one I intend to defend, links the denial of marriage rights to the cultural construction of gay men and lesbians as outsiders to the family who are *for that reason* defective citizens. In pursuing this third line of argument I will have a good deal to say about the House and Senate arguments supporting the Defense of Marriage Act.

## I. Marriage as Normative Ideal

One positive moral argument for same-sex marriage begins by recognizing that the legal institution of marriage is founded on an antecedent moral conception of marriage. On the moral conception of marriage, marriage is about the emotional and spiritual unity of two persons. Such unity requires monogamy, long-term commitment, and sexual fidelity. It is both a unity of companionship and an economic unity of mutual support. On natural law accounts, marital unity is partly expressed through procreation and child rearing; on more secular accounts, the stability of a relationship based on long-term commitment simply provides the ideal environment for child rearing. Understood morally, marriage is not simply one among many intimate relationships that people can voluntarily enter into. It is *the* normative ideal for how sexuality, companionship, affection, personal economics, and child rearing should be organized.

This moral conception of marriage provides the justification for state regulation of marriage. The state grants the legal right to marry, protects marital privacy, provides unique material benefits to marital couples, and regulates the dissolution of marriages because marriage is a basic personal and social good. Although state neutrality may require permitting other forms of intimate relationship, the state also has an obligation to promote valued ways of living. As Senator Byrd observed in the DOMA debates, '. . . humanity has discovered that the permanent relationship between man and woman is a keystone to the stability, strength, and health of human society'.[3] Promoting marriage is the point of giving state sanction to marriages.

---

[3] *Congressional Record*, 104th Cong., 2nd sess., 1996, 142, pt S10109.

In *The Case for Same-Sex Marriage*, William Eskridge, Jr. uses this sort of argument to defend same-sex marriage rights. In his view, 'the dominant goal of marriage is and should be *unitive*, the spiritual and personal union of the committed couple'.[4] Such unity requires long-term commitment, monogamy, and sexual fidelity. Eskridge argues for the value of long-term commitment in part by suggesting that commitment adds depth to a relationship[5], and in part by drawing on a communitarian view of the self as a relational self whose identity is constituted and sustained by ties to others.[6] Contemporary life, he claims, is increasingly hostile to the possibility of sustaining stable relations and a stable sense of self. The plurality of roles we now occupy, our geographical mobility and, often, our lack of stable employment all militate against a stable sense of self. In addition, liberal culture encourages us to think in terms of a 'marketplace of intimacies' where both entering and exiting relationships is a matter purely of individual choice. The result is that our identities are fluid, unstable, and fractured. Taking such fluidity and instability to be a bad thing, Eskridge concludes that some relationships should be viewed as unchosen, or at least not easily revisable once entered into. Marital relations and parent–child relations are cases in point. Because a stable sense of self is such an important good to the individual, using the law to protect marital and parenting relationships both from external intervention and internal dissolution is warranted.

Additional reasons for the importance of both long-term commitment and sexual fidelity might be drawn from the sort of argument given by cultural conservatives.[7] Cultural conservatives charge liberalism with breeding an excessive emphasis on personal choice, self-expression, and lifestyle experimentation. The consequence is that we now live in a 'sex-riddled, divorce-prone' culture that militates against the development of such personal and civic virtues as self-sacrifice, self-discipline, planning for the future, concern for others, responsible conduct, and loyalty.[8] Promoting, and to some extent coercively enforcing, the normative ideal of sexual fidelity and long-term commitment is designed to counteract this trend and to provide individuals with a context for cultivating and expressing the virtues of loyalty, self-discipline, self-sacrifice, and self-transcendence. This, it is assumed, will be good both for individuals and for society. Thus the answer to the question: 'Why

---

[4] William N. Eskridge, Jr., *The Case for Same-Sex Marriage: From Sexual Liberty to Civilized Commitment* (New York: Free Press, 1996), 91.

[5] Ibid. 72.

[6] William N. Eskridge, Jr., 'Beyond Lesbian and Gay "Families We Choose," ' in *Sex, Preference, and Family*, ed. David M. Estlund and Martha C. Nussbaum (New York: Oxford University Press, 1996), 277–89.

[7] Karen Struening, 'Feminist Challenges to the New Familialism: Lifestyle Experimentation and the Freedom of Association', *Hypatia* 11 (1996): 135–54.

[8] Stephen Macedo, 'Sexuality and Liberty: Making Room for Nature and Tradition?' in *Sex, Preference, and Family*, 86–101. Karen Struening surveys the main themes of cultural conservatives with respect to the family, focusing particularly on William Galston. See 'Feminist Challenges to the New Familialism'.

should anyone have the right to marry?' is that committed, monogamous, sexually faithful relationships contribute to personal and social flourishing.

On this type of viewpoint, one of the most important features of legal marriage is the costliness of dissolving a marriage. That costliness means that entering a marriage involves a higher level of personal commitment than, say, entering a domestic partnership. It also means that, once married, couples have an additional incentive to stay married. Eskridge hypothesizes that such incentives are especially important for gay men who are more likely than lesbians to be sexually promiscuous and thus to have difficulty sustaining committed relationships.

There is a good deal to object to in this argument for same-sex marriage. Let me begin with coercion. Under present no-fault divorce laws, the coercive pressures exerted on couples to marry and stay married are limited to the tax penalties imposed on couples who choose not to get legally married, and, once married, the costliness of divorce proceedings. However, any argument that appeals to the value of promoting *long-term* marriage clearly justifies toughening divorce laws, a move that is already underfoot in some states. Even if there is something to be said for committed relationships, it is hard to see how using the law to keep couples together could be justified. As Karen Struening has pointed out, basing state policy on the value of commitment elevates marital and familial stability to the status of the sole, or overriding good.[9] The values of personal and marital happiness, emotional and sexual intimacy, avoiding abusive or inegalitarian intimacies, and revising identities constituted through relationships all take a backseat to the overriding goal of stability. One might, however, wonder why stability provides a good reason to preserve either an identity or a relationship that has nothing else to recommend it. In addition, feminists have special cause for concern about what pressuring couples to stay together might mean for heterosexual women. Now that many women have the economic resources to leave unhappy marriages, they may find their way barred by restrictive divorce laws.[10] And, as Claudia Card has pointed out, because marriage includes the right to cohabit with one's spouse, it is more difficult for a married person to protect herself from battery and rape by a spouse since the spouse is entitled to reside where she does.[11] Placing obstacles to divorce exacerbates this vulnerability.

Equally troubling is the fact that coercion would be exerted in the name not just of commitment, but of a substantive moral conception of how people ought to organize their sexual, economic, parenting, and affectionate lives from which law and social practice have been retreating. Most states have eliminated fault-based divorce and criminal penalties for adultery and do not enforce criminal statutes against cohabitation. The divorce rate runs at about

---

[9] Karen Struening, 'Feminist Challenges to the New Familialism'.

[10] That the US has the highest divorce rate has recently been attributed to the fact that US women have the greatest economic independence.

[11] Card, 'Against Marriage and Motherhood'.

50 per cent. More people are cohabiting and marrying later. And parenting takes a variety of forms, from single-parenting, to joint custody, to parenting within divorce-extended families. It is, however, just this diminishing hetero-sexual compliance with the normative ideal of long-term, sexually faithful, two-parent families that has motivated a variety of suggestions for bolstering compliance. They have included restigmatizing divorce, toughening divorce laws for couples with children, punitive welfare policies for poor women who have children out of wedlock, and a return to some form of gender-structured marriage.[12] What is especially worrisome about this first argument for same-sex marriage rights, then, is its natural place within a larger cultural conversa-tion about the benefits of returning to a particular normative ideal of marriage and parenting. It is a return that requires using law and social policy to dissuade individuals from pursuing a plurality of conceptions of how intim-ate relationships ought to be organized.

Because this argument for same-sex marriage rights depends on the view that the state ought to promote one normative ideal for intimacies, it plays directly into queer theorists' and lesbian feminists' worst fears about what advocating same-sex marriage might mean. Queer theorists worry that pursu-ing marriage rights is assimilationist, because it rests on the view that it would be better for gay and lesbian relationships to be as much like traditional heterosexual intimate relationships as possible. To pursue marriage rights is to reject the value of pursuing possibly more liberating, if less conventional, sexual, affectional, care-taking, and economic intimate arrangements. Feminists worry that pursuing marriage rights will have the effect of endors-ing gender-structured heterosexual marriage, since the pursuit of marriage rights rests on an uncritical endorsement of traditional marriage.

Directed against the legal right to same-sex marriage, *no matter how defended*, these fears are, I think, misplaced. To claim that same-sex marriage would necessarily assimilate gays and lesbians to mainstream culture ignores the fact that many heterosexuals (who, of course, do have the right to marry) have been anything but assimilationists. Evolution in both marriage law and marital and parenting practices has been a result of heterosexuals' *resistance* to the legal and social conception of traditional marriage. And it is precisely heterosexual noncompliance that gives force to Representative Barr's remark during the DOMA debates that '[t]he flames of hedonism, the flames of narcissism, the flames of self-centered morality are licking at the very founda-tions of our society: the family unit'.[13] If having the right to marry has not prevented heterosexuals from challenging legal and social conceptions of marriage, there is no reason to suppose that gays and lesbians will cease think-ing critically about marital norms once granted a right to marry.

However, when extending marriage rights gets tied to the public policy goal

---

[12] Struening, 'Feminist Challenges to the New Familialism'.

[13] *Congressional Record*, 104th Cong., 2nd sess., 1996, 142, pt H7482.

of promoting one normative ideal for intimacy, queer theorists' objection is well placed. Marriage rights, so construed, ought not to have priority in a gay and lesbian political agenda. To endorse the goal of promoting one moral conception of marriage would, one might think, amount to deprioritizing securing legal rights—for example, the right to give proxy consent or the right to immigration preference—to those who are functioning as family members even if their families diverge from a conventional picture of family. But it is precisely legal rights for unconventional family arrangements that gays and lesbians may need most. Freed from conventional assumptions about what families and intimate relationships should look like, gays and lesbians have pursued alternative constructions of family involving extended networks of friends rather than biological kin. They have also pursued multiple parenting arrangements that sometimes involve more than the allotted two parents, because lesbian couples and gay couples may set up parenting arrangements with each other or with former spouses.[14] In short, to tie same-sex marriage rights to state promotion of one normative conception of marriage and family is to abandon the goal of critically rethinking which rights and benefits should be distributed to whom given a plurality of intimate and familial forms.

Similarly, the lesbian feminist argument that to pursue same-sex marriage is to endorse patriarchal gender-structured marriage is a bad argument when targeted at any possible defense of same-sex marriage. It ignores the fact that heterosexuals have resisted the gender-structuring of marriage, producing substantial changes in marital law that have included eliminating legal enforcement of separate husband–wife roles, fault-based divorce, long-term alimony, shared domicile requirements, and the like.[15] It also, oddly, ignores the fact that same-sex couples cannot replicate male–female power relations within marriage; and even if they do replicate gender structured marriage, it will be a gender structure decoupled from sexual difference. So it is hard to see how same-sex marriages could reinforce patriarchal marriage.

However, when extending marriage rights gets tied to the public policy goal of promoting one normative ideal for intimacy, the objection has some merit. What gets put into cultural circulation is a particular style of thinking about marriage. It is a style that resists any thoroughgoing departure from the most traditional normative ideal of marriage and family. It is a style that links marital-familial arrangements so tightly to the public good that state neutrality with respect to conceptions of the intimate good cannot go all the way down. And it is a style whose terms—procommitment, profamily, anti-promiscuity—are easily invoked to support moral norms and social policies that constrain women's reproductive, sexual, and relational liberty.

[14] See Nancy D. Polikoff, 'This Child Does Have Two Mothers', *Georgetown Law Journal* 78 (1990): 459–575.

[15] Of course, not all of these changes have been salutary for women, since the beneficial consequences of eliminating the formal gender structure of marriage depends in large part on the *actual* de-gendering of marital practices as well as gender equity in the paid workforce.

One last objection. To my mind, the greatest defect in arguments that defend same-sex marriage by appealing to a moral conception of marriage is that they ignore the connection between marriage bars and the system of heterosexual domination. On this view, a marriage bar simply denies gays and lesbians incentives to form and remain in long-term, monogamous, sexually faithful partnerships. Placing marriage rights on a gay and lesbian political agenda, however, requires a different sort of argument. In particular, we need a reason for supposing that denying same-sex marriage rights is integral to sustaining heterosexual domination. Arguments showing the connection between the denial of marriage rights and gender discrimination claim to do just that.

## II. Gender-based Arguments

A substantial body of largely legal literature is devoted to the claim that the marriage bar originates from a system of male dominance. Thus eliminating the bar challenges that system.[16] Arguments that connect same-sex marriage bars to male dominance are what I will call 'gender-based' arguments. According to gender-based arguments for same-sex marriage, cultural hostility to same-sex marriage derives from the fact that same-sex marriages are gender-free. A marriage between two women or two men cannot easily be organized around husband and wife roles. Blumstein and Schwartz's frequently cited study of American couples showed that gay and lesbian relationships do indeed tend to be more egalitarian than heterosexual ones.[17] This deviance from conventional marital gender norms by women, who happen to be lesbian, and men, who happen to be gay, presumably signifies the potential for similar gender deviance by all women and men, including those who happen to be heterosexual. This, it is claimed, explains the cultural hostility to same-sex marriage. To legalize same-sex marriage would be tantamount to declaring that gendered husband and wife roles are inessential to marriage—not only for lesbians and gays, but for heterosexuals as well. To sanction same-sex marriage legally would be to invite heterosexuals to model their own marriages on the already more egalitarian models adopted by lesbians and gay men.

Thus, as Cass Sunstein puts it, same-sex marriage bars are, like antimiscegenation laws, rooted in the assumption that there are 'only two kinds'.[18] Just

---

[16] See Sylvia Law, 'Homosexuality and the Social Meaning of Gender', *Wisconsin Law Review* 1988 (1988): 187–235; Cass R. Sunstein, 'Homosexuality and the Constitution', In *Sex, Preference, and Family*, 208–26; Andrew Koppelman, 'The Miscegenation Analogy: Sodomy Law as Sex Discrimination', *Yale Law Journal* 98 (1988): 145–64; 'Why Discrimination Against Lesbians and Gay Men is Sex Discrimination', *NYU Law Review* 69 (1994): 197–287; Nan D. Hunter, 'Marriage, Law, and Gender: A Feminist Inquiry', in *Sex Wars: Sexual Dissent and Political Culture*, Lisa Duggan and Nan D. Hunter (New York: Routledge, 1995), 107–22.

[17] Philip Blumstein and Pepper Schwartz, *American Couples: Money, Work, Sex* (New York: Morrow, 1983).

[18] Sunstein, 'Homosexuality and the Constitution', in *Sex, Preference, and Family*, 208–26.

as bars to interracial marriage were rooted in the idea that there are two distinct races whose differences must be preserved, so same-sex marriage bars are rooted in the idea that there are two distinct genders whose differences must be preserved. Just as the ideology of racial difference is the linchpin of white supremacy, so the ideology of gender difference is the linchpin of male supremacy. Thus, prohibiting same-sex marriage is a form of sex discrimination. That prohibition is simply a specific expression of a general intolerance to the blurring of gender difference anywhere, by anyone, including by heterosexuals in heterosexual marriages. The positive moral argument for same-sex marriage, then, is that same-sex marriage would make gender difference irrelevant within *all* marriages. It would thus contribute to the larger goal of producing a gender-just society.

Forging a link between same-sex marriage bars and sex discrimination was central to *Baehr v. Lewin*. Given that many states have laws prohibiting sex discrimination, but not sexual orientation discrimination, this particular argument for same-sex marriage rights seems most promising from a purely pragmatic point of view.

One particular advantage of arguing for same-sex marriage by showing that such rights would promote gender equality is that one need not make any substantive normative assumptions about the value of traditional marriage over other intimate relationships. Nor need one assume that the rights and benefits now distributed to married couples should not be distributed to others as well. Nor need one assume that the definition of marriage (e.g. as necessarily monogamous) and aims of marriage law (e.g. to coerce couples to stay together) are fixed and incontestable. This is an important point. Too often it is assumed that demanding the right to marry is equivalent to endorsing the traditional moral conception of marriage that was central to the first argument for marriage rights that we considered. Too often it is also assumed that any one demanding the right to marry must also support the present system of marital rights and benefits. This is not true. A person can want, for example, a right to equal opportunity within the present labor structure and still be highly critical of the labor system for being undemocratic and organized around categories of gender, race, and intellectual versus manual labor. Similarly, a person can want the right to marry and still be highly critical of, say, the lack of freedom of choice of marriage contract and the lack of state neutrality with respect to competing conceptions of the intimate and familial good. Only arguments for marriage rights that are based on the idea that the state should promote one form of intimacy equate the quest for marriage rights with endorsing one, typically traditional, moral conception of marriage.

However, the gender-based argument for same-sex marriage is not without its own defects. First, it provides a better reason for *heterosexuals* to make same-sex marriage a political priority than it does for gays and lesbians to do so. After all, the primary beneficiaries, on this view, would be heterosexual couples, particularly heterosexual women. Lesbians and gay men, it is assumed, are *already* not complying with gender norms and have *already* reconstructed their partnerships around more egalitarian ideals. It is heterosexuals who persist in imagining that gendered husband and wife roles are essential to marriage and who are deprived of a legally legitimated alternative model—to be provided by married lesbians and gays—for restructuring their own marriages.[19]

More importantly, the thesis that the principal aim of barring same-sex marriage is to enforce separate gender roles is simply not adequately supported by the full range of evidence. Typically, arguments for this thesis begin by observing that social animus is visited upon lesbians and gays because of their gender deviance.[20] Gay men are culturally stereotyped as having excessively feminine personalities, vocations, avocational interests, dress, and demeanor. Gay men also violate sexual gender norms by being willing to occupy the passive, penetrated role in sex. In adopting inferior female positions, particularly in sex, gay men debase themselves and fail to do their bit in sustaining male dominance. Similarly, lesbians are culturally stereotyped as having excessively masculine personalities, vocations, avocational interests, dress, and demeanor. They also violate sexual gender norms by refusing to occupy the passive, penetrated sexual role in relation to men. In making themselves sexually unavailable to men, lesbians insubordinately repudiate male right of sexual access to women. In short, by not complying with their assigned gender roles, gays and lesbians threaten the system of male dominance. For this, both are subjected to penalties ranging from discriminatory employment policies, to physical violence, to same-sex marriage bars. The idea that cultural aversion to homosexuality and lesbianism is connected to sexist conceptions of proper male and female behavior is supported by studies showing that people who have the most conservative gender role attitudes are also most homophobic.[21]

This evidence does indeed suggest that the point of same-sex marriage bars is to compel men to behave as men and women to behave as women. The problem is that arguments attributing same-sex marriage bars exclusively to sexism omit two important pieces of evidence. The omitted evidence suggests that sexism is not the primary, let alone sole, factor motivating same-sex marriage bars. Consider first the fact that lesbians and gays are not the only gender deviants. Heterosexual men and heterosexual women may also fail to conform to traditional gender roles. Heterosexual women, in particular, have

---

[19] Susan Moller Okin uses this role model argument in 'Sexual Orientation and Gender: Dichotomizing Differences', in *Sex, Preference and Family*, 44–59.

[20] For classic statements of this argument, see Andrew Koppelman, 'Why Discrimination Against Lesbians and Gay Men is Sex Discrimination', and Sylvia A. Law, 'Homosexuality and the Social Meaning of Gender'.

[21] Koppelman cites a variety of studies supporting this claim in 'Why Discrimination Against Lesbians and Gay Men is Sex Discrimination'.

had good reason to rebel against both feminine gender norms and the gender structure of traditional marriage. Were compelling men to behave as men and women to behave as women the primary rationale behind same-sex marriage bars, one would expect to see this same rationale at work in the legal regulation of heterosexual marriage. But this simply is not the case. Heterosexual marriages have largely been *de*-gendered under the law. All of the nineteenth- and early twentieth-century laws have been eliminated that made married women legally dead on the assumption that man and wife are one and that that one is the husband. The law no longer compels married women to adopt their husband's name, to share his domicile wherever he chooses it to be, to provide domestic services, and to submit to marital rape. The elimination of long-term alimony and the introduction of alimony for needy ex-husbands both resulted from abandoning the assumption that only husbands are economic providers within marriage. Repeated court refusal to employ sex-based classifications in family law has meant that all that is left of gender in marriage law are the constructs 'husband' and 'wife', evacuated of substantive content.[22] In addition, anti-discrimination laws which forbid formal and informal enforcement of gender differences in the workplace, education, access to housing, loans, and the like contribute to de-gendering the public sphere. In short, the law has taken a largely permissive attitude toward *heterosexual* gender deviance by refusing to enforce gender roles inside and outside of marriage. Thus, the claim that the law aims to enforce gender conformity by barring same-sex marriage is, at the very least, an overstatement. Whether the law takes a permissive or coercive approach to gender deviant intimate relationships appears to be a function of *whose* intimate relationships are at issue. Only specifically lesbian and gay intimate relations are subjected to legal control. This fact needs to be explained. Arguments that attribute same-sex marriage bars entirely to sexism fail to do this.

Second, those who argue that the principal aim of barring same-sex marriage is to enforce separate gender roles ignore evidence that in fact same-sex relations are not culturally interpreted as posing either a general threat to maintaining distinct gender roles for heterosexual men and women or a specific threat to preserving gender-structured heterosexual marriages. The only way that lesbian and gay behavior could threaten a system of gender roles and gender-structured marriage would be if their sexual orientation were irrelevant to their sex-gender categorization. That is, in order to imagine that lesbian gender insubordination represents a potential in *all* women, one would have to assume that there is no essential difference between lesbians and heterosexual women. Both are equally women. As a result, what some women (who just happen to prefer sex with women) do might readily be adopted by other women (who just happen to prefer sex with men). But this picture misrepresents how our culture thinks about sexual orientation. From

---

[22] Koppelman.

the early twentieth century to the present day, sexual orientation has been culturally interpreted as marking an *essential* difference between heterosexual women and lesbians and between heterosexual men and gays. Recall that at the turn of the century, sexologists accommodated the existence of lesbians and gay men by pluralizing sex-gender categories beyond the original two. Both gay men and lesbians were described as a third sex. Moreover, lesbian and gay difference from heterosexual men and women has persistently been interpreted as an immutable difference. Early sexologists claimed that true inversion was a congenital condition; Freudians traced homosexuality and lesbianism to early childhood experiences that made conversion to heterosexuality extremely difficult if not impossible; and contemporary scientific theories have attempted to locate a genetic origin for homosexuality and lesbianism. That is, lesbians and gay men have, for the past hundred years, been constructed as a kind of naturally fixed third sex for whom gender deviance is a uniquely constitutive and unavoidable part of their nature.

Because sexual orientation marks an essential difference between real men and women—who are also heterosexual—and those who by nature or early psychological development are not really men and women, lesbian and gay behavior does not signal a potential in heterosexual women and men. Quite the contrary, because lesbians and gays are members of a supposedly naturally gender-deviant third sex, their behavior will of course differ from real (heterosexual) women's and men's behavior. Lesbians' and gays' essential difference makes them incapable of significantly threatening either heterosexual gender roles or the gender structure of heterosexual marriage. Of course, since the end of the nineteenth century, it has been part of our cultural view that lesbians and gays might seduce and convert those who are not 'really' gay or lesbian.[23] However, such worries leave in place a basic assumption that heterosexuals can generally be relied on to conform to gender norms. That includes conformity to gender-structured heterosexual marriage.

In sum, looking at both the differential treatment of heterosexuals versus lesbians and gays within marriage law and the social construction of lesbians and gays as an essentially different type of person who is neither man nor woman suggests that same-sex marriage bars are not simply an expression of legal sexism. It also suggests that there is insufficient reason to suppose that removing same-sex marriage bars will have much of any impact on our gender expectations for heterosexual behavior inside and outside of marriage. It is possible, however, to construct a second gender-based argument that preserves the connection between same-sex marriage bars and sex discrimination, while

---

[23] Nineteenth-century sexologists distinguished between congenital and situational inverts. Judge Richard A. Posner has recently recast this distinction as one between preference homosexuals and opportunistic homosexuals ('The Economic Approach to Homosexuality', in *Sex, Preference, and Family*, 173–91). The concern about conversion has motivated, in the last decade, a series of what Nan Hunter aptly labels 'no promo homo' legislative initiatives. See 'Identity, Speech, and Equality', *Virginia Law Review* 79 (1993): 1695–719.

at the same time avoiding the problematic assumption that lesbian and gay gender deviance signals a potential in all men and all women. I turn now to this second possibility.

This argument might begin by recognizing that gays and lesbians are culturally constructed as beings for whom gender nonconformity is endemic. Hostility to this third sex derives from the view that the only normal, natural, healthy kinds of people are real women, who at least by nature have the capacity to conform to gender norms, and real men, who at least by nature have the capacity to conform to gender norms. Heterosexuals may not comply with gender norms, and that is a bad thing. But it is far worse to have on the social scene a whole category of persons who are not even naturally fit for gender norms.

Obviously, it is the gender ideology attached to our system of male dominance that makes being lesbian or gay so stigmatizing. Thus, even if lesbians and gays, as members of a third sex, are singled out for special mistreatment and legal regulation not visited upon gender-deviant heterosexuals, and thus even if we can meaningfully talk about the distinctive political relations between heterosexuals and nonheterosexuals (not just the political relations between men and women), it remains true that the special opprobrium felt toward lesbianism and homosexuality is ultimately rooted in gender ideology. Same-sex marriage bars may not be, precisely, sex discrimination, since they are not aimed at controlling all women. They are, nevertheless, of a piece with policies that discriminate on the basis of sex.

There is a good deal to be said for this second argument. It accounts for the special animus motivating mistreatment of gays and lesbians. Members of a third sex are not simply *noncompliant* with gender norms. They are distinctively *unfit* for incorporation in a society governed by gender norms. As a result, this argument explains why gays and lesbians would have a special political interest in challenging legal regulations that target them. In addition, this argument also accounts for the intimate connection between gay and lesbian subordination and male dominance.

Even so, I think this is the wrong argument for same-sex marriage rights— or at least it is seriously incomplete. All gender-based arguments start from an assumption that merits questioning. They assume that the fundamental inequality at stake in all gay rights issues is the inequality between men and women. On these arguments, male dominance alone accounts for both the oppression of women and the oppression of gays and lesbians. As a result, the possibility is never entertained that heterosexual domination might be a separate axis of oppression; nor is the possibility entertained that in maintaining same-sex marriage bars, in maintaining the liberty to discriminate against lesbians and gays in housing and employment, in controlling the normative content of school curricula and publicly funded artistic and scholarly endeavors, and in limiting gay and lesbian access to children, what is at stake is preserving heterosexuals' privileged socio-political status. That gender ideology factors into gay and lesbian oppression does not entail that it is the only factor. Gender ideology, as Andrew Koppelman has recently argued, also factored into anti-miscegenation laws that were aimed particularly at protecting white women from black male sexuality.[24] But the primary factor remained the system of white supremacy. If we are going to construct a positive moral argument for same-sex marriage rights, caution needs to be taken not to overlook systems of inequality that may play a more constitutive role in gay and lesbian oppression than male dominance does.

A central problem with gender-based arguments is that they under-describe the ideological construction of 'gay' and 'lesbian' as stigmatized social identities. Recall that both gender-based accounts assume that gay and lesbian gender deviance fully explains the stigmatizing of these identities. Now, it is true that cross-genderization was the defining feature of the third sex at the beginning of the twentieth century. It is also true that hostility to gender blurring continues to sustain part of the stigma attached to being gay or lesbian. This is manifested in, for example, fear that heterosexual soldiers will be subject to feminizing sexual advances from gay soldiers as well as fear that gay or lesbian parents will raise children who are themselves defectively gendered. However, gender deviance does not fully exhaust the content of what it culturally means to be gay or lesbian. Equally important in the cultural construction of gay and lesbian identities is the idea that gay and lesbian sexuality is dangerously uncontrolled, predatory, insatiable, narcissistic, and self-indulgent. As I will discuss at greater length in the next chapter, this aspect of gay and lesbian identity came to particular cultural prominence during the 1930s through 1960s—the era of both the sex crime panics and the formal exclusion of 'sex perverts' from all governmental service. Imagined to possess an excessive and unregulated sexuality, both gays and lesbians were claimed to pose a threat to heterosexual adults and to children, who might be either molested or seduced. This stigmatizing conception motivates policies barring gays and lesbians from adoption, foster parenting, employment as teachers, day care workers, and scout leaders, and also motivates some custody denials. In addition, because of their sexual insatiability, gays and lesbians were viewed as psychologically unable to maintain stable relationships. The idea that homosexuality is connected to undisciplined, self-indulgent sexual desire has recently been re-emphasized by natural law legal theorists who suggest that homosexual sex resembles solitary masturbation.[25] One natural law theorist argues that homosexuality should not be promoted in the public realm because the public realm is 'the milieu in which and by which all citizens are encouraged and helped, or discouraged and undermined, in their own resistance to being

---

[24] Koppelman, 'Why Discrimination Against Lesbians and Gay Men is Sex Discrimination', 224–34.

[25] John Finnis, 'Law, Morality, and "Sexual Orientation" ', *Notre Dame Journal of Law, Ethics and Public Policy* 9 (1995): 11–39, 25. See also Patrick Lee and Robert George, 'What Sex Can Be: Self-Alienation, Illusion, or One-Flesh Union', *The American Journal of Jurisprudence*, 42 (1997): 135–57, 138.

lured by temptation into falling away from their own aspirations to be people of integrated good character, and to be autonomous, self-controlled persons rather than slaves to impulse and sensual gratification'.[26]

Linking both the images of the gender deviant and the sex pervert is the culturally elaborated view that gays and lesbians are multiply unfit for marriage and family. Not only are they unfit for assuming gendered familial roles and producing properly gendered children, they are incapable of sustaining long-term stable relationships, pose a sexual threat to their own and others' children, and risk reproducing their own defects in a second generation.

As we will see in the next chapter, beginning in the 1980s, the stigmatizing conception of gays and lesbians as unfit for family life and as anti-family has begun to take on a life of its own, partially detached from its original roots in fears of gender deviance and sexual perversion. The increasing visibility of successful gay and lesbian families as well as the publicizing of empirical studies challenging, for example, the ideas that gays and lesbians constitute the majority of child molesters and that they are more likely to produce gay and lesbian children, have made it increasingly difficult to sustain the claim that gays and lesbians are unfit for family life. What remains an open possibility is to characterize gay and lesbians families as 'pretended family relationships'. That is, what remains an open possibility is the bald assertion that heterosexuality itself is the sole distinguishing feature of real versus pretended families.[27]

In sum, gender-based accounts of hostility to homosexuality and lesbianism take up only one theme in an historically complex construction of lesbian and gay identity. As a result, such accounts lack sufficient explanatory scope. They fail, for example, to explain why hostility to homosexuality and lesbianism crystallizes around marital and familial issues in the way that it does. Moreover, they fail to explain adequately the content of contemporary anti-gay discourse. If the gender-based account were correct, the House and Senate debates surrounding the Defense of Marriage Act should have focused on gays' and lesbians' unsuitability for fulfilling husband and wife roles, the possibility of producing gender- or sex-deviant children, the unnaturalness of men marrying men or women marrying women, and the importance of traditional gender-structured marriage. The DOMA debates, however, are strikingly *devoid* of any gender content. Instead, proponents of DOMA studiously—one might say deafly—refused to answer charges that heterosexuals were themselves posing the biggest threat to marriage through divorce, abandonment, spouse abuse, promiscuity, alcohol abuse, lack of marital

---

[26] John Finnis, 15.

[27] In 'Law, Morality, and "Sexual Orientation" ', John Finnis comes very close to this view, since the only reason why same-sex couples lack access to 'the marital good' and why their sex is no better than masturbation is that same-sex sex fails to unite biologically the reproductive organs of the couple in acts of a reproductive kind.

commitment, watching Sunday football, and having children out of wedlock. Rather than contrasting the *behavior* of heterosexuals to homosexuals, DOMA proponents insisted on a single definitional point: Real marriage requires one man and one woman.

I turn now to the Defence of Marriage Act debates and what I think the positive moral argument for same-sex marriage should be.

## III. DOMA's Defense of Heterosexual Status

Same-sex marriage bars are indeed predicated on the assumption that there are just 'two kinds'. But the relevant two kinds are not men and women. They are heterosexuals and nonheterosexuals. Same-sex marriage bars, sodomy laws, bars to adoption or foster parenting, and court denial of child custody are all predicated on stereotypes of nonheterosexuals' different relation to gender, sexual self-control, and the family. Specifically, they presuppose views about gays' and lesbians' gender deviance, lack of sexual self-control, and unfitness for family life. They thus assume that heterosexuals and nonheterosexuals are different kinds of people who should therefore be treated differently under the law. Anti-gay policies, however, differ in kind from racist or sexist policies. As we saw in the previous chapter, the aim of racist and sexist policies is to keep racial minorities and women *in their place*. Anti-gay policies, by contrast, aim to *displace* gays and lesbians from civil society by refusing to recognize that lesbians and gay men belong in either the public or the private sphere.

The same-sex marriage bar works in a particularly powerful way to displace gays and lesbians because we, as a culture, assume that married couples play a unique role in sustaining civil society. Within both specifically legal reasoning and broader cultural discourse, marriage and the family are typically construed as the bedrock on which social and political life is built. As Senator Faircloth put it during the DOMA debates: 'Marriage forms families, and families form societies. Strong families form strong societies. Fractured families form fractured societies. So all of us have an interest in seeing that strong families are formed in the first place'.[28] Proponents of DOMA repeatedly emphasized the foundational status of marriage in civil society: 'Marriage is the foundation of our society; families are built on it and values are passed through it'.[29] Marriage is 'the keystone in the arch of civilization'.[30] 'The time-honored and unique institution of marriage between one man and one woman is a fundamental pillar of our society and its values'.[31] '[T]hroughout

---

[28] *Congressional Record*, 104th Cong., 2nd sess., 1996, 142, pt S10117.

[29] Representative Lipinski of Illinois speaking for the Defense of Marriage Act (DOMA) to the House floor, H.R. 3396, 104th Cong., 2nd sess., *Congressional Record* (12 July 1996), 142, pt H7495.

[30] William J. Bennett, 'Not a Very Good Idea', qtd. in *Washington Post*, 21 May 1996, in the *Congressional Record*, 104th Cong., 2nd sess., 1996, 142, pt H7495.

[31] Representative Ensign of Nevada speaking for DOMA to the House floor, Ibid. pt H7493.

the annals of human experience, in dozens of civilizations and cultures of varying value systems, humanity has discovered that the permanent relationship between man and woman is a keystone to the stability, strength, and health of human society—a relationship worthy of legal recognition and judicial protection'.[32] And '. . . governments have recognized the traditional family as the foundation of prosperity and happiness, and in democratic societies, as the foundation of freedom'.[33]

The central concept of marriage being forwarded here is as a prepolitical institution. Although states may create the legal package of rights and benefits that attach to marriage and may set age, sex, biological relationship and other restrictions on who may marry, the state does not create the institution of marriage itself. 'There is no moment in recorded history when the traditional family was not recognized and sanctioned by a civilized society—it is the oldest institution that exists'.[34] In addition, while the state may choose to recognize and provide legal protections for a variety of voluntary relationships (e.g. domestic partnerships or labor unions), the state does not *choose* to recognize marriages. Since the very possibility of civil society depends on people entering marriages and forming families, the state *must* recognize marriages.

This conception of marriage as the prepolitical foundation of society has an important implication. It means that if a social group can lay claim to being inherently qualified or fit to enter into marriage and found a family, it can also claim a distinctive political status. To be inherently qualified for entering marriage is not like being inherently qualified for this or that cooperative endeavor that societies may or may not set up (as men, for example, have in the past claimed to be inherently qualified for being doctors, miners, and preachers). It is instead to be qualified for sustaining the foundation of civil society itself. Conversely, if a particular social group is deemed *un*fit to enter marriage and found a family, that group can then be denied this distinctive political status. Because they are incapable, as a group, of providing the necessary foundation for civil society, they are, ultimately, inessential citizens. At best, they are dependent citizens. Whatever social contribution they might make to civil society depends on the antecedent marital and familial labor of others.

For proponents of DOMA, the central debate was about *who* could lay claim to the political status that derives from being deemed qualified for marriage and the family.[35] The aim of proponents was to reaffirm, by

[32] Senator Byrd of West Virginia speaking for DOMA to the Senate floor, H.R. 3396, *Congressional Record*, 104th Cong., 2nd sess., 1996, 142, pt S10109.

[33] Senator Gramm of Texas speaking for DOMA to the Senate floor, Ibid., pt S10106.

[34] Senator Gramm, Ibid., pt S10105.

[35] Opponents clearly took the debate to be about something else, namely, about why, in practice, real families are not flourishing. Completely bypassing proponents' point, opponents instead focused on the misbehavior of heterosexual family members as well as inadequate health, education and day care, unemployment, the absence of a livable minimum wage, inability to afford single family homes, and loss of pensions, and insufficient Medicare payments.

constructing a federal definition of marriage, that only heterosexuals have this status.

Anxiety about what would happen to their own status if same-sex marriages were legally recognized ran very close to the surface. Many comments echoed Attorney General Bowers' assertion in his brief for *Bowers v. Hardwick* that '[h]omosexual sodomy is anathema of the basic units of our society—marriage and the family. To decriminalize or artificially withdraw the public's expression of its disdain for this conduct does not uplift sodomy, but rather demotes these sacred institutions to merely alternative lifestyles'.[36] Representative Smith, for example, asserted that '[s]ame-sex "marriages" demean the fundamental institution of marriage. They legitimize unnatural and immoral behavior. And they trivialize marriage as a mere "lifestyle choice". The institution of marriage sets a necessary and high standard. Anything that lowers this standard, as same-sex "marriages" do, inevitably belittles marriage'.[37] Others echoed this sentiment. '[I]t is vital that we protect marriage against attempts to redefine it in a way that causes the family to lose its special meaning'.[38] 'Should the law express its neutrality between homosexual and heterosexual relationships? Should the law elevate homosexual unions to the same status as the heterosexual relationships on which the traditional family is based, a status which has been reserved from time immemorial for the union between a man and a woman?'[39] 'Allowing for gay marriages would be the final straw, it would devalue the love between a man and a woman and weaken us as a Nation'.[40]

But exactly why would same-sex marriages devalue heterosexual love, belittle marriage, and render it a mere lifestyle choice? The obvious answer is that homosexuality is immoral. To recognize same-sex marriages legally would place the sacred institution of marriage in the disreputable company of immoral, unnatural unions, thus cheapening its status. This was surely part of the thinking. But it is not the whole story. For if concern about giving the same state seal of approval to immoral same-sex unions as to honorable heterosexual marriages were the primary concern, then one would expect proponents of DOMA to also be adamantly opposed to any legal protection of same sex unions. Yet Representative Lipinski, who thought that allowing gay marriages would be the final straw devaluing love between man and woman also observed that 'gays can legally achieve the same ends as marriage through draft wills, medical powers of attorney, and contractual agreements in the event that the relationship should end'.[41] Other proponents affirmed

---

[36] Qtd in Sylvia Law, 'Homosexuality and the Social Meaning of Gender', 219.

[37] *Congressional Record*, 104th Cong., 2nd sess., 1996, 142, pt H7494.

[38] Representative Weldon of Florida speaking for DOMA to the House floor, H.R. 3396, Ibid. H7493

[39] Representative Canady of Florida speaking for DOMA to the House floor, Ibid. H7491.

[40] Representative Lipinski, Ibid. H7495.     [41] Ibid. H7495.

the importance of guaranteeing the right to privacy[42] and pointed out that the law protects a variety of unions outside of marriage law (presumably potentially including same-sex ones).[43] These types of remarks suggest that the immorality of homosexuality was not the only issue.

The central concern instead seemed to be that recognizing same-sex unions as marriages would demote marriage from a naturally defined prepolitical institution to a state-defined contract. Senators Gramm and Byrd clearly express this concern. According to Gramm, '[h]uman beings have always given traditional marriage a special sanction. Not that there cannot be contracts among individuals, but there is something unique about the traditional family in terms of what it does for our society and the foundation it provides. . .'.[44] Byrd articulated a similar distinction:

Obviously, human beings enter into a variety of relationships. Business partnerships, friendships, alliances for mutual benefits, and team memberships all depend upon emotional unions of one degree or another. For that reason, a number of these relationships have found standing under the laws of innumerable nations.

However, in no case, has anyone suggested that these relationships deserve the special recognition or the designation commonly understood as 'marriage'.[45]

Reading between the lines, the underlying view seems to be this: Free, self-defining, sociable citizens may choose to enter a variety of voluntary relationships with each other. In deciding what legal protections might be in order for these relationships, a liberal political society that values freedom of association and the right to the pursuit of happiness must adopt a position of neutrality. Rather than giving priority to some of these relationships on moral grounds, the state instead assumes that citizens may reasonably choose any of these relationships on the basis of their own conception of the good. Thus, such voluntary associations might reasonably be dubbed 'lifestyle choices'. To call them 'lifestyle choices' is not to say that they are in fact morally equivalent. One might think that sodomy is immoral or that same-sex unions are immoral, but nevertheless think the state should adopt a neutral position, refraining from criminalizing sodomy and offering legal protection for same-sex unions under domestic partnership laws. To say that a particular form of relationship is a 'lifestyle choice', then, is simply to say that it falls within the category of relationships with respect to which state neutrality is appropriate.

What proponents of DOMA took pains to emphasize was that marriage falls in a different category. Marriage is not one among many voluntary associations that citizens might choose to enter. Nor is it one among many relationships whose nature free, self-defining persons might determine for themselves. Marriage constitutes the prepolitical foundation of society. To say

---

[42] Senator Burns of Montana speaking for DOMA to the House floor, H.R. 3396, 104th Cong., 2nd sess., *Congressional Record* (10 Sept. 1996), 142, pt S10117.

[43] Senator Byrd, Ibid. pt S10109.　　　　　　　　　[44] Senator Gramm, Ibid. pt S10106.

[45] Senator Byrd, Ibid. pt S10109.

that marriage is prepolitical is to say both that societies depend for their functioning on marriages and that the essential nature of marriage is fixed independently of liberal society—by God, or by human nature, or by the prerequisites for civilization. Consequently, state neutrality with respect to the definition of marriage involves a category mistake. State neutrality would involve treating a prepolitical institution as though it were a political institution, that is, as though it were an institution that must be compatible with multiple conceptions of the good. Since, on this view, it is not in fact a political institution, the appropriate legal treatment of marriage is instead to *insulate* marriage against revision according to liberal political principles. This is what DOMA does. Representative Seastrand summarized the point in her remark that '[a]s special interest pressure increasingly demands a tolerant and fluid definition of marriage, we progressively attempt to redefine marriage to fit social trends. . . . This bill will fortify marriage against the storm of revisionism'.[46]

In my view, then, what makes same-sex marriage rights so important is that marriage bars do not represent merely one among many ways that the state may discriminate against gays and lesbians by enacting laws based on stereotypes of lesbians' and gay men's gender deviance, undisciplined sexual desire, and unfitness for family life. They do, of course, rest on an underlying ideological construction of lesbians and gay men as unfit for stable relationships and child rearing. But marriage bars attach something else to that unfitness. That something else is political status—both the individual's political status as a citizen and the political status of particular kinds of relationships. Specifically, marriage bars enact the view that heterosexual love, marriage, and family have a uniquely prepolitical, foundational status in civil society. As a result, heterosexuals can claim for their own relationships not just moral superiority, but a uniquely privileged status beyond the reach of liberal political values. Marriage bars also enact the view that because only heterosexuals are fit to participate in this foundational marital institution, only heterosexuals are entitled to lay claim to a unique citizenship status. Heterosexuals are not *just* free, rational, self-defining persons. They are also naturally fit to participate in the one institution that all societies, liberal or otherwise, must presuppose. Thus they may lay claim to a citizenship status that *exceeds* what individuals are entitled to on the basis of being free, rational, self-defining persons. In addition to the rights of free association, including intimate association, to which all citizens are entitled, the special rights and privileges attached to marriage are set aside for heterosexuals only. And not only this.

Heterosexuals may also claim for themselves special entitlement to control future generations' ongoing commitment to heterosexuality and heterosexual marriage. Although children were infrequently mentioned in the DOMA

---

[46] Representative Seastrand of California speaking for DOMA to the House floor, H.R. 3396, 104th Cong., 2nd sess., *Congressional Record* (12 July 1996), 142, pt H7485.

debates, when they were, the primary concern was that the next generation might cease to think that heterosexual marriage and being heterosexual matters. Senator Coats, for example, proclaimed that '[t]he institution of marriage is our most valuable cultural inheritance. It is our duty—perhaps our first duty—to pass it intact to the future'.[47] Others insisted that '[w]e should not be forced to send a message to our children that undermines the definition of marriage as the union of one man and one woman'.[48]

Should Congress tell the children of America that it is a matter of indifference whether they establish families with a partner of the opposite sex or cohabit with someone of the same sex? Should this Congress tell the children of America that we as a society believe there is no moral difference between homosexual relationships and heterosexual relationships? Should this Congress tell the children of America that in the eyes of the law the parties to a homosexual union are entitled to all the rights and privileges that have always been reserved for a man and a woman united in marriage?[49]

Here are large political prizes. They explain both why it is reasonable to consider lesbian and gay subordination an axis of subordination separate from gender oppression and why same-sex marriage rights belong high up on a gay and lesbian political agenda. One of the major stumbling blocks to constructing a positive moral argument for same-sex marriage rights on the grounds that marriage bars are motivated by a desire to maintain a *sexual orientation* caste system analogous to racial and gender caste systems has been that it is not immediately obvious what heterosexuals might stand to gain from such a caste system. By contrast, it is far more obvious what men (and indeed some women) stand to gain from a gender caste system and what whites stand to gain from a racial caste system. What I have tried to argue here is that the gain takes the form of a unique citizenship status that grounds heterosexuals' claims to special state solitude for their private lives, a partial insulation of their legal privileges from liberal principles, and special entitlement to influence the evaluative commitments of future generations.

## Conclusion

The political significance of having a right to marry is, I have argued, a function of the fact that marriage itself is culturally taken to be a prepolitical institution. The bar to same-sex marriage thus plays such a central role in lesbian and gay subordination only because we, as a culture, assume that marriage is not like other voluntary associations that the state might choose to facilitate. We assume that marriages and families are essential to the functioning of any society in a way that other voluntary associations are not. Giving gays and

---

[47] *Congressional Record*, 104th Cong., 2nd sess., 1996, 142, pt S10114.

[48] Representative Delay of Texas speaking for DOMA to the House floor, H.R. 3396, 104th Cong., 2nd sess., *Congressional Record* (12 July 1996), 142, pt 7487.

[49] Representative Canady, Ibid. pt 7491.

lesbians the right to marry might, consequently, disrupt gay and lesbian oppression in one of two possible ways. On the one hand, we might continue to construe marriage as a prepolitical institution that plays a crucial role in society. Same-sex marriage rights would, in essence, affirm gays' and lesbians' fitness to participate in this foundational institution. On the other hand, we might reject the idea that marriage and family differ in any politically significant way from other voluntary associations. Same-sex marriage rights would, on this second view, disrupt gay and lesbian subordination not by incorporating them into a special, foundational institution, but by denying that marriage and family had any special political importance in the first place. Because marriage is similar to other voluntary associations, there is no good reason for the state to impose stricter regulations on marriage than on other voluntary associations. Thus there is no good reason to continue insisting that only a man and a woman may marry.

Both options are worth considering. If we take the first option, then we are agreeing, in part, with proponents of DOMA. Marriage, even if not heterosexual marriage, is unlike other possible voluntary intimate arrangements. That is, even if we have reason to think that marriages might take a wider array of forms than are presently recognized—for example, same-sex marriages, polygamous marriages, marriages where children have multiple mothers and fathers—we might still draw a distinction between associations called 'marriage' and other voluntary associations. And we might regard the arrangements labeled 'marriages' as prepolitical, foundational, and meriting special legal treatment. It is important to see here that it is possible to think that some forms of intimate and care-taking associations are critical to societies, in a way that other voluntary associations are not, and yet deny that traditional, heterosexual, two-parent families are the *only* intimate associations that fit this bill. However, any attempt to pick out which intimate associations are foundational would require that we endorse *some* (even if highly expanded) normative ideal for how persons should organize their intimate, affectional, personal economic, reproductive, sexual, and child rearing lives. The political task would be to determine which forms of (heterosexual, nonheterosexual, monogamous, polygamous, etc.) intimacy would be dignified with the label 'marriage' and the status of being regarded as foundational to civil society. In this case, the bid for same-sex marriage rights would amount to a demand to be deemed fit to participate in the foundational social institution and thus an essential citizen not dependent on the marital and familial work of others.

On the other hand, if we take the second option, we would reject the idea altogether that there are any prepolitical, foundational forms of intimacies. We might argue that civil societies depend only in the most general way on its citizens having the capacities for and interest in casting their personal lot with others and sharing, in voluntary private arrangements, sex, affection, reproduction, economic support, and care for the young, the infirm and the elderly.

But no one form or set of forms for doing so is foundational to civil society. Nor need all of these activities be consolidated within one relationship, as we standardly consolidate them within couples and couple-based families.[50] Parenting, the provision of emotional and economic support to an adult, and sex might take place in the context of different relationships rather than the same one. Nor need all of these activities be best undertaken through private arrangements, as we have up to this point typically thought to be true of the care of children and the provision of sex. Much more extensive public child support arrangements and the legal commercialization of sex might replace much of the traditional function of marriage and family. That is, we might envision a fully liberal society in which no private relationships are insulated from liberal principles. Whatever legal protection and support were provided for individuals' private intimate relations and the production of future generations would be predicated on the assumption that persons might choose a plurality of intimate arrangements in accord with their own conceptions of the good. In this case, the bid for same-sex marriage rights would amount to a demand to be deemed equal citizens within a fully liberal society that is simply committed to facilitating voluntary associations between people of whatever form people might choose. This would amount, in essence, to following a recommendation that Ruthann Robson has recently made that the legal categories of 'marriage' and 'family' be completely abolished. In that case, the state would interact with all citizens purely as individuals rather than as members (or nonmembers) of a particular intimate relationship.[51]

Which is the better option? To many, the obviously correct option is the second one. *Of course* the state should be neutral with respect to conceptions of the good. *Of course* it is always a bad thing for the state to promote any normative ideal of intimate relations. While I agree, I also find the choice of option two more difficult to make. Recall that at the beginning I said that I thought it was important *which* arguments get culturally circulated, not just *that* gays and lesbians get the right to marry. Liberal political reasoning that stresses state neutrality works best in societies that are *already* egalitarian, and where state neutrality serves to *maintain* equality. In inegalitarian societies, state neutrality often constrains interventions in the ideological status quo. For example, state neutrality on whether it would be a good or bad thing for adult men to have access to pornographic materials makes it more difficult to intervene in the sexual objectification of women. Defending same-sex marriage on grounds of state neutrality with respect to individuals' voluntary associations requires only that same-sex marriages be legally permitted *regardless* of how they are morally viewed. Genuine equality for gays and

[50] Will Kymlicka has argued for fully contractual intimate arrangements in 'Rethinking the Family', *Philosophy and Public Affairs* 20 (1991): 77–97.

[51] See both 'States of Marriage' and 'Resisting the Family: Repositioning Lesbians' in Ruthann Robson's *Sappho Goes to Law School* (NewYork: Routledge, 1998).

lesbians, however, requires more than merely coming to be tolerated. It requires that we, as a culture, give up the belief that gays and lesbians are unfit to participate in normatively ideal forms of marriage, parenting, and family. Only the first option permits us to put into cultural circulation legal arguments that directly challenge the ideology sustaining gays' and lesbians' social inequality.

I intend to leave open this question of whether we should continue treating marriage and the family as a prepolitical institution meriting special legal protections. As a matter of social fact, we do assign marriage and the family special social significance. What is most important to see is the effect that excluding gays and lesbians from marital and familial status has on maintaining a system of gay and lesbian subordination. In the next chapter, I will be arguing that portraying gays and lesbians as persons with traits that make them naturally unfit for family life has been central to the social construction of what it means to be lesbian and gay. Constructed as outlaws to the family, lesbians and gays have lacked the cultural authority that heterosexuals have to define and redefine what marriages and families are. I will be suggesting that *definitional authority* over what counts as a marriage or family is even more important than the right to same-sex marriage.

# 6

# Constructing Lesbians and Gay Men as Family's Outlaws

It remains to make good on two promissory notes from the previous chapter. As I mentioned at the outset of that chapter, lesbian feminists have constructed extensive and pointed arguments against lesbian marriage, motherhood, and family. Because those arguments are so compelling from a feminist perspective, they need to be addressed at length. Second, the previous chapter invoked, without defending, the thesis that being unfit for marriage and family has occupied a central position in the social construction of what it means to be gay or lesbian. Because putting the family at the center of lesbian and gay politics looks, on the surface, reactionary rather than revolutionary, some hefty evidence that the subordinating construction of gay and lesbian identity centers around their being family outlaws is in order.

In sections I and II, I summarize feminist and lesbian feminist critiques of family, marriage, and motherhood. In section III, I critique lesbian feminist reasons for eschewing a political agenda that endorses family, marriage, and mothering. There, I will pick up a theme central to Chapters 2 and 3. In lesbian feminist arguments against lesbian marriage, motherhood, and family, lesbians' *difference* from heterosexual women persistently drops from view because feminism has under-theorized lesbian and gay subordination as an axis distinct from gender oppression. In section IV, I trace the historical construction of lesbians and gays as outlaws to the family. There, I will suggest that heterosexuals' claim to be naturally fit for family life was purchased by promoting the view that gays and lesbians have in excess the very traits that threaten heterosexuals' abilities to maintain a family. Because the idea that lesbians and gay men are unfit for family is so central to the ideological construction of lesbian and gay identity, family issues belong at the very center of lesbian and gay politics. In the concluding section, I will argue that making family a political priority is not, as is sometimes argued, a conservative move. What is at stake is not the right to participate in a traditional form of family life but the right to *define* what counts as a family.

## I. Feminism and the Family

Feminist analyses of the family, marriage, and mothering have been driven by a deep awareness that the family has been a primary site of women's subordination to and dependence on men. Feminist analyses have also been driven by a deep awareness of the oppressive effects of gender ideology about women's natural place within the family as domestic caretakers, as reproductive beings, and as naturally fit for mothering. It has been the task and success of feminism to document the dangers posed to women by family, marriage, and mothering in their lived and ideological forms.

The ideology of the loving family often masks gender injustice within the family, including battery, rape, and child abuse. Women continue to shoulder primary responsibility for both child rearing and domestic labor; and they continue to choose occupations compatible with child care. Those occupations are often poorly paid and replaceable, and do not provide benefits and opportunities for career advancement. The expectation that women within families are first and foremost wives and mothers continues to offer employers a rationale for paying women less. Women's lower wages in the public workforce in turn make it seem economically rational for women to invest in developing their husband's career assets. Because no fault divorce laws now assume that men and women have equally developed career assets (or that those career assets could be developed with the aid of short-term alimony) and because they fail to treat the husband's career assets as community property, women exit marriage at a significant economic disadvantage.[1] Women's custody of children after divorce, their lower earning potential, the unavailability of low cost child care, the absence of adequate social support for single mothers, and, often, fathers' failure to pay full child support, all combine to reduce divorced women's economic position even further. The result is the feminization of poverty. The ideology that a normal family is a self-sufficient, two-income family is then mobilized to blame single mothers for their poverty, to justify supervisory intervention into their families, and to rationalize reducing social support.

This picture, although generally taken as a picture of women's relation to the family, is not, in fact, a picture of *women*'s relation to the family. It is a picture of *heterosexual* women's relation to the family. It is a picture whose outlines are determined by an eye ever vigilant for the ways that marriage, family, and mothering subordinate heterosexual women to men in the private household, in the public economy, and in the welfare state. It thus fails to grasp lesbians' relation to the family.[2]

It has instead been the task of lesbian-feminism from the 1970s through

---

[1] For discussions of women's vulnerability in marriage and after divorce, see Susan Moller Okin, *Justice, Gender, and the Family* (New York: Basic Books, 1989); and Lenore J. Weitzman *The Divorce Revolution: the Unexpected Social and Economic Consequences for Women and Children in America* (New York: Free Press, 1985).

[2] This is not to say that lesbians are entirely left out of the picture. Although drawn from a heterosexual viewpoint, this picture of the family, marriage, and mothering as a primary site of women's subordination and dependence is one that lesbians do nevertheless fit into in many ways. Lesbians, too, can find themselves in heterosexual marriages, undergoing divorce, becoming single parents, disadvantaged in a sex-segregated workforce that pays women less, without adequate child care or child support, vulnerable to welfare bureaucracies, and so on.

the 1990s to develop an analysis of lesbians' distinctive relation to the family. However, in its arguments for rejecting lesbian motherhood, lesbian marriages, and lesbian families, lesbian-feminism, too, has failed to make lesbian difference from heterosexual women central to its analyses. It is to the promise and, I will argue, the failure of lesbian-feminism to grasp lesbians' distinctive relation to the family that I now turn.

## II. Lesbian-feminism, the Family, Mothering, and Marriage

In evaluating lesbian marriage, motherhood, and families, lesbian feminists took as their point of departure feminist critiques of heterosexual women's experience of family, motherhood, and marriage. Lesbian feminists were particularly alive to the fact that lesbians are uniquely positioned to evade the ills of the heterosexual, male-dominated family. In particular, they are uniquely positioned to violate the conventional gender expectation that they, as women, will be dependent on men in their personal relations, will fulfill the maternal imperative, will service a husband and children, and will accept confinement to the private sphere of domesticity. Because of their unique position, lesbians can hope to be in the vanguard of the feminist rebellion against the patriarchal family and the institution of motherhood.

*Family*

As we saw in Chapter 2, in the 1970s and 1980s, lesbian feminists used feminist critiques of heterosexual women's subordination to men within the family as a platform for valorizing lesbian existence. Lesbian feminists like Monique Wittig and Charlotte Bunch argued that the nuclear family based on heterosexual marriage enables men to appropriate for themselves women's productive and reproductive labor.[3] Because lesbians do not enter into this heterosexual nuclear family, they can be read as refusing to allow their labor to be appropriated by men.

Lesbian feminists also used feminist critiques of heterosexual women's confinement to the private sphere of family and exclusion from the public sphere of politics and labor to argue for a new vision of lesbians' personal life. In that vision, lesbians would reject the private family. They would opt instead for a politicized life of connection to other women outside the family. Janice Raymond, for instance, argued for the feminist value of historical all-women's communities, such as the pre-enclosure nunneries and the nineteenth-century Chinese marriage-resisters' houses. There women combined intimate friendships, community, and work.[4] On Raymond's and others' view, passion-

---

[3] Monique Wittig, *The Straight Mind and Other Essays* (Boston: Beacon, 1992); Charlotte Bunch, 'Lesbians in Revolt', in *Passionate Politics, Essays 1968–1986* (New York: St. Martin's Press, 1987), 161–7.
[4] Janice G. Raymond, *A Passion for Friends* (Boston: Beacon, 1986).

ate friendships, centered around a common life of work, could and should replace the depoliticized, isolated life within the nuclear family.

As this emphasis on communities of friends suggests, lesbian feminists took its being a good thing that lesbians do not participate in *heterosexual*, male-dominated, private families to mean that lesbians should not participate in *any* form of family including lesbian families. For instance, lesbian feminist legal theorist Ruthann Robson rejects recent liberal legal efforts to redefine the family to include lesbian and gay families that are functionally equivalent to heterosexual ones.[5] She argues that, in advocating legal recognition of lesbian families, 'we have forgotten the lesbian generated critiques of family as oppressive and often deadly'.[6] In particular, we have forgotten the critiques of the family as an institution of the patriarchal state, of marriage as slavery,[7] and of wives as property within marriage.[8] Rather than seek to have lesbian families recognized and protected, Robson recommends resisting organizing lesbian relationships around the category of the family. In her view, the category 'family' should be abolished.

## Motherhood

Feminist critiques of heterosexual women's experience also supplied the point of departure for lesbian feminist critiques of lesbian motherhood. Lesbian motherhood, on this view, represents a concession to a key element of women's subordination—compulsory motherhood. By refusing to have children, or by giving up custody of their children at divorce, lesbians can refuse to participate in compulsory motherhood. They can thus refuse to accept the myth 'that only family and children provide [women] with a purpose and place, bestow upon us honor, respect, love, and comfort'.[9] Purpose and place is better found in political activities in a more public community of women. Sensitive to the power of the myth of female fulfillment through motherhood, lesbian feminists challenge lesbians contemplating motherhood to reflect more critically on their reasons for doing so, and on the political consequences of participating in the present lesbian baby boom. Ellen Lewin speculates that lesbian motherhood may simply serve to reinforce the gender ideology of women's fulfillment through motherhood. Thus, increasing media attention to lesbian mothers, in her view, may reflect 'the calcification of the old construction of gender in terms of motherhood and the simultaneous defusing of the threat to traditional gender categories the lesbian and gay movement and feminism seem to have achieved'.[10]

---

[5] Ruthann Robson, 'Resisting the Family: Repositioning Lesbians in Legal Theory', *Signs* 19 (1994): 975–96.

[6] Ibid. 977.                    [7] Ibid. 976.                    [8] Ibid. 986–7.

[9] Irena Klepfisz, 'Women Without Children/ Women Without Families/ Women Alone', in *Politics of the Heart: A Lesbian Parenting Anthology*, ed. Sandra Pollack and Jeanne Vaughn (New York: Firebrand, 1987), 55–65, 57.

[10] Ellen Lewin, *Lesbian Mothers: Accounts of Gender in American Culture* (Ithaca, NY: Cornell University Press, 1993), 192.

In resisting motherhood, lesbians not only reject the myth of women's fulfillment through motherhood. They are also freed to devote their lives to public political work for lesbians and women. Thus, resisting motherhood is seen by lesbian feminists as instrumental to effective political action. Nancy Polikoff, for instance, claims that '[t]o the extent that motherhood drains the available pool of lesbians engaging in ongoing political work, its long-term significance is overwhelming'.[11]

Finally, lesbian feminists have argued that resisting motherhood is politically important because being a mother disables lesbians from publicly occupying the identity 'lesbian'. Lesbian mothers are virtually automatically assumed to be heterosexual, because lesbianism and motherhood are culturally imagined to be incompatible. Thus, lesbian motherhood facilitates the closeting of lesbian existence. Even when lesbian mothers are careful not to pass as heterosexual, their motherhood works against their being publicly perceived as deviating from the category 'woman' in the way that lesbians are standardly thought to. 'My experience', observes Polikoff, 'is that straight women clearly feel that my choice to have a child *balances* my choice to be a lesbian and makes me more normal, easier to understand, woman, less of a challenge to their lives.'[12] And in her study of lesbian mothers, Ellen Lewin argues that motherhood enables lesbians to claim a less stigmatized place in the gender system; in particular, it enables them to claim for themselves the conventional womanly attributes of being altruistic, nurturant, and responsible—attributes that lesbians typically are stereotyped as lacking.[13] Because 'wanting to be a mother is a profoundly *natural* desire ... achieving motherhood implies movement into a more natural or normal status than a lesbian can ordinarily hope to experience otherwise'.[14]

## Marriage

In evaluating lesbian (and gay) marriage, lesbian feminists begin from the observation that, historically, the institution of marriage has been oppressively gender-structured. Lesbian feminists have been skeptical of the gender-based arguments for same-sex marriage discussed in Chapter 5. The historical and cross-cultural record of same-sex marriages does not in fact support the claim that same-sex marriages will revolutionize marriage. On the contrary, the same-sex marriages that have been legitimized in other cultures—for instance, African woman-marriage, Native American marriages between a *berdache* and a same-sex partner, and nineteenth-century Chinese marriages between women—have all been highly gender-structured. Thus, there is no

---

[11] Nancy D. Polikoff, 'Lesbians Choosing Children: The Personal is Political', in *Politics of the Heart*, 48–54, 51.  [12] Ibid. 53.
[13] Ellen Lewin, *Lesbian Mothers*, 16.  [14] Ibid. 74

reason to believe that ' "gender dissent" is inherent in marriage between two men or two women'.[15]

Lesbian feminists also assume that pursuing same-sex marriage rights will make it more difficult to critique the institution of marriage. In their view, proponents of marriage rights, if they hope to suceed, must necessarily offer nonrevolutionary and assimilationist arguments. They must stress the similarities of gay and lesbian relationships to conventional heterosexual ones rather than their differences.[16] By attempting to have specifically *marital* relationships recognized, marriage rights advocates reinforce the assumption that long-term, monogamous relationships are more valuable than any other kind of relationship. As a result, the marriage rights campaign, if successful, will result in privileging those lesbian and gay relationships that most closely approximate the heterosexual norm over more deviant relationships that require a radical rethinking of the nature of families.[17]

Finally, lesbian feminists have rejected the argument that lesbians and gays need marriage rights in order to have the same privileges that heterosexual couples now enjoy, such as access to a spouse's health insurance benefits.[18] Distributing basic benefits like health insurance through the middle class family neglects the interests of poor and some working class families, as well as single individuals, in having access to basic social benefits. If access to such benefits is the issue, then universal health insurance, not marriage, is what needs to be advocated.

### III. Lesbian Disappearance

The difficulty with the lesbian feminist viewpoint described above is that it is one from which lesbian difference from heterosexual women persistently disappears from view.

First, lesbian feminists judge the value of family and marriage for *lesbians* largely by looking at the *heterosexual* nuclear family's effects on *heterosexual* women. Lesbians are to resist family and marriage because heterosexual women have been treated as property and their labor appropriated by men within gender-structured heterosexual families. But to make this a principal reason for lesbians' not forming families and marriages of their own is to lose

---

[15] Nancy D. Polikoff, 'We Will Get What We Ask For: Why Legalizing Gay and Lesbian Marriage Will Not "Dismantle the Legal Structure of Gender in Every Marriage" ', *Virginia Law Review* 79 (1993): 1535–50, 1538.

[16] Polikoff, ibid.; Paula Ettelbrick, 'Since When is Marriage a Path to Liberation?' in *Lesbians, Gay Men, and the Law*, ed. William B. Rubenstein (New York: New Press, 1993), 401–6.

[17] Robson's objection to functionalist approaches to the family in legal thinking is precisely that functionalist approaches are inherently conservative and 'guarantee exclusion of the very relationships that might transform the functions', such as a sexual relationship between three lesbians (Robson, 'Resisting the Family', 989).

[18] Paula Ettelbrick, 'Since When is Marriage a Path to Liberation?' and Nancy Polikoff, 'We Will Get What We Ask For'.

sight of the difference between lesbians and heterosexual women. Lesbian families and marriages are not reasonably construed as sites where women can be treated as property and where their productive and reproductive labor can be appropriated by men. It thus does not follow from the fact that marriage and the family have been oppressive for heterosexual women that marriage and the family would be oppressive for lesbians. Patriarchy may be at work in gender-structured heterosexual marriages. It is not at work in lesbian marriages.

The alternative argument—that creating lesbian families will not *remedy* the gender structure in heterosexual families—drops lesbians from view in a different way. Here, *heterosexual* women's interests, not lesbians', provide the touchstone for determining what normative conclusions about the family and marriage lesbians should come to. Lesbians are to resist forming marriages and families of their own because heterosexual women's struggle against the institution of marriage and family will not be promoted, and may in fact be hindered if lesbians endorse the value of marriage and family. This line of reasoning ignores the possibility that lesbians may have interests of their own in marrying and forming families. Those interests may conflict with heterosexual women's political aims.

Second, resistance to sexist practices and oppressive gender ideology connected with the family is presented as a distinctively lesbian task within feminism. In fact it is a broadly feminist task whose burden should be equally shared by heterosexual women and lesbians. Both lesbians and heterosexual women have reason to resist the construction of mothering as an unpaid, socially unsupported task. Both have reason to reject women's confinement to the domestic sphere and reason to value participation in politically oriented communities of women. Both have reason to resist their gender socialization into the myth of feminine fulfillment through mothering. Both can have justice interests in objecting to a social and legal system that privileges long-term, monogamous relationships over all other forms of relationships and that does not provide universal access to basic benefits like health insurance. All of these are broadly feminist concerns. As a result, the lesbian feminist perspective does not articulate any distinctively *lesbian* political tasks in relation to the family, marriage, and mothering. Instead, lesbians are submerged in the larger category 'feminist'.

Finally, the specific forms that lesbian and gay subordination take and the related stigmatizing ideologies simply do not inform lesbian feminist analyses of lesbian families, marriage, and mothering. What governs the lesbian feminist perspective is above all the political relations between men and women. To a lesser extent, lesbian feminists also attend to class relations and the political relations between those who are in normative long-term, monogamous relations (whether heterosexual or nonheterosexual) and those who are not. As a result, the radicalness of lesbian and gay family, marriage, and parenting is measured on a scale that looks only at their power (or impotence) to transform gender relations, to remedy class-related inequities, and to end the privileging of long-term, monogamous relations. Not surprisingly, lesbian and gay families, marriages, and parenting fail to measure up. But this ignores the historical construction of lesbians and gays as outlaws to the natural family and their resulting displacement from a protected private sphere.

Unlike heterosexual women, lesbians have not been assumed to have a natural place within the family as domestic caretakers, reproductive beings, and naturally fit mothers. On the contrary, as I shall elaborate shortly, both lesbians and gays have been assumed to be unable to sustain long-term relationships and to be nonprocreative, dangerous to children, and ruled by sexual instincts to the exclusion of parenting ones. Moreover, unlike heterosexual women, it is not their powerlessness *within* the family that marks their subordination but rather their denial of access *to* a legitimated and socially instituted sphere of family, marriage, and parenting.

Among the array of rights related to marriage that heterosexuals enjoy, but gays and lesbians do not, are the rights to legal marriage, to live with one's spouse in neighborhoods zoned for single families only, and to secure US residency through marriage to a US citizen; the rights to social security survivor's benefits, to inherit a spouse's estate in the absence of a will, and to file a wrongful death suit; the rights to give proxy consent, to refuse to testify against one's spouse, and to file joint income taxes.

Lesbians and gays similarly lack access to the privileges and protections that heterosexuals enjoy with respect to biological, adoptive, and foster children. Sexual orientation continues to be an overriding reason for denying custody to lesbian and gay parents who exit a heterosexual marriage. Indeed, the heterosexual grandparents or other family members of the extended family may be given custody priority over lesbian or gay parents. Gays and lesbians who do gain custody of their children remain at continued risk of later losing custody if their sexual orientation was not made known to the court at the time of the original custody decision and later does become known.[19] And custody and visitation may be conditional on lesbian or gay parents' abiding by special restrictions.[20] Gays and lesbians fair equally poorly with respect to adoption and foster parenting. Even when adoption is successful, joint adoption generally is not—nor is adoption of a partner's biological child. As a result, lesbian and gay co-parents have neither legal rights to nor responsibilities for the children they parent. Should the adoptive or biological parent die, for instance, the co-parent has no legal claim to custody of the child.

---

[19] Custody decisions can be re-examined at any time if there have been material changes that affect the child's best interests. The discovery of the custodial parent's lesbianism or homosexuality is one ground for re-examining the custody award.

[20] For example, the courts may require that a gay or lesbian partner or lesbian and gay friends not be present when the child visits; and in the wake of AIDS one court forbade a lesbian parent from kissing her children. See Rhonda R. Rivera, 'Legal Issues in Gay and Lesbian Parenting', in *Gay and Lesbian Parents*, ed. Frederick W. Bozett (New York: Praeger, 1987), 199–227.

What comes into view in this picture of the legal inequities that lesbians and gay men confront is the fact that the family, marriage, and parenting is a primary site of heterosexual privilege. The family has historically been and continues to be constructed and institutionalized as the natural domain of heterosexuals only. It is a domain from which lesbians and gays are outlawed. This distinctively lesbian and gay relation to family is what fails to make its appearance within feminist critiques. But so long as the politics of denying lesbians and gay men access to the family remains out of view, distinctively lesbian and gay interests in family, marriage, and parenting cannot make their appearance; nor can distinctively lesbian and gay political goals in relation to the family

A constitutive feature of lesbian and gay oppression since at least the late nineteenth century has been the reservation of the private sphere for heterosexuals only. By 'private sphere', I do not here mean a zone of privacy beyond the reach of the law. I mean instead the domain of those intimate and familial relationships that are fundamental to western, industrialized societies' social structure and that stand, at least ideologically, in opposition to the public sphere of wage labor and politics. This is the sphere of romance, marriage, and the procreative family. Because lesbians and gays are ideologically constructed as beings incapable of genuine romance, marriage, or families of their own, and because those assumptions are institutionalized in the law and social practice, lesbians and gays are displaced from this private sphere. It is to the construction of lesbians and gays as outlaws to the family that I now turn.

## IV. Familial Outlaws

Like 'woman' and 'man', 'heterosexual' and 'homosexual'/'lesbian' are oppositional social categories. This is to say two things. First, articulating how women differ from men or how lesbians and homosexuals differ from heterosexuals is central to developing cultural understandings of what it means to be these kinds of persons. Thus, cultural articulation of the content of these paired categories proceeds in tandem. Second, because systems of subordination are organized around these categories, the differences that make a difference to how persons of these types are esteemed, what opportunities they are offered, and what restrictions are imposed on them are particularly central to the social construction of these identity categories. Thus, although social understandings of manhood or heterosexuality may shift over time, one may expect those shifts to be ones that preserve the higher standing of men and heterosexuals. In what follows, I want to suggest that the historical construction of the oppositional categories 'heterosexual' and 'homosexual'/'lesbian' has in large part been a matter of articulating their different relation to the family. In particular, the idea that lesbians and gay men differ in ways that make them outlaws to the family has been central to social understandings of what it means to be gay or lesbian. As we will see, the content of the social categories 'lesbian' and 'homosexual' shifted over time from an emphasis on gender deviance during the 1880s to 1920s, to an emphasis on sexual excess during the 1930s to 1960s, to an emphasis on 'pretending' familial relationships during the 1980s and 1990s. These shifts in emphasis make sense if we look at what was happening to the heterosexual family during each of these periods. In each period, different worries about the stability of the heterosexual nuclear family surfaced that were connected to family members' challenges to pre-existing familial norms. In the 1880s to 1920s it was especially norms governing (women's) gender behavior; in the 1930s to 1960s, it was most critically norms governing (male) sexuality; and in the 1980s and 1990s it was, above all, norms governing acceptable family composition that were most centrally challenged. In short, in historically specific ways, heterosexuals' violation of familial norms threatened to undermine the stability of the family. In the face of this, constructing lesbians and homosexuals as different from heterosexuals in a way that makes a difference to their social standing was accomplished by projecting on to gays and lesbians the most virulent forms of family disrupting behavior.

In tracking the correlation between historically specific worries about the stability of the heterosexual nuclear family and historically specific ideologies about gays' and lesbians' unfitness for family life, I do not mean to claim that anxiety about the family was the sole factor influencing social understandings of what it means to be lesbian or homosexual. I do mean to claim that it was an important factor. The construction of gay men and lesbians as highly stigmatized outsiders to the family who engage in family disrupting behavior allays anxieties about the potential failure of the heterosexual nuclear family by externalizing the threat to the family. As a result, anxiety about the possibility that the family is disintegrating from *within* can be displaced on to the specter of the hostile outsider to the family. One recent example of this phenomenon occurred during the US Defense of Marriage Act (DOMA) debates. In response to the view that recognizing same-sex marriages would undermine the family, opponents of DOMA pointed out that the threat to the family was being mistakenly displaced on to lesbians and gays. Opponents observed that the real threat was from heterosexual family members' misbehavior and from (presumably heterosexual) Congressmen's failure to install adequate social supports for the family in the form of health care, day care, employment, a livable minimum wage, and affordable single family homes.

The construction of gay men and lesbians as outsiders to the family also facilitates stigma-threatening comparisons between misbehaving members of the heterosexual family and gay men and lesbians. Such comparisons can be used to motivate heterosexual family members' compliance with gender, sexual, and family composition norms.[21] Lesbian baiting—that is, accusing

---

[21] Estelle B. Freedman also suggests that by locating the genuinely deviant, abnormal, perverse behavior outside the family, members of heterosexual families may have been enabled to adjust to new, liberalized norms for acceptable gender roles and sexual behavior within families. See ' "Uncontrolled

women who fail to comply with gender norms of being lesbian—is one famil-
iar example of such stigma-threatening comparisons.

## The 1880s to 1920s

This period witnessed significant challenges to the gender structure of
marriage. By the mid nineteenth century, the first wave of the feminist movement was underway, pressing for changes in women's gender roles within the
family. First wave feminists pushed for legal reforms that would recognize
women as separate individuals within marriage by, for example, securing
women property rights within marriage, and that would give women access to
divorce. They also pushed for increased access to higher education and
employment as well as for contraception, abortion, and (through the temper-
ance movement) control of male sexuality, all of which would free women
from a life devoted exclusively to child bearing and child rearing.

Women's push for greater economic independence and for the redefinition
of women's gender role coincided with a shift to an increasingly urbanized
and industrialized way of life and with it the organization of the family
around wages. While potentially liberating for women, the dependence of the
family on wages also threatened to undermine the family itself as it drew both
children and women into wage labor, and as men faced unemployment and
inability to support their families. As a result, the end of the nineteenth
century and the beginning of the twentieth saw a number of reforms designed
to protect the family against the effects of industrialization: child labor laws,
protective legislation for women limiting their hours and working conditions,
the growth of day care, the first official concern about unemployment.

First wave feminists' explicit critique of women's gender role within the
family, combined with the changes in children's, women's, and men's roles in
the family that resulted from the family's dependence on wage labor, posed a
challenge to the gender structure of the family. Because the early twentieth-
century gender ideology tied gender tightly to biology, women's violation of
gender norms was interpreted as having significant biological repercussions.
From the mid nineteenth century, physicians argued that 'unnatural'
women—that is, 'over' educated women, women who worked at gender atyp-
ical occupations, and women who practiced birth control or had abortions—
were likely to suffer a variety of physically based mental ailments including
weakness, nervousness, hysteria, loss of memory, insanity, and nymphoma-
nia.[22] Worse yet, their gender-inappropriate behavior might result in sterility

Desires": The Response to the Sexual Psychopath 1920–1960', in *Passion and Power: Sexuality in
History,* ed. Kathy Peiss and Christina Simmons with Robert A. Padgug (Philadelphia: Temple
University Press, 1989), 199–225.

[22] Carroll Smith-Rosenberg and Charles Rosenberg, 'The Female Animal: Medical and Biological
Views of Woman and Her Role in Nineteenth-Century America', in *Concepts of Health and Disease:
Interdisciplinary Perspectives,* ed. Arthur L. Caplan, H. Tristram Engelhardt, Jr., and James J. McCartney
(Reading, MA: Addison-Wesley, 1981), 281–303.

or inability to produce physically and mentally healthy offspring. In particular, they risked producing children who were themselves inappropriately gendered—effeminate sons and masculine daughters.

Not only could departure from women's traditional gender role as wife and mother have dire physical and mental consequences for both herself and her offspring, she herself might be suspected of being at a deep level not really a woman. Indeed, she might be suspected of being one of the third sex, a sexual invert. Although what distinguished the invert from 'normal' women was her gender inversion, what distinguished her from merely nonconforming women was the source of her gender deviance. Medical theorists postulated that, at a biological level, sexually inverted women were not real women. Some imagined that inverts were really hermaphrodites. Others, like Havelock Ellis, imagined that they possessed an excess of male 'germs'.[23] Others, like Krafft-Ebing imagined that the invert was a throwback to an earlier evolutionary stage of bisexuality (which for him meant bigenderization).[24]

The sexually inverted woman's attraction to other women was simply a natural result of her generally masculine genderization. The masculinization of her sexual desire entailed that the sexually inverted woman would play the part of a man in her sexual relationships with women. She would, as it were, wear the pants. If heterosexually married, she would adopt the masculine gender role with respect to her husband, who was himself likely to be sexually inverted and willing to play out a more feminine gender role.[25]

Because the discernible evidence of inversion was the nonconformity to women's conventional gender role, the line between the nonconforming sexual invert and the nonconforming feminist was often blurred. Feminist views and feminist-inspired deviance from gender norms might be both symptom and cause of sexual inversion. Like sexual inverts, feminists threatened to disrespect appropriate gender relations between women and men in marriage. One author of a 1900 *New York Medical Journal* essay, for instance, 'warned that feminists and sexual perverts alike, both of whom he classed as "degenerates", married only men whom they could rule, govern and cause to follow [them] in voice and action'.[26]

That excessive gender deviance rather than sexual excess or sexual orientation occupied center stage in constructions of lesbians' nature makes sense given the cultural context in which late nineteenth and early twentieth century medical theorizing occurred. The medical category of sexual inversion made it possible to condemn as pathological women's violations of conventional

---

[23] Havelock Ellis, *Studies in the Psychology of Sex, vol. II: Sexual Inversion* (Philadelphia: F. A. Davis, 1928).

[24] Richard von Krafft-Ebing, *Psychopathia Sexualis: A Medico-Forensic Study* (New York: Pioneer Publications, 1947).

[25] George Chancey, Jr., 'From Sexual Inversion to Homosexuality: The Changing Medical Conceptualization of Female "Deviance"', in *Passion and Power*, 87–117, 91–2.

[26] Qtd in George Chauncey, Jr., 'From Sexual Inversion to Homosexuality', 92.

gender norms, especially since the behavior of sexually inverted women and feminists was sometimes indistinguishable. At the same time, heterosexual women's social standing was preserved, despite their gender-deviant behavior, by attributing an excessive and biologically based gender inversion to inverted women.

The idea that this new medical category of sexual inversion was created in direct response to first wave feminists' challenge to gender norms is not new. Both Lillian Faderman and George Chauncey, Jr., for instance, have argued that given both the influence of feminist ideas and the burgeoning of economic opportunities for women, there was a cultural fear that women would replace marriages to men with Boston marriages or romantic friendships.[27] One response to that fear was greater attention to the ideal of companionate marriage, and thus to making marriage more attractive to women.[28] A second response, however, was a cultural backlash—or as Chauncey describes it, a heterosexual counter-revolution—against Boston marriages, romantic friendships, schoolgirl 'raves', and same-sex institutions. The pathologizing of both gender deviance and same-sex relationships brought what were formerly taken to be innocent and normal intimacies between women under suspicion of harboring degeneracy and abnormality.

The pathologizing of relations between women was not confined to medical literature. As Lisa Duggan has documented, newspapers sensationalized violent intimate relationships between women, such as the case of Alice Mitchell, a sexual invert, who intended to elope with and marry Freda Ward and to cross-dress as a man, adopting the name Alvin.[29] When their plan was discovered and the engagement forcibly terminated, Alice Mitchell murdered Freda so that no one else could have her. Duggan argues that Alice's clear intent to forge a new way of life outside the heterosexual, gender-structured family marked her as dangerous. In sensationalizing cases like Alice's,

[t]he late-nineteenth century newspaper narratives of lesbian love featured violence as a boundary marker; murders or suicides served to abort the forward progress of the tale, signaling that such erotic love between women was not only tragic but ultimately hopeless. . . . The stories were thus structured to emphasize, ultimately, that no real love story was possible.[30]

Not only was no real love story possible, no real family relation was possible either. The fully gender-deviant woman was someone who was not only

---

[27] George Chauncey, Jr. 'From Sexual Inversion to Homosexuality'; Lilian Faderman, *Surpassing the Love of Men: Romantic Friendship and Love between Women from the Renaissance to the Present* (New York: William Morrow, 1981); Lilian Faderman, 'Nineteenth-Century Boston Marriage as a Possible Lesson for Today', in *Boston Marriages: Romantic but Asexual Relationships Among Contemporary Lesbians*, ed. Esther D. Rothblum and Kathleen A. Brehony (Amherst: University of Massachusetts Press, 1993), 29–42.

[28] Chauncey, Jr., 'From Sexual Inversion to Homosexuality'.

[29] Lisa Duggan, 'The Trials of Alice Mitchell: Sensationalism, Sexology, and the Lesbian Subject in Turn-of-the-Century America' *Signs* 18 (1993): 791–814.　　　　　[30] Ibid. 808.

pathological and doomed to tragedy, but who was constitutionally unfit for family life. Her masculinity unfit her for the marital role of wife, unfit her for the task of producing properly gendered children, and unfit her for any stable, intimate relationships. The cultural construction of the lesbian was thus, from the outset, the construction of a kind of being who was, centrally, an outsider to marriage and motherhood. This image of the doomed, mannish lesbian could be used to motivate heterosexual women's compliance with gender norms. In addition, attributing the worst forms of gender deviance to a third sex externalized the threat to the heterosexual family, suggesting that the heterosexual family was not in fact being challenged from within by *real* women.

### The 1930s to 1960s

The US economic Depression of the 1930s and World War II in the 1940s created a new set of threats to the stability of the heterosexual family.[31] During the Depression, many men lost their traditional gender position in the family as breadwinners as a result of both massive unemployment and a drop in marriage rates. The sense of a cultural crisis in masculinity was reflected in numerous sociological studies of 'The Unemployed Man and his Family'.[32] Men's traditional position in the family and family stability itself was additionally undermined during World War II, which brought a rise in the frequency of prolonged separations, divorce, and desertion.[33]

Compounding the shifts in gender arrangements within the family, brought on by the Depression and World War II, were newly emergent understandings of women's, men's, and children's sexuality. Estelle B. Freedman argues that 'by the 1920s the Victorian ideal of innate female purity had disintegrated' and with it the symbolic power of female purity to regulate male sexuality.[34] The idea of female sexual satisfaction, the use of birth control, and the possibility of sexuality outside of marriage all gained increased acceptance. The 1930s Prohibition era speakeasy culture also contributed to a climate of increasing sexual permissiveness. And the publicizing of Freudian ideas underscored not only the sexuality of women, but the sexuality of children as well. The sexualizing of women and children meant that both might fail to be merely innocent victims of male sexual aggression; they might instead play a role in inviting male sexual transgressions.[35] Sexuality itself now posed a challenge to the stability of the family.

Heterosexual men's sexuality became a particular focus of concern. Partly

---

[31] See Estelle B. Freedman, ' "Uncontrolled Desires" '; John D'Emilio, 'The Homosexual Menace: The Politics of Sexuality in Cold War America', in *Passion and Power*, 226–40; and George Chauncey, Jr., *Gay New York: Gender, Urban Culture, and the Making of the Gay Male World, 1890–1940* (New York: Basic Books, 1994).

[32] Chauncey, *Gay New York*, 353–4.          [33] D'Emilio, 'The Homosexual Menace', 233.

[34] Freedman, ' "Uncontrolled Desires" ', 201.          [35] Ibid. 212.

in response to men's dislocation from their gender position within the family during the Depression, the cultural construction of masculinity underwent a shift from being gender-based to being sexuality-based. In his historical study of New York gay culture during the first third of the twentieth century, George Chauncey argues that sexual categories for men underwent a significant transformation during the 1930s and 1940s. The gender-based contrast between fairies (effeminate men) and men (who might be 'queer', 'trade', i.e. heterosexual men who accepted advances from homosexual men, or strictly heterosexual) gave way to the contemporary sexual binarism between homosexual and heterosexual. Real manhood ceased to be secured by simply avoiding feminine behaviors and instead came to rest on exclusive heterosexuality.[36]

The sexualizing of masculinity, however, meant that hypermasculinity could result in sexual excess. Symbolizing male heterosexual desire run amok, the figure of the heterosexual, psychopathic rapist became a focus of social concern during the sex crime panics of 1937–40 and 1949–55. But even if male heterosexual desire posed dangers, male homosexual desires risked greater excesses. During the sex crime panics, gay men were depicted as violent child molesters and seducers of youth. The image of the dangerously sexual homosexual received added reinforcement during the McCarthy era's purge of 'sex perverts' from governmental service on the grounds that they threatened not only the nation's children but its national security and the heterosexuality of its adult population as well.[37]

During the 1950s and 1960s, psychoanalytic descriptions of homosexual and (to a lesser extent) lesbian pathology further entrenched the equation of homosexuality with excessive sexuality. One particularly striking feature of psychoanalytic constructions of homosexuality was the insistence that, because of their multiple psychological defects, neither homosexuals nor lesbians were emotionally competent to experience genuine romantic love or sustain stable intimate relationships.

In 1962, Irving Bieber and his colleagues published the results of a nine year study, begun in 1952, of 106 male homosexuals and 100 male heterosexuals who were undergoing psychoanalysis.[38] Conducted by the Research Committee of the Society of Medical Psychoanalysts, the study claimed to find that homosexuals are 'compulsively preoccupied with sexuality in general and with sexual practices in particular'.[39] Not only are gay men fixated on sex, but what they want out of sex is not a romantic relationship but escape from the

---

[36] George Chauncey, *Gay New York*. One of his central aims in this work is to argue that the hetero-homosexual binarism is a significantly more recent invention than generally acknowledged.

[37] John D'Emilio, in 'The Homosexual Menace', points out that there was virtually no evidence supporting McCarthy era allegations that lesbians and gays were vulnerable to blackmail and hence unsuitable for government employment. He suggests that the massive efforts to counter the 'homosexual menace' can only be explained as a result of the depression and war's disruption of family life, gender arrangements, and patterns of sexuality.

[38] Irving Bieber, *Homosexuality: A Psychoanalytic Study* (New York: Basic Books, 1962).

[39] Ibid. 252 (italics in original).

anxieties produced by heterosexual contact, a substitute for the affection never received from father, and, above all, a large penis. As evidence for sexual desire's overshadowing place in gay men's emotional subjectivity, Bieber observed that 'homosexuals were more often excessively preoccupied with sexuality in childhood',[40] and '[s]ignificantly more homosexuals start sexual activity before adolescence than do heterosexuals and more homosexuals are *more frequently* sexually active during pre-adolescence, early adolescence, and adulthood'.[41]

Compounding this obsessive preoccupation with sex, were crippling anxieties that meant that homosexuals' attempts to do more than sexually couple would inevitably be undermined by feelings of fear, hostility, rage, and jealousy toward their partners. Bieber observed that the 'warmth, friendship, concern for the other's welfare and happiness' that occurs in heterosexual relationships are, for gay men, unsustainable:

[I]n the homosexual pairing, hostile and competitive trends (overt and covert) often intrude to prevent a stable relationship with a partner. We found many homosexuals to be fearful, isolated, and anxious about masculinity and personal acceptability. Ambivalence leads to impermanence or transiency in most homosexual contacts. The inability to sustain a relationship frequently arises from an inability to bring social and sexual relations into a unity. This problem is well illustrated by the superficial and evanescent quality of social activities often carried on at bars and in 'cruising'.[42]

Bieber's teammate, Cornelia Wilbur, issued the same judgment about lesbian relationships:

Female homosexual relationships are characterized by great ambivalence, by great longing for love, by intense elements of hostility, and by the presence of chronic anxiety. They do not contribute to the individual's need for stability and love:[43]

They cannot do so because the frequency of hostile eruptions, verbal and physical fighting, and general destructiveness within these relationships renders those relationships impermanent.[44] That same-sex relationships are destructive and impermanent was not a view peculiar to the Research Committee. It was shared by psychoanalysts generally during the 1950s and into the 1960s. Writing in the late 1960s, Charles Socarides, a psychotherapist equally as influential as Bieber and even more unsympathetic, condemned same-sex relationships for their 'destruction, mutual defeat, exploitation of the partner and self, oral-sadistic incorporation, aggressive onslaughts, attempt to alleviate anxiety and a pseudo solution to the aggressive and libidinal urges'.[45]

---

[40] Ibid. 193.          [41] Ibid. 189.          [42] Ibid. 253.

[43] Cornelia Wilbur, 'Clinical Aspects of Female Homosexuality', in *Sexual Inversion: The Multiple Roots of Homosexuality*, ed. Judd Marmor (New York: Basic Books, 1965), 281.

[44] Ibid. 279.

[45] Qtd in Ronald Bayer, *Homosexuality and American Psychiatry* (Princeton: Princeton University Press, 1987), 36.

Again, the point I want to underscore is that shifting gender and sexual patterns within the heterosexual family were integrally connected with the social construction of gay men and lesbians as family outlaws. That sexual excess occupied center stage in constructions of gay men's and lesbians' nature makes sense given the cultural context in which theorizing occurred. For a variety of reasons, including the rise of Freudianism, the dangers of sexuality for family life and for children became culturally prominent. Attributing a distinctly pathological, child-endangering, and relationship-destroying sexuality to gay men and lesbians was central to constructing lesbians and gays as different in a way that makes a difference. Even if heterosexual families risked disruption by the potentially excessive or violent sexuality of its own members, the dangers of heterosexuality still fell well short of those posed by homosexuality and lesbianism. In addition, locating the sexual danger to children outside the family in 'sex perverts' allayed anxiety that the family risked disruption from within.

In short, from the 1930s through the 1960s, gay men's and lesbians' nature was constructed as one that made them fundamentally unfit for family life. Constitutionally prone to uncontrolled and insatiable sexuality, gay men and lesbians could not be trusted to respect prohibitions on adult-child sexual interactions.[46] Nor, given the compulsive quality of their sexual desire, could gay men or lesbians be expected to maintain stable relationships with each other. Thus, even the sympathetic author of a 1951 text arguing for decriminalization of homosexuality, nevertheless found extension of marriage rights unnecessary. For, as he observed of male and female homosexual couples who live together as though married, '[t]he quality of emotional instability encountered in homosexuals, both male and female, makes them continually dissatisfied with their lot' and hence these relationships rarely last.[47]

## The 1980s to 1990s

This more recent period posed a different challenge to the family. Technological, social, and economic factors combined to produce an explosion of new family and household forms that undermine the nuclear, biology-based family's claim to be *the* natural, normative social unit.

Increasingly, sophisticated birth control methods and technologically assisted reproduction using *in vitro* fertilization, artificial insemination, surrogate motherhood, fertility therapies, and the like undermine cultural understandings of the marital couple as a naturally reproductive unit, introduce nonrelated others into the reproductive process, and make it possible for women (and men) to have children without a heterosexual partner. The

---

[46] Fear that the child will be sexually molested is one reason for denying lesbians and gay men custody of their children.

[47] Morris Ploscowe, *Sex and the Law* (New York: Prentice Hall, 1951), 205.

institutionalization of child care, as mothers work to support families, involves nonfamily members in the familial task of raising children. Soaring divorce rates have made single-parent households a common family pattern—so common that Father's Day cards now include ones addressed to mothers, and others announcing their recipient is 'like a dad'. The high incidence of divorce has also meant an increase in families constituted through remarriage that combine children from previous marriages. Divorce also offers the opportunity for creating divorce-extended families, incorporating grandparents and other kin from former marriages as well as former spouses who may retain shared custody or visitation rights.[48] As a result of remarriage, semen donation, and surrogacy, the rule of one-mother, one-father per child (both of whom are expected to be biological parents) that has dominated legal reasoning about custody and visitation rights has ceased to be adequate to the reality of many families. Multiple women and/or multiple men become involved in children's lives through their biological, gestation, or parenting contributions.[49] The extended kinship networks, including 'fictive kin', of the black, urban poor, that enable extensive pooling of resources have become increasingly common in the working class, as the shift from goods to service production and the decline of industrial and unionized occupations has made working class persons' economic position increasingly fragile.[50] And the impoverishment of single-parent households has increasingly involved welfare agencies in family survival. In short, as Judith Stacey observes:

No longer is there a single culturally dominant family pattern to which the majority of Americans conform and most of the rest aspire. Instead, Americans today have crafted a multiplicity of family and household arrangements that we inhabit uneasily and reconstitute frequently in response to changing personal and occupational circumstances.[51]

We now live, in her view, in the age of the postmodern family. It is an age where one marriage and its biological relations have ceased to determine family composition. Choice increasingly appears to be the principle determining family composition: choice to single parent, choice of fictive kin, choice to combine nuclear families (in extended kin networks or in remarriage or in divorce-extended families), choice of semen donors or surrogate mothers, choice to dissolve marital bonds, choice of who will function as a parent in children's lives (despite of the law's failure to acknowledge the parental status of many functional parents). That is, what Kath Weston

---

[48] Judith Stacey cites one San Francisco study of divorced couples as revealing that one-third of them sustained kinship ties with former spouses and their relatives: *Brave New Families: Stories of Domestic Upheaval in Late Twentieth Century America* (New York: Basic Books, 1990], 254. 'Divorce-extended' is her term.

[49] For an exhaustive discussion of the inadequacies of the one-mother, one-father assumption to both heterosexual and gay/lesbian families see Nancy D. Polikoff, 'This Child Does have Two Mothers', *The Georgetown Law Journal* 78 (1990): 459–575.

[50] Stacey, *Brave New Families*.

[51] Ibid. 17

describes as a distinctively gay and lesbian concept of 'chosen families', contrasted to heterosexuals' biological families, in fact characterizes the reality of many heterosexual families who fail in various ways to construct a nuclear family around a procreative married couple.[52]

As family forms multiply, the traditional, heterosexual and procreative, nuclear family delimited by bonds of present marriage and blood relation and capable of sustaining itself rather than pooling resources across households has ceased to be the natural family form.[53] Not only has the pluralizing of family forms undermined the credibility of the claim that the traditional family is the most natural family form, it has also highlighted the failure of the traditional family to satisfy individual needs better than other personal relationships or alternative family forms. As Jeffrey Weeks observes,

[t]he existence of a diversity of family and household forms is . . . perhaps the most challenging issue of all [those presently confronting the family], because it poses in an acute fashion the question of value: not only the empirically verifiable issue of what is changing in the family, or families, but the more critical question of what ought to change, and what are the most appropriate means of satisfying individual and collective needs.[54]

As in previous periods, cultural understandings of what was threatening the stability of the traditional, nuclear family set the terms for how gay and lesbian difference would be articulated. In the 1980s and 1990s, references to lesbian and gay lifestyles that undermine family values gained widespread circulation. In its more modest formulation, the idea that lesbians and gays challenge family values has involved portraying lesbian and gay unions and parenting relationships as 'pretend' families. For instance, recall from Chapter 4 that in the late 1980s Britain passed Clause 28 of the Local Government act that forbade local authorities from promoting 'the teaching in any maintained school of the acceptability of homosexuality as a pretended family relationship'.[55] The pretended nature of gays' and lesbians' family relationships has, in the United States, been repeatedly underscored in court rulings affirming that marriage requires one man and one woman. The pretend nature of lesbian motherhood has also been underscored in custody rulings that have assumed that being parented by a lesbian is not in a child's best interests—because the

---

[52] Kath Weston, *Families We Choose: Lesbians, Gays, Kinship* (New York: Columbia University Press, 1991).

[53] Indeed, it has become doubly denaturalized. First, in failing to be repetitively enacted by individuals creating families, the heterosexual, procreative, nuclear family has lost its appearance of being the natural family form. That is, just as gender is 'naturalized' through repeated performances: Judith Butler, *Gender Trouble: Feminism and the Subversion of Identity* (New York: Routledge, 1990), so too one might imagine that the family itself is naturalized through being repetitively enacted. Second, family composition extends well beyond those 'naturally' linked by blood and those whose marital coupling 'naturally' issues in progeny.

[54] Jeffrey Weeks, 'Pretended Family Relationships', in *Against Nature: Essays on History Sexuality and Identity* (London: Rivers Oram, 1991), 134–56, 143.

[55] Qtd in Jeffrey Weeks, 'Pretended Family Relationships', 137.

child may be molested, or may fail to be socialized into her or his appropriate gender or into heterosexuality, or may be harmed by the stigma of having a lesbian parent.[56]

One particularly clear example of the attempt to construct lesbian and gay families as pretend families occurs in the recent work of family law scholar Lynn Wardle.[57] Wardle argues against legalizing same-sex marriage and argues for a legal presumption against awarding custody, visitation rights, and adoption to anyone engaged in an 'ongoing homosexual relationship' on the grounds that lesbian and gay families are not in fact functionally equivalent to heterosexual families. Lesbians and gays, he claims, come to partnerships with such different expectations that their unions should be regarded as, in fact, anti-marriage no matter how much lesbians and gays themselves may invoke the ideals of commitment, fidelity, and love. In words reminiscent of 1960s psychoanalytic literature, Wardle asserts that 'sexual fidelity is not an expected or typical characteristic in same-sex relationships'; those relationships lack a romantic foundation;[58] and they are chronically unstable.[59] In his view, same-sex unions are so different from real, heterosexual marriages that 'legalization of same-sex marriage entails a radical rejection of marriage by redefinition and replacement'.[60] In his view, same-sex parenting is, similarly, not functionally equivalent to heterosexual parenting. In particular, it poses potential dangers to children that heterosexual parenting does not. In his list of possible worrisome impacts that lesbian and gay parenting might have on children, Wardle echoes concerns raised in earlier historical periods about lesbian and gay gender deviance and its effects on children as well as concerns about the impact of lesbian and gay sexual excess on children. He raises the specter of boys becoming deficiently masculine, girls cross-dressing and being unable to relate to men in later life, and both boys and girls being more likely to turn out gay. He also raises the specter of various sexual dangers—exposing children to adultery and sexual activity, child molestation, and incest.[61]

---

[56] Although courts are moving to the assumption that the mother's lesbianism *per se* is not a bar to her fitness as a parent, this did not prevent the Virginia Supreme Court in the 1995 case of *Bottoms v. Bottoms* (249 Va. 410, 1995) from ruling that, even so, *active* lesbianism on the part of the mother could be a bar to her fitness.

[57] Lynn D. Wardle, 'The Potential Impact of Homosexual Parenting on Children', *University of Illinois Law Review* 1997 (1997): 833–99; 'Legal Claims for Same-Sex Marriage: Efforts to Legitimate a Retreat from Marriage by Redefining Marriage', *South Texas Law Review* 39 (1998): 735–68; and 'Fighting with Phantoms: A Reply to Warring with Wardle', *University of Illinois Law Review* 1998 (1998): 629–41.

[58] Wardle, 'Legal Claims for Same-Sex Marriage', 759–60.

[59] Wardle, 'The Potential Impact of Homosexual Parenting on Children', 862.

[60] Wardle, 'Legal Claims for Same-Sex Marriage', 761.

[61] He does not in fact say that gays and lesbians are more prone to sexual excess than heterosexuals. However, given that no mention is ever made of the reasonableness of instituting a presumption against heterosexual parenting on the grounds that heterosexuals may engage in all these activities, and that he is arguing for a presumption against homosexual parenting, it is only logical to infer that he thinks (or wishes his readers to think) that sexual dangers are distinctively connected to lesbianism and homosexuality.

His aim is not only to foreground the nonequivalence between heterosexual and nonheterosexual families. It is also to motivate heterosexual compliance with traditional family norms. Wardle offers fairly explicit stigma-threatening comparisons between misbehaving members of heterosexual families and lesbian and gay families; and he does so for the purpose of rallying increased heterosexual commitment to the ideal of long-term, monogamous marriage. Divorce, domestic violence, child bearing out of wedlock, and other dysfunctions in the heterosexual family may have, in his view, many of the same effects on children that lesbian and gay parenting does. In response to childhood traumas within these defective heterosexual families, including over-controlling mothers and weak fathers, children may turn out gay who would otherwise be heterosexual.[62] They may also come to share what he takes to be a distinctively lesbian and gay view of marriage, namely, a rejection of the naturalness of traditional marriage and family in favor of 'radical and dangerous substitutes'.[63] The explicit message is that misbehaving heterosexuals are responsible for cultivating a social climate that contributes to producing a new generation of lesbian and gay children, to undermining family values, and to fueling lesbian and gay claims to same-sex marriage. To avoid being like lesbian and gay pretend families, heterosexuals need to increase their compliance with traditional marital norms.

In its more extreme form, the idea that lesbians and gay men challenge family values has involved portraying gay men and lesbians not only as beings whose marriages and families fail to be the genuine article, but as beings who, simply by being publicly visible or mentionable, assault family values. As a result, anti-discrimination measures are equated with hostility to the family, even though ending workplace discrimination or punishing hate crimes would appear to have little to do with advocating one family form rather than another. This view has been defended with particular vigor by the leading natural law legal theorist, John Finnis.[64] Finnis argues that even though gay men and lesbians might imitate the sexually faithful, lifelong, monogamous marriages of heterosexuals, these relationships differ in kind from heterosexual marriages. That difference enables him to read same-sex marriages as in fact hostile to real marriage. Same-sex partners, he argues, are incapable of engaging in acts of 'the reproductive kind' which biologically unite two people in one flesh and are oriented toward reproduction. But it is a marriage's orientation toward producing and rearing children that ultimately provides the rationale for lifelong, monogamous, sexually faithful commitment. Thus, in his view, there is no good reason for same-sex couples to strive for this ideal. 'For them, the permanent, exclusive commitment of marriage . . . is [ration-

---

[62] Wardle, 'Legal Claims for Same-Sex Marriage', 765.                [63] Ibid. 767.

[64] John M. Finnis, 'Law, Morality, and "Sexual Orientation" ', *Notre Dame Journal of Law, Ethics, and Public Policy* 9 (1995): 11–39, 32; and 'The Good of Marriage and the Morality of Sexual Relations: Some Philosophical and Historical Observations', *American Journal of Jurisprudence* 42 (1997): 97–131.

ally] inexplicable.'[65] Group marital and parenting arrangements would make as much sense for gays and lesbians as long-term monogamous ones. Because same-sex sexuality is not intrinsically connected to long-term, sexually faithful, monogamous marriage in the way that heterosexual sexuality is, Finnis concludes that gay sexuality is 'deeply hostile to the self-understanding of those members of the community who are willing to commit themselves to real marriage.'[66] He makes it clear that any policy protecting a 'gay lifestyle' threatens the stability of the family, and for that reason should be rejected:

A political community which judges that the stability and protective and educative generosity of family life is of fundamental importance to that community's present and future can rightly judge that it has a compelling interest in denying that homosexual conduct—a 'gay lifestyle'—is a valid, humanly acceptable choice and form of life, and in doing whatever it *properly* can, as a community with uniquely wide but still subsidiary functions, to discourage such conduct.[67]

One of the main strategies that the community can validly use, in his view, is to refuse to protect gay men and lesbians against discriminatory treatment.

So threatening to the family are gay men and lesbians sometimes taken to be that even protecting them against hate crimes may be interpreted as dangerously close to attacking the family. Thus, the Hate Crimes Act passed by Congress in 1990 (which covers sexual orientation) includes the affirmation that 'federal policy should encourage the well-being, financial security, and health of the American family', and that '[n]othing in this Act shall be construed, nor shall any funds appropriated to carry out the purpose of the Act be used, to promote or encourage homosexuality'[68]

That being anti-family should now occupy center stage in constructions of gay men's and lesbians' nature makes sense given the cultural context in which these constructions are being developed. The gay liberation movement, begun in the 1970s, brought with it a rise in lesbian custody suits and in litigation contesting the denial of marriage licenses to same-sex couples.[69] At the same time that gay men and lesbians were publicly claiming to have genuine marriages and families of their own, it was becoming increasingly clear that heterosexuals were deviating in multiple ways from the conventional model of the two-parent, nuclear family. As in previous periods, constructing lesbians and gay men as dangerous outlaws to the family served to externalize the threat to the heterosexual, procreative, nuclear family, diverting attention from heterosexuals' own choices to create multiple, new family arrangements that undermine the hegemony of the traditional family. In addition, the equation of heterosexuality with family values and homosexuality and lesbianism

---

[65] Finnis, 'The Good of Marriage and the Morality of Sexual Relations', 131.
[66] Finnis, 'Law, Morality, and "Sexual Orientation" ', 32.
[67] Ibid. 32–3.
[68] 28 U.S.C. #534, qtd in Robson, 'Resisting the Family', 981 fn. 16.
[69] For 1970s marriage cases, see *Lesbians, Gay Men, and the Law*.

with hostility to the family serves to motivate loyalty to a traditional conception of the family. It also renders suspect some of the alternative family arrangements that heterosexuals might be inclined to choose, such as supportive, family-like relationships between women involved in single-parenting. Finally, constructing gay men and lesbians as anti-family works to preserve heterosexuals' social standing. No matter how much heterosexual families may deviate from the traditional ideal, they nevertheless qualify as nonpretend families, formed by people who are capable of genuine commitment to family life.

## V. The Right to define what Counts as a Family

I have argued for the existence of a historical pattern in which anxiety about the stability of the family goes hand-in-hand with the ideological depiction of gay men and lesbians as unfit for marriage, parenting, and family. The construction of lesbians and gay men as natural outlaws to the family and the masking of heterosexuals' own family-disrupting behavior results in the reservation of the private sphere for heterosexuals only.[70]

It is because being an outlaw to the family has been so central to the social construction of lesbianism and homosexuality, that I think the family belongs at the center of lesbian and gay politics. Because being denied access to a legitimate and protected private sphere has been and continues to be central to lesbian and gay oppression, the most important scale on which to measure lesbian and gay political strategies is one that assesses their power (or impotence) to resist conceding the private sphere to heterosexuals only. On such a scale, the push for marriage rights, parental rights, and recognition as legitimate families measures up. Indeed, on the historical backdrop of the various images of family outlaws—the mannish lesbian, the homosexual child molester, and their pretended family relationships—putting same-sex marriage, lesbian motherhood, and the formation of lesbian and gay families off or at the margins of a lesbian and gay political agenda looks suspiciously like a concession to the view of lesbians and gay men as family outlaws.

All this is not to say that there is no merit in lesbian feminists' concern that normalizing lesbian motherhood will reinforce the equation of 'woman' with 'mother'. Overcoming the idea that lesbian motherhood is a contradiction in terms may very well result in lesbians' being expected to fulfill the maternal imperative just as heterosexual women are. But this is just to say that lesbian and gay subordination is structurally different from gender oppression. Thus, strategies designed to resist *lesbian* subordination (such as pushing for the

---

[70] Justice White, in *Bowers v. Hardwick* (478 U.S. 186, 1986) argued that homosexual sodomy is not protected by the right to privacy because, in his view, the right to privacy protects the private sphere of family, marriage, and procreation and he opined that there was no connection between family, marriage, and procreation on the one hand, and homosexuality on the other.

legal right to co-adopt) are not guaranteed to counter *gender* oppression (which might better be achieved by resisting motherhood altogether). In gaining access to a legitimate and protected private sphere of mothering, marriage, and family, lesbians will need to take care that it does not prove to be as constraining as the private sphere has been for heterosexual women.

Nor have I meant to claim that there is no merit in both lesbian feminists' and queer theorists' concern that normalizing same-sex marriage will reinforce the distinction between good, assimilationist gays and bad gay and heterosexual others whose relationships violate familial norms (the permanently single, the polygamous, the sexually nonmonogamous, the member of a commune, etc.). Overcoming the idea that lesbian and gay marriages are merely pretended family relationships may very well result in married lesbians and gays being looked upon more favorably than those who remain outside accepted familial forms. But this is just to say that countering lesbians' and gays' family outlaw status is not the same thing as struggling to have a broad array of social relationships recognized as (equally) valuable ones.

It may, however, still seem to many that advocating lesbian and gay families is a dangerously conservative strategy. In countering the subordinating effects of lesbians' and gays' family outlaw status, would it not be better to demote the cultural importance assigned to family life rather than bid for lesbian and gay access to the very institution that has systematically been invoked against gays and lesbians? Why think that lesbian and gay interests would be better served through incorporation into the traditional family rather than through repudiating the family? Two related assumptions underpin these challenges to centering the family in lesbian and gay politics. Both merit scrutiny. They are, first, that bidding for access to the family means bidding for access to the traditional family; and second, that lesbian and gay intimate relations are so essentially different from heterosexual families that bidding for access to the family would not secure for lesbians and gays what they most need, namely, socio-legal recognition of their unique private arrangements.

The idea that bidding for access to the family *necessarily* means bidding for access to the traditional family is not a supportable assumption. As has often been observed, the 'traditional' nuclear, self-sufficient family composed of two parents and their biological children, is a historically specific, ideological construct. It characterizes neither dominant cultural conceptions of the family at all historical moments, nor actual families during historical periods where the ideal image of the nuclear family has in fact reigned. As I have argued, heterosexual families have failed to conform to the family composition norms defining the traditional family. In addition, heterosexuals have persistently violated the gender and sexual norms that have, at various historical moments, been taken to be definitive of conventional families. This has not prevented heterosexuals from claiming that, their deviancy notwithstanding, they still have real marriages and real families, and are themselves naturally suited for marriage and parenting. On the contrary, because heterosexuals are assumed to be naturally fit for family life, they have had cultural authority to contest dominant familial norms that were not serving their interests. Heterosexual women, for example, have had cultural authority as heterosexuals (if not as women) to object to the equation of family with hierarchical gender roles for husbands and wives. Thus, it is important not to exaggerate the level of conformity involved in having familial status.

Moreover, to think that pressing for marriage rights and socio-legal recognition of lesbian and gay families means advocating an Ozzie and Harriette ideal for lesbians and gay men is to misunderstand, in a fundamental way, what having *familial status* means. To have familial status is not to have applied to oneself one highly conventional family form. Having familial status means having the privilege that heterosexuals alone have heretofore had, namely the privilege of claiming that *despite their multiple deviations* from norms governing the family, their families are nevertheless *real* ones and they are themselves naturally suited for marriage, family, and parenting *however* these may be defined and redefined. It also means having the cultural authority to challenge existing familial norms, to redefine what constitutes a family, and to demand that the preferred definition of the family be reflected in cultural and legal practices. Centered within a liberatory lesbian and gay politics, the bid for access to the family is the bid for the right to exercise definitional authority with respect to the family.

Even in this highly modified form, it may still seem that the family ought not to be at the center of lesbian and gay politics. Lesbian and gay 'families', it might be objected, differ so radically from any existing version of heterosexual families that it would be strategically better to advocate demoting the cultural status of the family rather than trying to force same-sex relationships into any model of family life, even a highly revised one. In her investigation of competing discourses on and ideological representations of the family, for example, Kath Weston oppositionally positions reproductive, biological kin-based, heterosexual families against lesbian and gay families composed of chosen, adult, supportive relationships among individuals who are neither married nor in the business of procreating:

The very notion of gay families asserts that people who claim nonprocreative sexual identities and pursue nonprocreative relationships can lay claim to family ties of their own without necessary recourse to marriage, child bearing, or child rearing.[71]

On this view, lesbian and gay families lack the procreative and biological boundaries of heterosexual families. Kin are chosen, not biologically determined. Given the different principles—biology versus choice—underlying heterosexual versus lesbian and gay families, it might seem strategically wiser not even to describe lesbian and gay relationships as families at all. The political problem

---

[71] Weston, *Families We Choose*, 35.

for lesbians and gay men is precisely, one might think, that the 'natural', biologically based family has been granted socio-legal priority over the plurality of alternative, chosen, intimate associations that individuals might prefer to enter into.

Though forceful, this objection to centering the family in lesbian and gay politics depends on overdrawing the contrast between heterosexual families on the one hand, and lesbian and gay intimate associations on the other. First, it is important to keep in mind that, in opposing the biological, reproductive family to 'families we choose', Weston claimed to be articulating competing *discourses* or *ideological representations* of the family. The contrast between biological and chosen families that she develops is a contrast between different ways of talking about the family, not necessarily differences in the real composition of families or differences in the actual organizing principle of families.

Even if, ideologically, the traditional family gets depicted as a procreative, biologically linked unit, in practice that family is partially governed, and increasingly so, by the principle of choice. As we saw earlier, heterosexual families incorporate chosen, nonbiologically related individuals into their kinship structure in a variety of ways. The most obvious example is marriage. Marriage is the choice of kinship, including in-law kinship and (in the case of remarriage) step-kinship, with a set of persons who are not biologically one's kin. Adoption as well as procreation via semen or egg donation are also choices to make nonbiologically related children kin. In foster parenting, individuals choose temporary kinship to nonbiologically related children. Additional nonrelated kin can be brought in as godparents and honorary 'aunts' and 'uncles'. Weston herself mentions that there are racial and cultural differences in the extent to which families include fictive kin.

Traditional families also employ the principle of choice to terminate or deny kinship status. Divorce is the most obvious example. But kin can also be disinherited, disowned, and barred from family events, as is too often the consequence of coming out to families. Families can also refuse to acknowledge marriages, denying in-law kinship—again, a common experience of gay men and lesbians whose families do not acknowledge their partners and partners' families as kin.

In addition to using the principle of choice to determine who is or is not kin, traditional families make choices about the role and status of kin. Aunts, sisters, and grandparents may be assigned primary or partial parenting responsibilities. And distinctions can be drawn between close and distant relatives on subjective grounds without regard to biological closeness.

Finally, the increasing acceptability of single-parent families, including never married parents, as well as the acceptability of media presentations of alternative families represents less a 'queering' of the traditional family than a natural extension of the principle of choice already in operation.

The point here is that the family as *conventionally* understood permits kinship to be determined by choice as well as biology. Indeed, Kath Weston observes that gay and lesbian discourse about chosen family was in large measure *derived* from the behavior of heterosexual families who clearly made choice rather than biology the basic determinant of kinship when they threatened to expel gay and lesbian members.

On the other side of the fence, even if gay men and lesbians differ from heterosexuals in choosing to incorporate more fictive kin and in assigning them primary family status, gay and lesbian families continue to employ procreative and biological conceptions of the family. Even when exiled from biological families, gay men and lesbians often continue thinking of biological family as kin. When not exiled from biological families, the kinship status of biological relatives goes unquestioned. Gay men and lesbians also continue to operate on the conventional assumption that they will be kin to their (heterosexual) children's children. Furthermore, even if lesbians and gay men do not feel subject to the procreative *imperative*, two-thirds of Weston's interviewees wanted children; some already had children from previous heterosexual marriages; and the much publicized lesbian baby boom was in part made possible by gay men who contributed semen and sometimes chose to co-parent as well. This is all to say that procreation, parenting, and biologically determined kinship all play a role in gay and lesbian conceptions of family.

It would seem, then, that both straight families and gay and lesbian families employ both the principle of choice and procreatively secured biological ties to determine kinship. Differences between the two sorts of families arise because they use the two principles to do different things. For example, straight families use the principle of choice to expel gay men and lesbians, while gay men and lesbians may use the principle of biological relatedness to challenge their expulsion. Straight families typically use biological parentage to assign parenting roles, while gay and lesbian families make greater use of the principle of choice to assign parenting roles.

If both sorts of families are using both principles, then proclaiming an essential difference between heterosexual families and gay and lesbian intimate associations seems misguided. The central political problem is not that the conventional understanding of family excludes the principle of choice, but that lesbians and gay men are denied social and legal entitlement to use *either* kinship principle. Social and legal arrangements are built on the assumption that kinship, *however determined*, is for heterosexuals only.

That gay men and lesbians are not entitled to use the principle of choice is patently obvious in the denial of marriage and joint adoption rights, in straight families' refusal to acknowledge partners, and in the discriminatory policies of adoption, foster care, and alternative insemination agencies. That gay men and lesbians cannot get the kinship of friends or alternative co-parenting arrangements recognized is simply an extension of the general prohibition against gays and lesbians choosing their kin no matter how conventional and assimilationist those choices may be.

That gay men and lesbians are not entitled to use the principle of biological relatedness is obvious in child custody decisions where heterosexual orientation may count for more than biological closeness. It is also evident in straight families' refusal to accept biology as grounds for claiming kinship with gay men and lesbians.

These observations suggest that unless heterosexuals' exclusive right of access to the family (*however* family membership and structure is determined) is directly confronted, the primary beneficiaries of demoting the cultural status of the family are unlikely to be lesbians and gay men.

Finally, emphasizing an essential difference between heterosexual families and gay and lesbian intimate associations concedes too much to the ideology of gays and lesbians as family outlaws, unfit for genuine marriage and dangerous to children. Describing families that depart substantially from traditional family forms as distinctively gay also conceals the queerness of many heterosexual families. I have tried to show that, historically, gay men and lesbians have become family outlaws not because *their* relationships and families were distinctively queer, but because *heterosexuals'* relationships and families queered the gender, sexual, and family composition norms. The depiction of gays and lesbians as deviant with respect to family norms was a product of anxiety about that deviancy within heterosexual families. Thus, claiming that gay and lesbian families are (or should be) distinctively queer and distinctively deviant helps conceal the deviancy in heterosexual families, and thereby helps to sustain the illusion that heterosexuals are specially entitled to access to a protected private sphere.

## Conclusion

Throughout this book I have argued that lesbian and gay oppression is not a mere byproduct of sexism; nor is it structurally similar to racial oppression and gender oppression. Instead, lesbian and gay oppression is a separate and distinctive axis of oppression. Getting clear about the nature of lesbian and gay subordination enables us to answer more accurately the question: Which liberties do lesbians and gays *really* need most in order to be fully equal citizens?

I have argued that lesbian and gay oppression is above all distinguished by the phenomenon of *displacement* from civil society. Specifically, lesbians and gay men are displaced from the public sphere, from the private sphere, and from our social future. Given his, three liberties are particularly crucial:

(1) the liberty to represent one's identity publicly
(2) the liberty to have a protected private sphere, and
(3) the liberty to equal opportunity to influence future generations.

In Chapter 4, I argued that the practice of penalizing openly lesbian and gay people forces lesbians and gays to adopt pseudonymous heterosexual identities if they want full access to the public sphere. In effect, the only individuals who are permitted to speak and act in the public sphere are heterosexuals—both real and pseudonymous. If gay men and lesbians are to become fully equal citizens, one of the liberties we need most is the right to be *publicly* lesbian and gay.

In this and the previous chapter, I have argued that if gay men and lesbians are to become fully equal citizens, their private lives must be equally protected. Our culture connects full citizenship with being married and having a family. We assume that the family is a bedrock on which social and political life is then built and that citizens thus support civil life by getting married and having families. When lesbians and gays are contructed as outlaws to the family and are told that they cannot marry, they are being told that they are not capable of doing the work of citizens. Thus, lesbians and gays will not be fully equal until the law recognizes same-sex marriages and equally protects lesbian and gay family life.

In Chapters 4 and 6, I argued that an important aspect of the construction of lesbians and gays as outlaws to the family is the idea that lesbians and gay men are bad for children. They are incapable of socializing children into proper gender roles and a heterosexual orientation; they cannot be trusted not to molest or seduce the young; and they cannot offer children more than a pretended family relationship. Laws and policies built on these ideologies reduce gays' and lesbians' contact with children. In essence, such laws and policies hand over to heterosexuals exclusive entitlement to determine the character of future generations. This seriously undermines lesbian and gay equality. Being able to help shape our social future is, like being able to speak one's mind or having the opportunity to improve oneself, a basic interest that people have. Lesbians and gays will not be fully equal citizens until they have the equal liberty to influence who our future citizens will be.

In sum, these three liberties—the liberty to represent one's identity publicly, to marry and have a family, and to equally influence future generations—constitute the center of lesbian and gay politics. They are not the liberties that feminists have thought it most important for *women* to have. But, as I argued in Chapters 1, 2 and 3, it is important not to assume that feminist politics and lesbian politics are identical. Whether lesbians can occupy the center of feminist theorizing depends on whether feminism can find a space for the lesbian not-woman who shares with gay men the experience of a distinctive form of oppression.

# Bibliography

Addelson, Kathryn Pyne. 'Words and Lives'. *Signs* 7 (1981): 187–99.

Allen, Hillary. 'Political Lesbianism and Feminism—Space for a Sexual Politics?' *m/f* 7 (1982): 15–34.

Allen, Jeffner, ed. *Lesbian Philosophies and Cultures*. Albany, NY: State University of New York Press, 1990.

APA (American Psychiatric Association). *Diagnostic and Statistical Manual of Mental Disorders*. 3rd edn. Washington, DC: APA, Inc., 1980.

—— *Diagnostic and Statistical Manual of Mental Disorders*. 3rd rev. edn. Washington, DC: APA, 1987.

Bayer, Ronald. *Homosexuality and American Psychiatry*. Princeton: Princeton University Press, 1987.

Bennett, Jo. 'Same-Sex Sexual Harassment'. *Law & Sexuality: A Review of Lesbian, Gay, Bisexual, and Transgender Legal Issues* 6 (1996): 1–29.

Bensinger, Terralee. 'Lesbian Pornography: The Re/Making of (a) Community'. *Discourse: Journal for Theoretical Studies in Media and Culture* 15 (1992): 69–93.

Berube, Allan. *Coming Out Under Fire: A History of Gay Men and Women in World War II*. New York: Plume, 1990.

Bieber, Irving. *Homosexuality: A Psychoanalytic Study*. New York: Basic Books, 1962.

Blackstone, William, Esq. *Commentaries on the Laws of England* 8th edn. Oxford: Clarendon Press, 1778.

Blumstein, Philip and Schwartz, Pepper. *American Couples: Money, Work, Sex*. New York: Morrow, 1983.

Boswell, John. 'Categories, Experience and Sexuality'. In *Forms of Desire: Sexual Orientation and the Social Constructionist Controversy*, edited by Edward Stein. New York: Routledge, 1992.

Brownmiller, Susan. *Against Our Will: Men, Women, and Rape*. New York: Bantam, 1976.

Bunch, Charlotte. *Passionate Politics, Essays 1968–1986*. New York: St. Martin's Press, 1987.

Butler, Judith. 'Gendering the Body: Beauvoir's Philosophical Contribution'. In *Women, Knowledge, and Reality: Explorations in Feminist Philosophy*, edited by Ann Garry and Marilyn Pearsall. Boston: Unwin Hyman, 1989.

—— *Gender Trouble: Feminism and the Subversion of Identity*. New York: Routledge, 1990.

—— 'Imitation and Gender Insubordination'. In *Inside/Out: Lesbian Theories, Gay Theories*, edited by Diana Fuss. New York: Routledge, 1991.

Cain, Patricia A. 'Tensions and Possibilities within Contemporary Feminism: Lesbian Perspective, Lesbian Experience, and the Risk of Essentialism'. *Virginia Journal of Social Policy & the Law* 2 (1994): 43–74.

Calhoun, Cheshire. 'Denaturalizing and Desexualizing Lesbian and Gay Identity'. *Virginia Law Review* 79 (1993): 1859–75.

—— 'Making Up Emotional People: The Case of Romantic Love'. In *The Passions of Law*, edited by Susan Bandes. New York: New York University Press, 1999.

Card, Claudia. *Lesbian Choices*. New York: Columbia University Press, 1995.

—— 'Against Marriage and Motherhood'. *Hypatia* 11 (1996): 1–23.

—— 'Radicalesbianfeminist Theory'. *Hypatia* 13 (1998): 206–213.

Case, Mary Anne. 'Couples and Coupling in the Public Sphere: A Comment on the Legal History of Litigating for Lesbian and Gay Rights'. *Virginia Law Review* 79 (October 1993): 1643–94.

Case, Sue-Ellen. 'Toward a Butch-Femme Aesthetic'. In *The Lesbian and Gay Studies Reader*, edited by Henry Abelove, Michele Aina Barale, and David M. Halperin. New York: Routledge, 1993.

Caserio, Robert L. 'Supreme Court Discourse vs. Homosexual Fiction'. In *Displacing Homophobia: Gay Male Perspectives in Literature and Culture*, edited by Ronald R. Butters, John M. Clum, and Michael Moon. Durham, NC: Duke University Press, 1989.

Chauncey Jr., George. 'From Sexual Inversion to Homosexuality: The Changing Medical Conceptualization of Female "Deviance" '. *Passion and Power: Sexuality in History*, edited by Kathy Peiss and Christina Simmons with Robert A. Padgug. Philadelphia: Temple University Press, 1989.

—— *Gay New York: Gender, Urban Culture, and the Making of the Gay Male World, 1890–1940*. New York: Basic Books, 1994.

Chodorow, Nancy. *The Reproduction of Mothering: Psychoanalysis and the Sociology of Gender*. Berkeley: University of California Press, 1978.

Christensen, Craig W. 'Legal Ordering of Family Values. The Case of Gay and Lesbian Families'. *Cardozo Law Review* 18 (January 1997): 1299–416.

Clark, Danae. 'Commodity Lesbianism'. In *The Lesbian and Gay Studies Reader*, edited by Henry Abelove, Michele Aina Barale, and David M. Halperin. New York: Routledge, 1993.

Cohen, Ed. 'Legislating the Norm: From Sodomy to Gross Indecency'. In *Displacing Homophobia: Gay Male Perspectives in Literature and Culture*, edited by Ronald R. Butters, John M. Clum, and Michael Moon. Durham, NC: Duke University Press, 1989.

Collins, Patricia Hill. *Black Feminist Thought: Knowledge, Consciousness and the Politics of Empowerment*. New York: Routledge, 1990.

Coombs, Mary. 'Between Women/Between Men: The Significant for Lesbianism of Historical Understanding of Same-(Male)Sex Sexual Activities'. *Yale Journal of Law & the Humanities* 8 (1996): 241–61.

Creet, Julia. 'Daughter of the Movement: The Psychodynamics of Lesbian S/M Fantasy'. *Differences* 3 (1991): 135–59.

Crosby, Christina. 'Dealing with Differences'. In *Feminists Theorize the Political*, edited by Judith Butler and Joan W. Scott. New York: Routledge, 1992.

Cuomo, Chris J. 'Thoughts on Lesbian Differences'. *Hypatia* 13 (1998): 198–205.

Daly, Mary. *Gynecology*. Boston: Beacon Press, 1978.

Davidson, Arnold. 'Sex and the Emergence of Sexuality'. In *Forms of Desire: Sexual Orientation and the Social Constructionist Controversy*, edited by Edward Stein. New York: Routledge, 1992.

D'Emilio, John. 'The Homosexual Menace: The Politics of Sexuality in Cold War America'. In *Passion and Power: Sexuality in History*, edited by Kathy Peiss and Christina Simmons with Robert A. Padgug. Philadelphia: Temple University Press, 1989.

Dover, Kenneth. *Greek Homosexuality*. New York: Vintage, 1980.

Duberman, Martin. *Cures: A Gay Man's Odyssey*. New York: Dutton, 1992.

Duggan, Lisa. 'The Trials of Alice Mitchell: Sensationalism, Sexology, and the Lesbian Subject in Turn-of-the-Century America'. *Signs* 18 (1993): 791–814.

Editors of the Harvard Law Review. *Sexual Orientation and the Law*. Cambridge: Harvard University Press, 1989.

Eisenstein, Zillah R., ed. *Capitalist Patriarchy and the Case for Socialist Feminism*. New York: Monthly Review Press, 1979.

—— *The Radical Future of Liberal Feminism*. New York: Longman, 1981.

Ellis, Havelock. *Studies in the Psychology of Sex, vol. II: Sexual Inversion*. Philadelphia: F. A. Davis, 1928.

English, Jane, ed. *Sex Equality*. New York: Prentice Hall, 1977.

Eskridge, William. 'A History of Same-Sex Marriage'. *Virginia Law Review* 79 (1993): 1419–513.

—— *The Case for Same-Sex Marriage: From Sexual Liberty to Civilized Commitment*. New York: Free Press, 1996.

—— 'Beyond Lesbian and Gay "Families We Choose" '. In *Sex, Preference, and Family*, edited by David M. Estlund and Martha C. Nussbaum. New York: Oxford University Press, 1996.

Ettelbrick, Paula. 'Since When is Marriage a Path to Liberation?' In *Lesbians, Gay Men, and the Law*, edited by William B. Rubenstein. New York: New Press, 1993.

Faderman, Lillian. *Surpassing the Love of Men: Romantic Friendship and Love between Women from the Renaissance to the Present*. New York: Morrow, 1981.

—— *Odd Girls and Twilight Lovers: A History of Lesbian Life in the Twentieth Century*. New York: Penguin, 1992.

—— 'The Return of Butch and Femme: A Phenomenon of Lesbian Sexuality of the 1980s and 1990s'. *Journal of the History of Sexuality* 2 (1992): 578–96.

—— 'Nineteenth-Century Boston Marriage as a Possible Lesson for Today'. In *Boston Marriages: Romantic but Asexual Relationships Among Contemporary Lesbians*, edited by Esther D. Rothblum and Kathleen A. Brehony. Amherst: University of Massachusetts Press, 1993.

Ferguson, Ann. 'Patriarchy, Sexual Identity, and the Sexual Revolution'. In 'Viewpoint: On "Compulsory Heterosexuality and Lesbian Existence": Defining the Issues', by Ann Ferguson, Jacquelyn N. Zita, and Kathryn Pyne Addelson, *Signs* 7 (1981): 158–99.

—— 'On Conceiving Motherhood and Sexuality: A Feminist Materialist Approach'. In *Mothering: Essays in Feminist Theory*, edited by Joyce Trebilcot. Totowa: Rowman & Allanheld, 1983.

—— 'Cheshire Calhoun's Project of Separating Lesbian Theory from Feminist Theory'. *Hypatia* 13 (1998): 214–23.

Finnis, John M. 'Law, Morality, and "Sexual Orientation" '. *Notre Dame Journal of Law, Ethics, and Public Policy* 9 (1995): 11–39.

—— 'The Good of Marriage and the Morality of Sexual Relations: Some Philosophical and Historical Observations', *American Journal of Jurisprudence* 42 (1997): 97–131.

Firestone, Shulamith. *The Dialectic of Sex*. New York: Morrow, 1970.

Foucault, Michel. *The History of Sexuality, vol. I: An Introduction*. New York: Vintage, 1990.

Fraser, Nancy. *Unruly Practices: Power, Discourse, and Gender in Contemporary Social Theory*. Minneapolis: University of Minnesota Press, 1989.

Freedman, Estelle B. ' "Uncontrolled Desires": The Response to the Sexual Psychopath 1920–1960'. In *Passion and Power: Sexuality in History*, edited by Kathy Peiss and Christina Simmons with Robert A. Padgug. Philadelphia: Temple University Press, 1989.

Friedan, Betty. *The Feminine Mystique*. New York: Norton, 1963.

Frye, Marilyn. *The Politics of Reality*. Freedom, CA: Crossing Press, 1983.

—— 'A Response to *Lesbian Ethics*: Why Ethics?' In *Feminist Ethics*, edited by Claudia Card. Lawrence: University Press of Kansas, 1991.

—— *Willful Virgin: Essays in Feminism 1976–1992*. Freedom, CA: Crossing Press, 1992.

Garber, Marjorie. *Vested Interests: Cross-Dressing and Cultural Anxiety*. New York: Harper Perennial, 1993.

Goldstein, Anne B. 'Reasoning about Homosexuality: A Commentary on Janet Halley's "Reasoning about Sodomy: Act and Identity In and After *Bowers v. Hardwick*" '. *Virginia Law Review* 79 (1993): 1781–804.

Gordon, Michael R. 'Pentagon Spells Out Rules for Ousting Homosexuals'. *New York Times*, 23 December 1993, p. A1, A14.

Hacking, Ian. 'Making Up People'. In *Reconstructing Individualism: Autonomy, Individuality, and the Self in Western Thought*, edited by Thomas C. Heller *et al.* Stanford, CA: Stanford University Press, 1986.

Haddock, David D. and Polsby, Daniel D. 'Family as a Rational Classification'. *Washington University Law Quarterly* 74 (1996): 15–46.

Halberstam, Judith. *Female Masculinity*. Durham, NC: Duke University Press, 1998.

Hale, Jacob. 'Are Lesbians Women?' *Hypatia* 11 (1996): 94–101.

Hall, Jacquelyn Dowd. ' "The Mind that Burns in Each Body": Women, Rape, and Racial Violence'. In *Race, Class, and Gender*, edited by Margaret L. Andersen and Patricia Hill Collins. Belmont: Wadsworth, 1992.

Halley, Janet E. 'The Construction of Heterosexuality'. In *Fear of a Queer Planet: Queer Politics and Social Theory*, edited by Michael Warner. Minneapolis: University of Minnesota Press, 1993.

—— 'Reasoning About Sodomy: Act and Identity In and After *Bowers v. Hardwick*'. *Virginia Law Review* 79 (1993): 1721–80.

Halperin, David M. 'Is There a History of Sexuality?' In *The Lesbian and Gay Studies Reader*, edited by Henry Abelove, Michele Aina Barale, and David M. Halperin. New York: Routledge, 1993.

Hart, Nett. 'Lesbian Desire as Social Action'. In *Lesbian Philosophies and Cultures*, edited by Jeffner Allen. Albany, NY: State University of New York Press, 1990.

Hartmann Heidi. 'The Unhappy Marriage of Marxism and Feminism: Toward a More Progressive Union'. In *Feminist Frameworks: Alternative Theoretical Accounts of the Relations between Women and Men*, 2nd edn, edited by Alison M. Jaggar and Paula Rothenberg Struhl. New York: McGraw-Hill, 1984.

Hewlett, Sylvia Ann. *A Lesser Life: The Myth of Women's Liberation in America*. New York: Morrow, 1986.

Hoagland, Sarah Lucia. *Lesbian Ethics: Toward New Value*. Palo Alto, CA: Institute of Lesbian Studies, 1988.

Hooks, Bell. *Feminist Theory: From Margin to Center*. Boston: South End Press, 1984.

Hunter, Nan D. 'Identity, Speech, and Equality.' *Virginia Law Review* 79 (l993): 1695–719.

—— 'Marriage, Law, and Gender: A Feminist Inquiry'. In *Sex Wars: Sexual Dissent and Political Culture*, by Lisa Duggan and Nan D. Hunter. New York: Routledge, 1995.

Jaggar, Alison M. *Feminist Politics and Human Nature*. Totowa: Rowman & Allanheld, 1983.

Kaplan, Morris. 'Constructing Lesbian and Gay Rights and Liberation'. *Virginia Law Review* 79 (1993): 1877–902.

—— *Sexual Justice: Democratic Citizenship and the Politics of Desire*. New York: Routledge, 1997.

Katz, Jonathan. *The Invention of Heterosexuality*. New York: Dutton, 1995.

Kitzinger, Celia. *The Social Construction of Lesbianism*. London: Sage, 1987.

Klepfisz, Irena. 'Women Without Children/ Women Without Families/ Women Alone'. In *Politics of the Heart: A Lesbian Parenting Anthology*, edited by Sandra Pollack and Jeanne Vaughn. New York: Firebrand Books, 1987.

Koppelman, Andrew. 'The Miscegenation Analogy: Sodomy Law as Sex Discrimination'. *Yale Law Journal* 98 (1988): 145–64.

—— 'Why Discrimination Against Lesbians and Gay Men is Sex Discrimination'. *NYU Law Review* 69 (1994): 197–287.

Krafft-Ebing, Richard von. *Psychopathia Sexualis: A Medico-Forensic Study*. New York: Pioneer Publications, 1947.

Kymlicka, Will. 'Rethinking the Family'. *Philosophy and Public Affairs* 20 (1991): 77–97.

Lauritsen, John and Thorstad, David *The Early Homosexual Rights Movement, 1864–1935*. New York: Times Change Press, l974.

Law, Sylvia A. 'Homosexuality and the Social Meaning of Gender'. *Wisconsin Law Review* 1988 (1988): 187–235.

Lee, Patrick and George, Robert 'What Sex Can Be: Self-Alienation, Illusion, or One-Flesh Union'. *The American Journal of Jurisprudence* 42 (1997): 135–57

Lewin, Ellen. *Lesbian Mothers: Accounts of Gender in American Culture*. Ithaca, NY: Cornell University Press, 1993.

Linden, Robin Ruth *et al.*, ed. *Against Sadomasochism: A Radical Feminist Analysis*. San Francisco: Frog in the Well, 1982.

Lorde, Audre. 'Uses of the Erotic: the Erotic as Power'. In *Sister Outsider: Essays and Speeches by Audre Lorde*. Trumansburg, NY: Crossing Press, 1984.

Macedo, Stephen. 'Sexuality and Liberty: Making Room for Nature and Tradition?' In *Sex, Preference, and Family*, edited by David M. Estlund and Martha C. Nussbaum. New York: Oxford University Press, 1996.

Martin, Biddy. 'Sexual Practice and Changing Lesbian Identities'. In *Destabilizing Theory: Contemporary Feminist Debates*, edited by Michele Barrett and Anne Phillips. Stanford, CA: Stanford University Press, 1992.

—— 'Lesbian Identity and Autobiographical Difference[s].' In *The Lesbian and Gay Studies Reader*, edited by Henry Abelove, Michele Aina Barale, and David M. Halperin. New York: Routledge, 1993.

Millett, Kate. *Sexual Politics*. New York: Doubleday, 1969.

Nestle, Joan. 'Butch-Femme Relationships: Sexual Courage in the 1950s'. In *A Restricted Country*. Ithaca, NY: Firebrand Books, 1987.

Newton, Esther. 'The Mythic Mannish Lesbian: Radclyffe Hall and the New Woman'. *Signs* 9 (1984): 557–75.

Okin, Susan Moller. *Justice, Gender, and the Family*. New York: Basic Books, 1989.

—— 'Sexual Orientation and Gender: Dichotomizing Differences'. In *Sex, Preference, and Family*, edited by David M. Estlund and Martha C. Nussbaum. New York: Oxford University Press, 1996.

Ortiz, Daniel R. 'Creating Controversy: Essentialism/Constructivism and the Politics of Gay Identity'. *Virginia Law Review* 79 (1993): 1833–57.

Penelope, Julia. 'Heteropatriarchal Semantics and Lesbian Identity: The Ways a Lesbian Can Be'. *Call Me Lesbian: Lesbian Lives, Lesbian Theory*. Freedom, CA: Crossing Press, 1992.

Peterson, Cynthia. 'Envisioning a Lesbian Equality Jurisprudence'. In *Legal Inversions: Lesbians, Gay Men, and the Politics of Law*. Philadelphia: Temple University Press, 1995.

Phelan, Shane. 'The Woman-Identified Woman'. In *Identity Politics: Lesbian Feminism and the Limits of Community*. Philadelphia: Temple University Press, 1989.

—— 'Sadomasochism and the Meaning of Feminism'. In *Identity Politics: Lesbian Feminism and the Limits of Community*. Philadelphia: Temple University Press, 1989.

Ploscowe, Morris. *Sex and the Law*. New York: Prentice Hall, 1951.

Polikoff, Nancy D. 'Lesbians Choosing Children: The Personal is Political'. In *Politics of the Heart: A Lesbian Parenting Anthology*, edited by Sandra Pollack and Jeanne Vaughn. New York: Firebrand Books, 1987.

—— 'This Child Does have Two Mothers'. *The Georgetown Law Journal* 78 (1990): 459–75.

—— 'We Will Get What We Ask For: Why Legalizing Gay and Lesbian Marriage Will Not "Dismantle the Legal Structure of Gender in Every Marriage" '. *Virginia Law Review* 79 (1993): 1535–50.

Posner, Hon. Richard A. 'The Economic Approach to Homosexuality'. In *Sex, Preference, and Family*, edited by David M. Estlund and Martha C. Nussbaum. New York: Oxford University Press, 1996.

Radicalesbians. 'The Woman Identified Woman'. In *Radical Feminism*, edited by Anne Koedt *et al*. New York: Quadrangle, 1973.

Raymond, Janice G. *A Passion for Friends: Toward a Philosophy of Female Affection*. Boston: Beacon Press, 1986.

—— 'Obstacles to Female Friendship'. In *A Passion for Friends*. Boston: Beacon Press, 1986.

—— 'Putting the Politics Back into Lesbianism'. *Women's Studies International Forum* 12 (1989): 149–56.

Reskin, Barbara F. and Hartmann, Heidi I. ed. *Women's Work, Men's Work: Sex Segregation on the Job*. Washington, DC: National Academy Press, 1986.

Rich, Adrienne. 'Compulsory Heterosexuality and Lesbian Existence'. In *The Signs Reader: Women, Gender, and Scholarship* edited by Elizabeth Abel and Emily K. Abel. Chicago: University of Chicago Press, 1983.

Rich, B. Ruby. 'Feminism and Sexuality in the 1980s'. *Feminist Studies* 12 (1986): 525–61.

Rivera, Rhonda R. 'Legal Issues in Gay and Lesbian Parenting'. In *Gay and Lesbian Parents*, edited by Frederick W. Bozett. New York: Praeger, 1987.

Robson, Ruthann. 'Resisting the Family: Repositioning Lesbians in Legal Theory'. *Signs* 19 (1994): 975–96.

—— *Sappho Goes to Law School.* New York: Columbia University Press, 1998.

Rubin, Gayle. 'The Traffic in Women'. In *Toward and Anthropology of Women*, edited by Rayna Reiter. New York: Monthly Review Press, 1975.

—— 'The Leather Menace: Comments on Politics and S/M'. In *Coming to Power*, edited by Samois. Boston: Alyson, 1981.

Rush, Sharon Elizabeth. 'Breaking with Tradition: Surrogacy and Gay Fathers'. In *Kindred Matters: Rethinking the Philosophy of the Family*, edited by Diana Tietjens Meyers, Kenneth Kipnis, and Cornelius F. Murphy. Ithaca, NY: Cornell University Press, 1993.

Sedgwick, Eve Kosofsky. *Epistemology of the Closet.* Berkeley: University of California Press, 1990.

—— 'How to Bring Your Kids up Gay'. In *Fear of a Queer Planet*, edited by Michael Warner. Minneapolis: University of Minnesota Press, 1993.

Sidel, Ruth. *Women and Children Last: The Plight of Poor Women in Affluent America.* New York: Viking, 1986.

Smith-Rosenberg, Caroll. 'The Female World of Love and Ritual: Relations between Women in Nineteenth-Century America'. *Signs* 1 (1975): 1–29.

—— and Rosenberg, Charles. 'The Female Animal: Medical and Biological Views of Woman and Her Role in Nineteenth-Century America'. In *Concepts of Health and Disease: Interdisciplinary Perspectives*, edited by Arthur L. Caplan, H. Tristram Engelhardt, Jr., and James J. McCartney. Reading, MA: Addison-Wesley, 1981.

Spelman, Elizabeth V. *Inessential Woman: Problems of Exclusion in Feminist Thought.* Boston: Beacon Press, 1988.

Stacey, Judith. *Brave New Families: Stories of Domestic Upheaval in Late Twentieth Century America.* New York: Basic Books, 1990.

Star, Susan Leigh. 'Swastikas: The Street and the University'. In *Against Sadomasochism: A Radical Feminist Analysis*, edited by Robin Ruth Linden *et al.* San Francisco: Frog in the Well, 1982.

Stein, Edward. 'The Essentials of Constructionism and the Construction of Essentialism'. In *Forms of Desire: Sexual Orientation and the Social Constructionist Controversy*, edited by Edward Stein. New York: Routledge, 1992.

—— *The Mismeasure of Desire: The Science, Theory, and Ethics of Sexual Orientation.* New York: Oxford University Press, 1999.

Stoltenberg, John. 'Sadomasochism: Eroticized Violence, Eroticized Powerlessness'. In *Against Sadomasochism*, edited by Robin Ruth Linden *et al.* San Francisco: Frog in the Well, 1982.

Struening, Karen. 'Feminist Challenges to the New Familialism: Lifestyle Experimentation and the Freedom of Association'. *Hypatia* 11 (1996): 135–54.

Sunstein, Cass R. 'Homosexuality and the Constitution'. In *Sex, Preference, and Family*, edited by David M. Estlund and Martha C. Nussbaum. New York: Oxford University Press, 1996.

Towell, Pat. 'Nunn Offers a Compromise: "Don't Ask/Don't Tell" '. *Congressional Quarterly Weekly Report* 51 (1993): 1240.

Trebilcott, Joyce. 'Conceiving Women: Notes on the Logic of Feminism'. In *Women and Values: Readings in Feminist Philosophy*, edited by Marilyn Pearsall. Belmont, CA: Wadsworth, 1986.

Vicinus, Martha. ' "They Wonder To Which Sex I Belong": The Historical Roots of the

Modern Lesbian Identity'. In *The Lesbian and Gay Studies Reader*, edited by Henry Abelove, Michele Aina Barale, and David M. Halperin. New York: Routledge, 1993.

Wagner, Sally Roesch. 'Pornography and the Sexual Revolution: The Backlash of Sadomasochism'. In *Against Sadomasochism: A Radical Feminist Analysis*, edited by Robin Ruth Linden *et al*. San Francisco: Frog in the Well, 1982.

Wardle, Lynn D. 'The Potential Impact of Homosexual Parenting on Children'. *University of Illinois Law Review* 1997 (1997): 833–99.

—— 'Legal Claims for Same-Sex Marriage: Efforts to Legitimate a Retreat from Marriage by Redefining Marriage'. *South Texas Law Review* 39 (1998): 735–68.

—— 'Fighting with Phantoms: A Reply to Warring with Wardle'. *University of Illinois Law Review* 1998 (1998): 629–41.

Weeks, Jeffrey. 'Pretended Family Relationships'. In *Against Nature: Essays on History, Sexuality, and Identity*. Concord, MA: Paul & Company, 1991.

Weitzman, Lenore J. *The Divorce Revolution: The Unexpected Social and Economic Consequences for Women and Children in America*. New York: Free Press, 1985.

Weston, Kath. *Families We Choose: Lesbians, Gays, Kinship*. New York: Columbia University Press, 1991.

—— *Render Me, Gender Me*. New York: Columbia University Press, 1996.

Wilbur, Cornelia. 'Clinical Aspects of Female Homosexuality'. In *Sexual Inversion: The Multiple Roots of Homosexuality*, edited by Judd Marmor. New York: Basic Books, 1965.

Wittig, Monique. *The Straight Mind and Other Essays*. Boston: Beacon Press, 1992.

Wollstonecraft, Mary. *A Vindication of the Rights of Woman*. New York: W.W. Norton, 1967.

Woods, James D. and Lucas, Jay H. *The Corporate Closet: The Professional Lives of Gay Men in America*. New York: Free Press, 1993.

Young, Iris Marion. *Justice and the Politics of Difference*. Princeton: Princeton University Press, 1990.

# Index

## DATE DUE

| | | | |
|---|---|---|---|
| | | | |
| | | | |
| | | | |
| | | | |
| | | | |
| | | | |
| | | | |
| | | | |
| | | | |
| | | | |
| | | | |
| | | | |
| | | | |

Campus Women's Center
800 Langdon Street
4th Floor Memorial Union
Madison, WI  53706